Questioning Ireland

Fergal O' Connor, RTÉ Late Late Show 1973

QUESTIONING IRELAND

Debates in Political Philosophy and Public Policy

Edited by

Joseph Dunne, Attracta Ingram
and Frank Litton

Celebrating Fergal O'Connor OP
Teacher and Philosopher

INSTITUTE OF PUBLIC
ADMINISTRATION

First published 2000
by the Institute of Public Administration
57-61 Lansdowne Road
Dublin 4

ISBN 1 902448 34 0

British Library Cataloguing in Publication Data
A catalogue record of this book is available from the
British Library

Cover design by Jan de Fouw
Typeset in Garamond 10/11.5
by Wendy A. Commins, The Curragh
Printed by ColourBooks Ltd., Dublin

Contents

Notes on Contributors

Fergus Armstrong practises law at the firm of MacCann Fitzgerald in Dublin where he has previously served as managing partner and chairman. He studied at UCD and the Harvard Law School and was formerly solicitor at Aer Lingus.

John Baker is Senior Lecturer in Politics at UCD where he was Director of the Equality Studies Centre between 1996 and 1998. He studied at the Universities of Oxford and Toronto. He is author of *Arguing for Equality* (London: Verso, 1987).

John Barry is a political theorist at Keele University in the UK. He studied at UCD and the University of Glasgow. He is author of *Rethinking Green Political Theory: Nature, Virtue and Progress* (London: Sage, 1999) and *Environment and Social Theory* (London: Routledge, 1999).

Maeve Cooke is a Senior Lecturer in the Department of German at UCD. She studied at UCD and the University of Konstanz. In 1994-95 she was a Research Fellow at the von Humboldt Foundation in Bonn. She is author of *Language and Reason: A Study of Habermas's Pragmatics* (Cambridge Ma: MIT Press, 1994) and editor of a collection of Habermas's writings on language and communication, *On the Pragmatics of Communication* (Boston: MIT Press, 1998).

Joseph Dunne teaches philosophy in the Education and Human Development programmes at St Patrick's College, Dublin City University. In 1998 he was visiting professor of philosophy at Duke University in the US. He studied at UCD, and is author of *Back to the Rough Ground: Practical Judgment and the Lure of Technique* (Notre Dame and London: Notre Dame University Press, 1997).

Austin Flannery OP is a Dominican priest, manager of Dominican Publications and editor of *Religious Life Review*. He is a founder member and one-time president of the Irish Anti-Apartheid Movement. He has edited the collections, *Vatican Council ll: Constitutions, Decrees, Declarations* (1996) and *Vatican Council ll: More Post-Conciliar Documents* (1998), both published in Dublin by Dominican Publications.

Iseult Honohan teaches political philosophy at UCD. She studied at UCD and Georgetown University. Her academic interests include feminism and civic republicanism, on which she is writing a book for Routledge.

Attracta Ingram is Associate Professor of Politics at UCD. In 1993-94 she was Jean Monnet Fellow at the European University Institute in Florence. She studied at UCD and Trinity College Dublin. She is author of *A Political Theory of Rights* (Oxford: Clarendon Press, 1993) and co-editor (with Gerard Quinn and Stephen Livingstone) of *Justice and Legal Theory in Ireland* (Dublin: Oaktree Press, 1995) and (with Maria Baghramian) of *Perspectives on Pluralism* (forthcoming from Routledge).

Frank Litton teaches Politics and Public Policy-making at the Institute of Public Administration in Dublin. He studied at UCD and is editor of *Unequal Achievement* (Dublin: IPA, 1982) and *The Irish Constitution, 1937 to 1987* (Dublin: IPA, 1988).

Rory O'Donnell is a former Director of the National Economic and Social Council and is now Jean Monnet Professor of European Business Studies at UCD. He studied at UCD and the Universities of London and Cambridge. His publications include *Adam Smith's Theory of Value and Distribution* (London: Macmillan, 1990) and (with Bridget Laffan and Michael Smith) *Europe's Experimental Union: Rethinking Integration* (London: Routledge, 1999).

Shane O'Neill is Reader in Politics at the Queen's University Belfast. He studied at UCD and the University of Glasgow. He is author of *Impartiality in Context: Grounding Justice in a Pluralist World* (New York: SUNY Press, 1997) and co-editor (with Iain MacKenzie) of *Reconstituting Social Criticism* (London: MacMillan, 1998).

Philip Pettit is Professor of Social and Political Theory at the Research School of Social Sciences at the Australian National University in Canberra. He studied at Maynooth and at Queen's University Belfast and lectured in Politics at UCD. His publications include (with John Braithwaite): *Not Just Deserts: A Republican Theory of Criminal Justice* (Oxford: Oxford University Press, 1990), *The Common Mind: An Essay on Psychology, Society and Politics* (New York: Oxford University Press, 1993) and *Republicanism: A Theory of Freedom and Government* (Clarendon Press, 1997).

Denys Turner is Norris Hulse professor of Divinity at the University of Cambridge. He studied at UCD and Oxford and taught at UCD and the Universities of Bristol and Birmingham. He is author of *Marxism and Christianity* (Oxford: Blackwell, 1983) and *The Darkness of God: Negativity in Christian Mysticism* (Cambridge: Cambridge University Press, 1995).

Introduction

Joseph Dunne, Attracta Ingram, Frank Litton

This volume of essays has two main objectives: first, to pay tribute to Fergal O'Connor, who taught political philosophy for over thirty years in University College Dublin; and second, to build a bridge between the world of political theory and everyday thinking about important issues in Irish politics and society.

The essays share one central preoccupation: how to understand and assess our rapidly changing society as we enter the new millennium. The authors provide a variety of perspectives on the processes, institutions and values of this society. In doing so, they spell out connections between our ways of thinking about matters of public interest and basic concepts of political theory – justice and rights, the common good, democracy, the state and its relationship to the economic, cultural and domestic spheres. In addition, they seek to propose alternative ways of thinking that may be helpful in shaping our responses to practical problems, while at the same time being alive to the theoretical and practical implications of these alternatives.

The volume is written in a political and social context much changed from de Valera's Ireland. Our state is no longer exposed to charges of theocracy and moral paternalism. Our national identity is no longer seen as homogeneous. It is regarded as more open and adaptive, more hospitable to the inclusion of a plurality of rival views about who we are and how to live. We have abandoned our irredentist claim to the North. We have become secure enough about sovereignty to engage in its pooling and functional division as members of the European Union. We have a successful open economy driven by the skills of a young educated workforce. We have loosened many traditional assumptions about what counts as a family unit, the roles of men and women, and national destiny.

We have, also, a society in which there are grounds for discontent. There are great disparities in wealth, effective inequality of opportunity, and a large underclass of marginalised and unrepresented people. Less visible are the gnawing anxieties of many people about the kind of society we seem set to become – cynical about politics, disengaged from civic participation, and insensitive to the costs to family, neighbourhood and nation of the unravelling moral fabric of community. All this, and apparently little collective control over the forces that govern our lives.

In such circumstances, we need to raise some fundamental questions about what our society is and should be. What should democracy mean today – within the political arena, and within civil society? How are we to define the state in conditions of pluralism? How does, and should, it relate to the ethnocultural nation? What is the relationship of state to civil society, that is, to those areas of social life – the domestic sphere, the economic world, cultural activities, and political parties and movements – that are organised by individuals and groups outside the direct control of the state? How are we to understand the function of the public service, operating as it does between state and society? What should be the role of education in the midst of sweeping cultural and economic changes? How should we deal with those whose behaviour puts them on the wrong side of the criminal law? Is the idea of a more free and equal society compromised by the growth of market individualism? How should we think about the relationship between human needs and interests and the environment? What are the dynamics of interest group interaction with policy-makers and within the corporate business culture? What is the fate of religion in our brave new Ireland – is there a role for church in relation to society and state, mediated perhaps by a realignment of 'lay' and 'clerical' roles? Each of the essays in this volume explores aspects of these and related questions.

Since the book is a *Festschrift* for an inspiring teacher, we begin with education. Clearly there is a lot more of this now than there used to be – and a good thing too, we must surely think. Far greater numbers of students stay on much longer at schools and colleges, on which the government spends a great deal more money than ever before. Nor is this money badly spent: not only has much of the recent success of the Irish economy been rightly attributed to the quality of our school-leavers and graduates but the school has also been properly identified as a key site in tackling socioeconomic disadvantage and bringing about greater social equity. But the very worthiness of these social functions of schools and universities can eclipse another question: what is education for? As well as helping students to make a living, can it challenge them about how to live? Can it integrate intellectual development with a deepening of moral concern and provide occasions for personal transformation as well as social critique?

In the first essay Joseph Dunne deals with these issues by reflecting on the educative practice of Fergal O' Connor. He shows how in Fergal's classes engagement with canonical authors could unsettle students' opinions and attitudes and develop awareness of the kind of testing through which knowledge-claims must pass. If the aim of this teaching was not the transmission of authoritative doctrine, neither was it simply the development of sceptical skills. It was, rather, that students should experience the kind of search for truth that is itself animated by a care for the good. This aim is deeply at odds with much that now dominates not only our educational system but our whole society; and its very possibility is contested by much postmodernist theory. Dunne reveals the significance of Plato's writing in making sense of Fergal O' Connor's pedagogic practice. But he also tries to show how this practice illuminates central elements of Platonic theory – those elements that were inspired by the witness of Socrates, the central figure in Plato's dialogues. It is a similar witness, Dunne suggests, that we find in Fergal's life as a teacher, and his essay is an attempt both to display the Socratic parallels and to canvass their power to enliven our own educational imaginations.

The essay by Shane O'Neill addresses the question of how a liberal democratic state should respond to the social fact of pluralism, that is the existence within it of people committed to a variety of different, and ultimately irreconcilable, religious, moral and philo-sophical doctrines. The state in such circumstances cannot impose one of the rival doctrines without giving up on its own basis of legitimacy – the reasonable consent of all citizens. Instead, it must in its constitution and laws remain impartial as between the rival views. Such a neutral state, O'Neill argues, need not be morally vacuous or passive. In addition to protecting a standard set of individual rights it can make room for justice and equality for individuals and groups in the expression of their particular identities. In this vision of the state, democratic politics opens up informal public spheres through which groups – especially minority or disadvantaged groups – can clarify their needs and struggle for the conditions necessary to fulfil them. This is a modified liberalism in which tolerance and respect for difference gives substance to common citizenship.

In her essay Attracta Ingram argues that pluralism, together with forces of globalisation, has a further entailment for liberal democracy – a major realignment of the nation-state relationship. She argues that the primacy of the ethnic or cultural nation in providing the unified political people for the modern nation-states of Europe must be discarded in favour of the nation of citizens. This civic nation is separated from the ethnocultural nation, on the model of the privatisation move that separates church and state in the conception of the modern state. The political project we should pursue in Ireland, Ingram argues, is a common post-nationalist citizenship. This is a vision of civic identity that depends not on the social unity of the pre-political nation, but rather on a shared commitment to human rights and democracy as these are given effect in the living constitution that we make and remake together.

The arguments of O'Neill and Ingram are framed by a commitment to political liberalism. The essays by Iseult Honohan and Denys Turner contest liberalism in part or as a whole. A proper conception of the common good, Honohan argues, need not have authoritarian implications and offers the possibility of a richer politics than liberal premises ordain. In rejecting this kind of politics liberals ignore the extent to which certain substantial human goods are inherently social, their value deriving from the fact that they are shared by people who, through this very sharing, are constituted as members of a community. Examples of the kind of goods Honohan has in mind are a natural heritage such as the Burren, or a social institution such as marriage. Attention to goods of this kind, she suggests, enhances rather than curtails our autonomy as individuals.

To the extent that his version of liberalism emphasises the

interactive nature of human experience and the importance of group membership in the formation of personal identity, O'Neill has common ground with Honohan. But Honohan rejects his liberal image of the neutral state. She argues for a positive role for the state in supporting certain common goods, while allowing that these are matters of ongoing interpretation, deliberation and debate. Such debate cannot be confined to 'private' arenas, leaving politics to operate on the premises of an allegedly universal 'public reason'. Liberal banishment of substantive moral convictions from the public forum leads to a truncated politics by foreclosing on a democratic space where citizens can articulate their actual positions, expose their differences, and test their views through the deliberative process.

While leading versions of liberal theory are currently governed by an effort to reconcile the ideals of freedom and equality, liberalism may remain, in the end, a politics of individual self-interest, dressed up to look like the interests of all. This at any rate is the conclusion that seems to issue from Denys Turner's critique of neo-liberal politics: that latter-day followers of Locke, Mill and Berlin do little more than put an acceptable face on a social reality whose ugliness was already brutally exposed by Hobbes. Hobbes plays a crucial role in Turner's analyis as a proto-Thatcherite who, with much greater lucidity than Thatcher herself, sees that the naked pursuit of self-interest not only licences an untrammelled market but also – if the destructive effects of this pursuit are to be curbed – justifies absolute state power. The only alternative to the Hobbesian prescription, Turner suggests, is the very one that the liberal-pluralist ethic disallows: an acknowledgement of commonalities that are deeper than consciously projected self-interest and more substantial than a mere agreement to disagree.

For Turner it is Plato – or rather 'Fergal O' Connor's Plato' – who offers the most powerful vision of this alternative. The image of the Cave in the *Republic* is political, symbolising a systematically structured state of illusion endemic to a whole society. This is Plato's own Athenian society undergoing a transition from traditionally accredited norms to a new abstract cosmopolitanism; but, in Turner's reading, it is our society too. Plato's chief targets were the sophists, 'modernisers' unencumbered by commitment to any truth that might get in the way of convenient accommodation and the free flow of commodities and ideas. And Turner remains similarly suspicious of contemporary neutralists – of modern or 'postmodernist' hue – who put moral issues beyond the pale of rational discussion. For him, their refusal to countenance any moral foundations does not detract from the fact that the capitalist market remains the foundation of our actual society – and that its actual effects belie their own benign rhetoric.

Whether or not one agrees with Turner's diagnosis of modern capitalist society, one fact stands out in this kind of society: the existence of widespread inequality. In Ireland some 15.3 per cent of the population live in 'human poverty', according to the United Nations *Human Development Report* for 1999. However this category is defined, the glaring contrasts between rich and poor are there for anyone to see on the streets of our capital city and around the country. 'Inequality', John Baker writes, 'is as obvious as the pubs and Georgian streetscapes … a striking part of the background of our lives'. And taken almost entirely for granted. But inequality, he observes, is not a fact of nature, but a human creation, something we can redress if we have the will, and, first of all, the imagination.

Can we imagine an Ireland without inequality? Baker's essay sketches the main lines of what an egalitarian society would look like. It would be a society in which everyone's basic needs are met; everyone has equal respect; current massive inequalities in income and wealth are compressed; there is legal and political equality; and relations of domination and oppression among social groups are undone. Full equality may be far off, but for Baker it is not a utopian ideal. Ireland could be a much more equal society long before it became a fully equal one. We can fight for degrees of equality along the way, starting with provision for people's basic rights and most urgent needs, moving to such objectives as toleration of difference, basic income for all, worker participation, extensions of democracy, protections against discrimination. At the core of this project, for Baker, are groups of women, disabled people, Travellers, gays and lesbians, unemployed people, political activists, and some voices from the areas of religion and the media. Politics, the economy and education are the three key sites in which such groups operate. But equality, Baker insists 'is not the business of any one group of people in one area of life. It is the business of us all.'

In arguing the case for equality (or some other account of justice) there is a standard assumption that justice is universal and impartial in the sense of requiring social goods – liberties, opportunities, rights, and material goods – to be distributed on the same basis to all. Justice focuses on what is common to human beings (or citizens of this or that polity) rather than what divides us. Differences of race, culture, creed, class, gender, and so on, are regarded as irrelevant from a moral point of view. For purposes of law and politics, therefore, they are put out of court. But there are growing claims, made in the name of justice, for at least some differences to be taken into account. Respect for people, it is claimed, involves respect for them as the people they are – bearers of particular cultural/social identities. This claim raises issues that that are now widely discussed in the currently fashionable literature on multiculturalism, or the politics of difference. But it was feminist reflections on justice, since roughly the 1960s (second-wave feminism), that opened and developed the seam of work now more widely taken up in this literature.

In her essay Maeve Cooke lays out the main lines of argument that have gone into the making of one powerful strand of feminist critique of the received universalist view of justice. Cooke notes that an important question in this feminist debate is whether the struggle to end women's oppression should emphasise what women have in common with men or should focus instead on women's 'distinctiveness' as bearers of a different 'feminine' experience or even 'nature'. The first approach is a basis for the political objectives of equal opportunities, entitlements and rights. The second approach leads to a more contextual understanding of equality, with the general political aim of achieving recognition of feminine difference. The problem of how, if at all, to reconcile the demands of universality with attention to concrete difference emerges as urgent and difficult to resolve.

Cooke examines the background and argumentative strategy of one promising feminist response to the problem. This response focuses on the procedures that govern participation by socially embedded individuals (and groups) in moral-political debate about justice. Given a fair process for arriving at social norms and principles, outcomes are deemed fair or valid even though they may not be the product of a universal consensus. Cooke points out that there is a price to be paid for taking a procedural approach. If the morality of claims depends on the validity of the way of reaching a decision, any idea that the validity of a moral view rests on its grounds is undermined. What is lost by this move is a dimension of criticism addressed to the grounds of moral claims. Consequently, the capacity for moral, social and political criticism, and for moral insight, is considerably weakened. This must be a serious concern for feminists who write on behalf of the disadvantaged and oppressed. Cooke leaves us not with a solution but a better picture of the challenge facing a feminist theory of justice: how to retain the universalist ideas of liberty and equality while acknowledging the concrete demands of context and particular needs, but in a way that retains possibilities for moral insight and critique.

Debates about justice and its implications have traditionally been 'anthropocentric', focused entirely on obligations between human beings. But clearly we have some obligations in respect of the non-human world also. How are we to understand our obligation to protect the environment? And how does such an obligation fit in with human reasons and interests? These are the questions raised in John Barry's analysis of green politics. Radical greens reject anthropocentrism in favour of an 'ecocentric' world-view that privileges protection of the environment over human uses of it. Barry criticises this position and proposes an idea of ecological stewardship as a way of combining responsibility for nature with human concerns. In laying out this idea Barry argues that steward-ship is best understood and cultivated as a disposition of character, a matter of sensitivity to the non-human world that does not lapse into romanticism. This virtue-ethics approach is not about attempting to get a technological 'fix' on human-nature relations, thereby 'solving' or eliminating our problems. It is about coping and adapting to the contingencies and uncertainties of our condition. 'A proper regard for the non-human world would be one that is scientifically informed but also leaves room for emotional attachments to particular ecosystems, land forms, species or individual animals.' Like several of the other contributors to this volume, Barry sees the expansion of participatory democracy as the key institutional development for supporting the attitudes and practices of a desirable social transformation. 'Green citizenship becomes a way of transforming urban dwellers into ecological stewards, giving those who have no direct experience of nature some responsibility for managing the relationship between society and the environment.'

As we move from the world of political ideas to the world of institutions and public policy the issues that arise have to do with understanding the interplay of political forces, interests and processes that influence the generation and implementation of policy. These become matters of lively debate when reform of decision-making processes is seen as necessary. The next four essays give us analyses of some of the dynamics operating in public policy-making and business culture. Philip Pettit examines why imprisonment remains the chief response to crime in many western democracies despite the well-established fact that prisons do not serve the cause of combating crime. He argues that reform in this area is blocked by 'the scandal machine' which makes political judgment the hostage of public outrage. This operates as 'an invisible foot' ensuring that there can be no move away from the pattern of unproductive imprisonment that dominates our current response to crime. The solution Pettit offers is to 'depoliticise'. Gag the politicians and entrust the decisions to non-political bodies of expert and impartial committees. This kind of solution may seem 'undemocratic'. Not so, Pettit argues, at least if we accept what he calls a critical or contestatory theory of democracy. The kernel of this theory is that what matters for democracy is not essentially where public decisions come from, but that the people retain the ability to make an effective challenge to those decisions. If we agree with this view, a proposal for the depoliticisation of penal policy need not be ruled out in principle as undemocratic. Taking decisions away from politicians need not lessen the people's power.

From the late 1950s the Irish state pursued a more or less explicit social democratic vision, actively intervening in the management of the economy and extending schemes for social welfare. In the 1970s and 1980s it became clear that the vision had failed to deliver steady economic growth and high rates of employment, and the New Right emerged to challenge its coherence. New Right protagonists pointed to the failure as evidence of social democracy's fundamentally flawed understanding of the state's capacity. They wanted us to see that those who directly control the state, or work for it, have an interest in expanding its activities beyond its indispensable role in sustaining law and order. Interest groups willingly collude with this ambition and are rewarded with dispensations from the rigours of market discipline. As a consequence economic inefficiencies multiply, the economy stagnates, welfare bureaucracies trap a growing underclass in poverty, and the public suffers.

The civil service, which plays so important a role in the formulation and implementation of policy, must be a major villain in this story. Frank Litton in his essay criticises two powerful analyses that support this belief. He finds they have too limited a view of the possible motivations of interest groups and civil service policy-makers. He argues that the interaction between interest groups and policy-makers can, at least in some circumstances, be the pursuit of the common good. However, this is the case only provided the institutions for policy-making allow the necessary motivations. This analysis has an obvious bearing on present efforts to reform the public service which have their source in New Right critiques.

Ireland has escaped from the economic doldrums, its fiscal crisis surmounted and its unemployment problems pretty well resolved. How and why the Celtic tiger emerged remains a matter for debate. It is, to say the least, highly likely that changes in the pattern of public policy-making played an essential role. To be sure, the play of economic interests constrains and directs public policy. But since 1987 a succession of national agreements has altered the way the 'game' is played. Partnership, at national and local levels, exercises an increasingly important role in the formulation of policy. Without this, policies sustaining present economic success would not have gained the necessary support. This development, widely recognised as one of the most significant initiatives in public policy-making in Europe, is the subject of Rory O'Donnell's essay.

O'Donnell examines the problems encountered in making partnership work and argues that the solutions are to be found by recognising the novelty of what is happening in Ireland. The fact that we moved from a pluralist free-for-all to a more structured process of interest group interaction with government is not unusual. Other states have moved in the same direction, supplementing pluralist politics with neo-corporatist institutions. The Irish move is distinctive both because of the range of interests it includes and the scope of the problems it addresses. Its efforts to resolve conflicts about the distribution of the national product in a manner that does not inhibit further growth are joined by concern to overcome problems of social exclusion that deny substantial numbers an equitable share. Novel institutional arrangements and pragmatic problem-oriented understandings can be discerned which may presage a new design for democracy in Ireland.

Ireland is now an industrialised, largely urbanised, society, a fully fledged member of the world capitalist order. But the character of its business culture has hardly received the attention its merits. In his essay Fergus Armstrong examines that culture. He finds that it has much in common with what prevails in the Anglo-American business world, with heavy emphasis on the value of a company as it is assessed in capital markets. This encourages a short-term perspective and rewards deal-making as assets are primed for market trading. Both these characteristics are well matched to long-established traits in Irish culture. But this way of conducting business has come under increasing criticism in the US and the UK where it has been observed that directors' and managers' obsession with accounting profit all too often lead them to overlook other elements essential to the long-term prosperity of their companies. A shift in corporate ethos is required which would replace a conception of the company as (in Tony Blair's words) 'a mere vehicle for the capital market to be traded, bought and sold as a commodity' by a vision of it as 'a community or partnership in which each employee has a stake, and where the company's responsibilities are more clearly delineated'.

The search is on for new forms of company governance that would achieve a better balance between all the stakeholders – the employees and customers as well as the shareholders. Armstrong argues that the proposals so far are an inadequate answer to the problem. And his essay is an attempt to develop a better understanding of what constitutes a humanly rewarding endeavour and the relationships that sustain it – whatever the inescapable tensions between this reward and the profit imperative.

In the final essay Austin Flannery OP brings us back to the occasion of this volume: the engagement of a priest in teaching political philosophy – and thus inevitably in politics. Ask people now in their twenties or thirties for their views on priests and politics. The chances are that – if they have any views – they are negative. To pose the question seems to invite return to a past when religious observance was well-nigh universal and the church was closely intertwined with the state, its teachings accepted without question as the default norms of the whole society. This past seems now to be truly a 'foreign country', as substantial numbers practise no religion, give little heed to church teachings, and view the church's declining authority and status as a welcome liberation.

To see the question of the 'Priest in Politics' in this light, however, is to take far too narrow a perspective. It is to concede too much to present prejudices and specifically Irish experience – and to ignore much that has been positive in this experience. Flannery explores the question in a much wider context, showing how experiences of the church across the world have encouraged an understanding very different from that suggested by the parochial, and temporary, condition of post-independence Ireland. He examines how the church now understands its relation with the state and demonstrates how it has opened space for a new stance by clergy and laity. The church has always been concerned, for example, with the poor. But whereas its efforts were once directed to bettering their lot it is now concerned with changing the structures that cause poverty – a concern that can hardly avoid bringing it into conflict with established political authority. Flannery explores the implications of this move – and in doing so throws light on an important part of the context in which Fergal O'Connor found his orientation as a political philosopher.

All the essays have been specially written for this volume, ten by former students of Fergal's, two by former colleagues of his at UCD, and one by a close Dominican confrere. The book is presented to him with admiration, affection, and appreciation of all that he has contributed by his teaching in the university, his more public voice in the media, and the example of his work for disadvantaged groups. Differences among the various contributors will make it clear that agreement – either with each other or with Fergal – has not been our aim. And we realise in advance that the book will have no more acute critic than the man to whom it is dedicated. Still, it will have achieved its purpose if it reflects even a small portion of his intellectual passion and of the depth of his critical concern for our society and politics.

CHAPTER 1

Figures of the Teacher:
Fergal O'Connor and Socrates

Joseph Dunne

I t is a source of regret to Fergal O'Connor that in contemporary discussions, in the media and elsewhere, fascination with 'personalities' has so much displaced critical analysis of issues. If this essay, then, focuses a fair bit on Fergal himself I hope it may escape his strictures to the extent that in doing so it also seeks to explore an 'issue' that has been of special concern to him: the nature of teaching. The best approach in analysing human affairs, according to Aristotle, is not to prescribe how things should be done on the basis of some prior formula but rather, having consulted our experience of best practice, to forge concepts that do justice to the exemplars of excellence with which we are already familiar. If you want to understand practical wisdom, attend less to a treatise on the subject than to a person who is practically wise – the most worthwhile treatise in any case will be the one that best captures the quality of such a person. Similarly with the case of teaching: if you are lucky enough to have had a good teacher then you are better placed to say what good teaching is.

Well, for me, like very many others fortunate enough to have attended his courses in political philosophy at UCD, Fergal's greatness as a teacher is indisputable, the impact of his lectures unforgettable. And so the reflection on teaching I shall present here arises out of memories of him in his element in the old Earlsfort Terrace (to be made a venue for music was not the worst imaginable fate for that dear place). As an avowed Platonist of course, Fergal will find little comfort in thus being made grist for an Aristotelian mill. But philosophical justice may be served by the fact that his main company in the following pages will be that of Plato's Socrates. He and Socrates throw an interesting light on each other; and both together, as I hope to show, do much to enlarge and enliven our understanding of a teacher's calling.

Back to the lecture hall

In introducing us to the great figures of political philosophy, Fergal eschewed the conventional role of first presenting their views and then offering dispassionate assessment of their merits and weaknesses. When he lectured on Hobbes, he *was* Hobbes, unleashing the full power of the latter's thought and defending it against allcomers. The disconcerting effect was realised only later when, now that many of us had become convinced Hobbesians, Fergal metamorphosed before our eyes in the next set of lectures as Rousseau, the human world now being reconfigured so that only Jean-Jacques truly divined its secrets. When, later again, Rousseau suffered the earlier fate of Hobbes, and newly enthusiastic Rousseauians were exposed to the unrelenting force of Hegel's social vision, Fergal's sorcery was in full view and the question of what *he* thought had become acute. But if we were now gripped by a desire to know his mind – that many other teachers might have envied and been only too eager to gratify – Fergal was not about to provide ready answers. What really mattered – a hard learning, perhaps for the first time in our whole education – was what *we* thought.

Not that Fergal's inscrutability was in the service of a studentcentred pedagogy for which 'thinking for oneself' could be a sufficient goal. He was indeed adept at eliciting our immediate prejudices and understandings, but only so that they could be tested by exposure to the master whose mask he had temporarily assumed; the whole point of being introduced to a succession of great thinkers, after all, was to have one's own thinking stretched or deepened, or sometimes overturned, by theirs. Fergal's exposition of the ideas of these thinkers was extraordinarily lucid, won by long hours of patient study (*un*blear-eyed wisdom out of midnight oil) but also fruit of a mind natively sinuous and uncluttered. 'Exposition', however, is not quite the right word here. For Fergal's way of opening up classic texts enabled him at the same time to scrutinise current issues and prevailing assumptions in their light. Far from distracting from the texts, this scrutiny served only to confirm their continuing interpretative and critical power; to read these texts with Fergal was at the same time to be read *by* them.

His doctoral dissertation had been on Aquinas's understanding of the role of imagination as the crucial hinge between perception and feeling ('sense') on one side and concept and argument ('intellect') on the other. And the imaginativeness of his own teaching enabled the perceptions and feelings of students to become less blind (to paraphrase another philosopher, Kant) in the act of his showing that the concepts and arguments of the philosophers were not empty. The young followers of Socrates had been both perplexed and captivated by his way of raising the deepest questions about human existence while still talking about 'pack asses, or blacksmiths, or cobblers, or tanners' (Plato, 1989, 221 E). And Fergal's thought retained a similar footing in the 'life-world': in his lectures, Plato's allegory of the cave or Rousseau's concept of *amour propre* or Hegel's analysis of the master-slave dialectic shared mental space with references to fashions in student clothing, a row in Fianna Fáil, an ongoing strike by a group of workers, a pending piece of legislation, or a recent judgment in the courts. Such were these juxtapositions – or rather inter-penetrations – that it was hard to say which was more brilliantly illuminated: the universal reach of the present event or the very particular saliency of the classic text.

The 'lectures' in which all this went on were immensely lively, even theatrical. The drama of ideas in which students got caught up owed its momentum to the peculiar, and in some respects paradoxical, gifts of the teacher. Although politics is inevitably about power – who has it and for what – he seemed happy to give away whatever power lay in his position as lecturer (he frequently offered the lectern to anyone who would propose a counter-position) and to rely only on the power of the better argument. Though bound to the disciplines of a religious order, he seemed to have the freest, most unfettered mind in the university. He delighted in argument and was fearless in provoking it, goading and teasing his listeners – usually in direct proportion to their complacency and cocksure-ness. Still, the sharpness of his dialectical rapier never took away from his gentleness; he had no need to hurt. And while irony pervaded a great deal of what he said, he never seemed cynical. To the contrary, his thinking was generous, not only in the sympathy it brought to his chosen authors but also in the imaginative vistas it opened up; the sting most often lay in the dawning sense of how much less we are than what we might be.

For all the personal gifts that made Fergal's style so attractive, there was a rigorous impersonality in his teaching. Irony served him as a mode of self-effacement, of directing attention to the texts and, beyond them, to the truth of the matter – ultimately the truth about us as humans – with which they were concerned. Winning us over to the point of view of his chosen authors, however, was not Fergal's purpose in expounding them. For, despite the clarity of his presentation and the flair of his defence of a specific text, his espousal of it could always be subverted by his subsequent partisanship on behalf of *another* text. Long before the word had made its appearance, then, 'deconstruction' – indirect and cumulative – was part of his pedagogical arsenal: apparently well-earned positions broke down and thinking became 'disseminated' in an ongoing movement of 'deferral'. Still, Fergal's teaching was different from what has come to be practised under the rubric of decon-struction. For the latter, the act of unmasking, or of showing every reading to be necessarily a misreading, is enough; since texts can be about nothing except other texts, the energy of endless deferral can be taken as its own end. This taboo on any reference by texts to a reality beyond themselves, which they might be *about,* is also a disavowal of truth; texts no longer make truth-claims which constrain a reader's assent or challenge him or her to justify dissent. Deprived, then, of their own truth-claims, texts are also displaced as realities about which interpretations might, or might not, be true. Under the rule of 'intertextuality', and freed from the tyranny of truth, interpretations can succeed just by proving themselves interesting or inventive. Now Fergal's own interpretations were never less than interesting or inventive – the playfulness and mobility of his mind enabled him to conjure up and entertain hugely disparate ideas and perspectives. But playfulness was never a substitute for pursuing truth; it was, rather, the most fruitful way of making this pursuit.

While Fergal's commitment to a truth to be pursued distinguished him from exponents of deconstruction, his playfulness distinguished him no less from zealous custodians of a truth already achieved. There was no trace of a hectoring tone in his teaching nor even of – what some might have regarded as a proper – earnestness. Instead, a lightness of touch and ease in banter bespoke something of that 'joyful kind of seriousness and that wisdom full of roguishness' that Nietzsche sees as the 'finest state of the human soul' (Nietzsche, 1986, p. 332). Indeed our responses to Fergal seemed to confirm another of Nietzsche's sayings (in oblique allusion to Socrates): that 'nothing better or happier can befall a person than to be in the proximity of one of those who, precisely because they have thought most deeply, must love what is most alive' (Nietzsche, 1984, p. 136). His combination of neither appearing to have designs on what we *should* think nor of being threatened by what we *did* think dissipated resistance; with him, stereotyped reaction against authority-figures did not get its usual purchase. Not that we didn't react strongly, sometimes fiercely, to what he said – given the frequent outrageousness of his baiting, how could we not have done so? But this reaction had none of the indifference or sullenness of withdrawal. It was rather an expression of engagement, evidence of being already 'hooked'. And here was no trivial gamesmanship on Fergal's part but rather something that he saw as indispensable to the teacher's role: the arousal (in Plato's words) of *eros* in a student's soul. This *eros* is a desire for understanding, which may eventually become that love of wisdom which is not only a prelude to but rather (as etymology attests) the very heart of philosophy itself.

Negative dialectics

Fergal took it from Aquinas that the intellect, being in harmony with reality, is naturally fitted for the pursuit of truth. But if this picture suggests an ultimately secure goal for the human mind it by no means indicates that its essential task can be immediately or easily accomplished. According to the early Greek philosopher, Heracleitus, 'nature loves to hide' – an idea which gave rise to the conception of truth as an unconcealment brought about only through a process of outwitting what otherwise escapes notice. In one form or another, this notion of truth, not as given to immediate apprehension but as the prize of an arduous quest, has been deeply embedded in western thought. It is reflected for instance in the notion of dialectic, as the process through which the mind is extended and tested in a back and forth movement towards knowledge, first elaborated by Plato. It still echoes in Aquinas's own mode of inquiry, which proceeds only through recurrently posing and then unpicking difficulties or 'objections' that arise at every turn, as well as in Hegel's account of the reconciliation between 'subject' and 'object' as achieved only through the cumulative overcoming of contradictions along the way. It is found also in thinkers who attend less to the explicit content of their writing than to the difficulty of any straightforward communication of this content to their readers. While these are less systematic thinkers, they are also more self-consciously pedagogical, even therapeutic. Their mode of address is complicated by their sense that if what they have to say is true then *ipso facto* their readers may not be well disposed to receive it. And so there are the strategies and ruses of Kierkegaard's mode of 'indirect communication': 'One can deceive a person for the truth's sake, and – to recall old Socrates – one can deceive a person into the truth. Indeed, it is only by this means, i.e. by deceiving him, that it is possible to bring to the truth one who is in illusion' (Kierkegaard, 1962, pp. 39-40). Or there is the unsettling angle of Witttgenstein's writing, as an exercise in conceptual therapy, an attempt to break the 'bewitchment' of thought by language or, in his striking metaphor, 'to show the fly the way out of the fly-bottle' (Wittgenstein, 1973, 309). And, unsurprisingly, these styles of writing find strong equivalents in oral practices: for example the dialectical traps and ironic dissimulations through which Socrates is supposed to have led on his interlocutors or, in the psychoanalytic exchange, the tactical struggles of the analyst in attempting to outmanoeuvre the 'resistances' of the client.

If, in all these cases, Socrates is the original – and still exemplary – figure, this is because the kind of knowledge they involve is the one that he first canonised in the West: *self*-knowledge. Here the nature that 'loves to hide' is our own; and so gaining insight into it calls for a form of instruction and learning that is nothing less than a *psyches therapeia,* a practice of caring for the soul. This practice is characterised by a strong element of negativity, manifest in both method and content. In method it appears in the oppositional nature of dialectic, in the fact that the path is neither linear nor smooth but advances only by confronting mistakes, problems, objections, tensions and conflicts – and by correcting, resolving or overcoming them. And it appears too in a pedagogical approach that values unlearning more than learning – or rather that sees precisely in unlearning the most important form of learning. What has to be unlearned is the 'knowledge' we suppose ourselves already to possess and that is all the more debilitating – and difficult to dislodge – just in so far as our possession of it (or rather its possession of us) hides from us our need to search for what better deserves to be called knowledge. Hence the intention of Socrates' pedagogy was not that students should acquire his knowledge but rather that they should come to recognise their own ignorance. It was not indeed clear that Socrates credited even himself with any knowledge higher than this clear-eyed acknowledgement of ignorance – an acknowledgement that was in any case valuable for his interlocutors precisely in so far as it freed them from the tyranny of false or half-baked ideas and gave them, instead of their mistaken sense of already possessing truth, a greater keenness in *searching for* it.

⸱ The negativity of this method resides not only in the paradoxical character of its outcome – a truthful state of ignorance rather than a deceived state of knowledge – but also in the pain that is inseparable from it as a process. Aeschylus had spoken of 'learning through suffering' as Shakespeare would speak of knowledge making 'a bloody entrance'. And while Socratic pedagogy, insulated as it was within a virtual arena of speech, fell short of the tragic exposures of lived experience, it was still people's live convictions – and not any merely academic opinions they might hold – that were put to the test when they were exposed to Socrates' questioning. The pressure to shed these convictions, and implicitly to admit the gullibility that had allowed one to entertain them, could only be painful. It was not for nothing that Socrates had characterised himself as a gadfly constantly exciting an itch, nor was it surprising that the discomfort of this itch to his fellow countrymen should eventually have driven them to bring charges against him that were to cost him his life. For what one was being forced to relinquish, often enough, was not only particular views but a whole posture of mind that had made one vulnerable to these views in the first place. Rather than being easily detachable from oneself, such a posture can seem to constitute one's very self or, as we say, to confer one's identity.

It is perhaps evidence enough of Fergal's Socratic credentials that on at least one occasion a member of the Oireachtas publicly denounced him as a corrupting influence on young minds, just as a bishop attempted more discreetly to have him banished from the airwaves when memorable appearances on the 'Late Late Show' had extended the spirit of his seminars to the living rooms of the nation. I mentioned above, though, a negativity not only of method but also of content; and I still need to say something about how the latter, too, was manifest in Fergal's teaching. Here it is not only a matter of the implicit negations of positions he had earlier seemed to support, which we have already seen to follow from his espousal – rather than simple exposition – of each consecutive figure who appeared on his syllabus. Nor is it only a matter of his systematic dissent from whatever views appeared at the time to be dominant – so that, while he might have been taken for a 'liberal' in his earlier years as a teacher, when liberal pieties ('freedom', 'rights', 'tolerance') themselves became orthodox, both in the academy and the media, they too became targets of his critique. This dissent was linked to what seemed an instinctive distrust of 'public opinion' (or the 'great beast' as Plato called it [Plato, 1979, 493]). But the distrust in turn was only a consequence of deeper intuitions about the kind of creatures we are, or what lies in 'human nature' itself.

Insistent in Fergal's teaching, at any rate, was a note of deflation. To be sure, attendance at his lectures could be a heady experience and as students we were not mistaken to pick up, and often to be fired by, an emancipatory impetus in his words. But this impetus did not derive from any neo-Pelagian (or 'Californian') conviction about our irrefragable goodness. In his class one could not forget that it was human beings – 'enlightened' human beings of the twentieth century – who were agents of the Holocaust and the Gulag. The extremity of these evils was not allowed to distract from the fact that we ourselves might be capable of them, as we were in any case caught up in the pettiness and foibles of the ordinary human scene. In disabusing us of any facile utopianism, Fergal was of course helped by the particular authors whose voices he so effortlessly assumed: Hobbes on the rapaciousness generated by an elemental fear, Rousseau on the vanity – and potential for violence – implicit in the comparative basis of our self-esteem and, perhaps most of all, Plato (especially through the characters of Thrasymachus and Callicles in the *Republic* and the *Gorgias*) on the thinness of the veneer of 'morality' and the strength of unreformed egoism and will to power often lurking beneath it.

But, as I have already intimated, Fergal's real force as a teacher lay in his ability not so much to expound these authors as to show the terrible plausibility of their respective accounts: their plausibility, that is to say, precisely as accounts of *ourselves* and of our many twisted ways of relating with each other.

Despite the darkness of these pictures it was often a comic note that prevailed in Fergal's classes. This created space for the intimacy of the pictures to strike home – for us to realise that they were really mirrors in which to catch our own image. The fact that our frequent laughter was not at the expense of others perhaps freed it from knowing superiority. But how, on the other hand – if it carried the smack of such chastening self-recognition – did it avoid being the expression of disillusionment or defeat? Corrosive cynics who know the value of nothing or no one – including students – are not unknown in universities, and how was Fergal not one of them? How was his *via negativa* not a path to nihilism?

The search for the good

As we have already seen, deconstruction – or to use his own term, criticism – did not amount, in Fergal's hands, to a denial of truth; rather its intention was, in exposing counterfeits, to quicken a search for what is genuine. The distinction that holds here is the Platonic one between *seeming* or mere appearance and the real. It is our own propensity to be taken in by appearances – the fact that 'humankind cannot bear very much reality' – that imposes the rigours of dialectical search. The latter is undertaken, then, in the service of truth and not as a demonstration of its unattainability. The affirmative stance that energised the negative movement of thought did not lie only in an inclination towards truth, however. I have spoken already of an *eros* in the soul that, when awakened, drives us in the pursuit of truth. But in Fergal's Platonic perspective truth is not the ultimate source of attraction nor does it, on its own, arouse this *eros*. What does? The answer is: the good – which itself cannot in the end be separated from the beautiful. The ultimate question for such beings as ourselves is not 'how or what can we know?' but rather 'how shall we live?' – which entails not only 'how should we act?' but what 'kind of persons should we become and what kind of society should we create?' It is the 'good' that presides over these questions, drawing us on to search for answers to them. We are committed to truth in so far as we desire these answers to be adequate. More generally, searching for and finding the truth (about non-human matters, too) is our good as intellectual beings.

With regard to the good, two contrasting factors have to be held together: on the one hand its power – magnified by the allure of a beauty that attends it – to draw us ever onwards, beyond where we are now; and on the other hand the fact that even where we are now – wherever that may be – we are *already* in the grip of the good. Let us get some grounding here by first looking at the latter of these two factors. What it reveals is the ordinariness, one might say the democracy, of the good – its non-confinement to an elite, intellectual or otherwise. All of us are well attuned to it, at least in some areas of our lives: we may like a good steak, enjoy a good 'pint', appreciate finely-cut clothes or a well-designed house, admire a brilliant footballer or a virtuoso fiddler. In these and similar cases – some firmly embedded in our lives, others more discretionary – we exercise choice or judgment: but only as drawn towards, or even compelled by, standards whose power of attracting or of binding does not derive from the mere fact that they accord with our taste. Rather, they enshrine the good, and the judgment we ourselves have – or are educated to acquire – is itself good just in so far as it accords with *them*. Many disparate domains, then, exhibit this structure of a 'good' and, correlatively, of a bad or indifferent. But beyond all these separate domains – or, rather, by and through our judgments, choices, and actions in and across all of them – we enact a whole life which is similarly exposed to evaluation with respect to the good. The shape and burden of our lives is such that, no matter how reflective or unreflective we may be, we cannot avoid an overall pattern of preference or aversion that betrays some notion of the human good. As human beings we must have *some* bearings in relation to this good. It is these bearings that orientate us in moral space, determining what matters to us or what we care about, as well as what we despise or find abhorrent. Just as, bodily, we would be radically disorientated without some sense of front and behind or above and below so, without these bearings, we would be no less disorientated as persons in moral – that is to say human – space.

A concern with the good, then, if only as what keeps us going in times of difficulty or despondency, is universal and inescapable. And yet, for Socrates, it is only too possible for people to be most exacting in their requirements regarding, for example, a horse or a saddle or, more personally, a dietary regime – and still to be careless with regard to the overall pattern of their lives. Not that this pattern could avoid revealing *some* conception of the human good; but this may be a distorted or false conception. We are prone then to be both mistaken about and heedless of our own true good. And so Socrates' understanding of his role as a teacher was to instruct people about, and to arouse in them a concern for, this good. His role was paradoxical, however, in that he disavowed being a teacher or having any instruction to offer. The image of himself he offered instead – following his mother's profession – was that of a midwife. His function was only to help people – his friends, fellow citizens or just anyone who cared to join in his conversations – to bring forth and nurture something that was already potentially alive in themselves: a susceptibility to, or weakness for, the good.

Here, then, we touch on the other aspect of the good – its reality less as an immediate presence than as a horizon of aspiration, an ever-receding vista that draws us on. To a great extent the world we inhabit is ruled by necessity and not by the good; and between these two poles there is an 'infinite distance' (Weil, 1976, p. 142; Plato, 1979, 293C). 'Necessity' here connotes not just the blind and impersonal forces through which, for example, diseases or natural disasters are visited on human beings. It also includes a kind of entropy in the human world itself, whether in horribly predictable regularities of oppression suffered by whole groups, or in random afflictions that blight the lives of many scattered individuals. It comes to reside in the logic of social structures and institutions (for example, the market), dictating their survival in spite of casual cruelties they inflict or high social costs they exact. And it can become a form of rationalisation – a cover for expediency and violence – that presents itself as unblinking recognition of the workings of 'the real world'. Given the strong entrenchment of this necessity, then, the good becomes fragile, having to work against a constant gravitational pull. And yet, however fragile, the good maintains its own counter-attraction – which has perhaps never been more starkly expressed than in Socrates' proposition: 'it is better to suffer evil than to inflict it'.

Several points follow from this way of seeing the good. First, it involves an always problematic dialectic between an individual and his or her society. On the one hand it is within individual souls that a sensitivity to the good must be awakened, a point all the time made by Socrates both in the highly individuated way in which he lived his own life and through the directly personal way in which he related to each of his interlocutors. On the other hand Socrates was first and last a citizen of Athens, a city to which he committed his life and at the hands of which he did not try to escape death. Both Plato and Aristotle take their cue from Socrates in seeing ethics as inseparable from politics, that is to say in seeing the good life not as something to be achieved in isolation but as requiring a community held together by a shared ethos which animates its laws and institutions. By following these Greek thinkers Fergal found himself at odds with contemporary 'liberals' who deem pursuit of the good to be only the private affair of individuals, while the polity must (as it were by 'necessity') resign itself to a lower-level neutrality undisrupted by conflict between rival versions of the good. From a Platonic perspective the good cannot be thus confined; and liberal politics, just like any politics, will itself willy-nilly enshrine *its* version – an inadequate one, as it must seem to a Platonist. The inadequacy derives from the fact that as an individual one cannot realise the good on one's own, since community is not external to or imposed on one but rather already implicit in one's very reality as a person.

If Fergal was not a liberal, neither was he a 'communitarian' – at least not of the type that provides an easy target for liberal critics. For he did not believe that any society could be secure enough in its possession of the good to be entitled to define it pre-emptively for individual members. The ever-present threat of authoritarianism – no less than the danger that this 'good' would anyhow be distorted – distanced him from enthusiasts for established *Gemeinschaft*. Still, as I have just suggested, his love of liberty – his instinctive recoil from coercion in any matter really concerning the spirit – did not make him a 'liberal'. For privatising the good, in his view, was only too likely to remove it from the arena of rational discussion and thus to reduce it to the *fiat* of individual preference. And the beneficiaries, all too predictably, of this moral *laissez faire*, he believed, will be the strong and powerful at the expense of the weak and vulnerable. What distinguished him from *both* liberals and communitarians, then, was his commitment to the search for the good. Indeed for him this search was not just a path towards the good but was rather already at least partly constitutive of it: 'The good life for man is the life spent in seeking for the good life' (MacIntyre, 1984, p. 219). It was in the nature of this search, for Fergal as for Socrates, that it could best be conducted not on one's own but with others. And if one were to ask what education is for Fergal, I believe the precise answer would be: the conduct by teacher and students together of this search for the good.

Education despite the university

It follows from all this that Fergal saw the university (or at least the *good* university) as a space in which each student could raise fundamental questions for herself or himself, with the great advantage of being able to do so *with* others, *and* in which the society to which they all belonged – and to which they owed some obligation just in virtue of being beneficiaries of a university education – could be subjected to thoroughgoing critique. Fergal went on pursuing this understanding of a university in his own practice even as it became increasingly clear that the university's actual role in society was becoming that of just another industry governed by the logic of 'the bottom line' – as, for individual students, enhancement of their prospects in a competitive economy was becoming the overwhelming purpose of their education. As a place increasingly devoted to efficient dissemination of information within ever narrower and more fragmented specialisms, the university had become an inhospitable space for Fergal's kind of educative practice – all the more so when the radicalism of those in the Humanities most likely to be critics of this debasement had often succumbed to a postmodernist rhetoric that was itself more a symptom than a critique of 'late capitalism'. But what *was* this practice and how, against such odds, did he sustain it? The answer to the first of these questions makes the answer to the second one all the more remarkable. Or rather it shows that Fergal's practice has been even more deeply uncongenial to the reality of a contemporary university than I have thus far made apparent – so that it is something of a miracle that he has sustained it at all.

Fergal's teaching was of course about much more than trans-mitting information. He wanted students to acquire capacities to think rigorously – to follow out the implications of a position or to identify the assumptions lying behind it, to be alert to inconsistencies in argument, to understand the kind of evidential grounds required to justify claims and to recognise whether or not in particular cases they are available. He also wanted our minds to become more adventurous, being carried to unfamiliar places by a free play of ideas, undeterred by fear of novelty or the pressure of immediate 'reality-checking'. And he wanted us, too, to develop interpretative sensitivity, a feel for context, an ability to enter sympathetically into the shaping concerns of individual thinkers and to experience the force of their particular perspectives on the world. He wanted us to become intimate with these thinkers and to see that their ideas *mattered*. By exposing us in a year to several of them he wanted us to be challenged by the conflicts between them and thereby to learn the complexity and many-sidedness of the human condition. But he knew, too, that the result of such exposure can all too easily be the sceptical conclusion that these thinkers simply cancel each other out by their conflicts, leaving nothing to trump the received 'common-sense'; and he wanted us, beyond this, to come to some deep and tested convictions of our own. To be sure these are very ambitious goals, which it might seem portentous to relate to undergraduate teaching. And yet – parochial and literal-minded though most of us undoubtedly were when we entered his class – they really did seem to inspire Fergal's teaching. And of course they were goals that required, intrinsically and not as a mere option, a particular style of pedagogy: one that constantly elicited the voices of students so that they came into play with Fergal's own voice and, through it (and often as indistinguishable from it), with the voices of his chosen philosophers. Following Socrates and Plato he saw thinking as the 'dialogue of the soul with itself'; and like them, too, he saw actual dialogue, live and unscripted with face-to-face others, as the very best medium in which thinking is learned.

But 'learning to think' could never in itself be the sufficient aim of Fergal's teaching. For there was a style of thinking which had beguiled the minds of Socrates' youthful followers and which Socrates himself, with Plato, saw as the lethal enemy of philosophy as the pursuit of wisdom. This was the sophistry – or, in its more combative forms, the eristic – which, transcending the specific densities of particular areas of knowledge, offered itself as a powerful tool for delivering success in *any* area. As masters of the arts of persuasion, sophists could deploy arguments with deadly cleverness and skill – but with success, not truth, as the defining norm of their advocacy. Here dialectic was a weapon to be used – with suitable manipulation of images and appeal to the emotions – to prove whatever case was required. The great sophists were intellectual mercenaries, hired guns who could assure victory in the law-courts, the assembly, or any relevant forum; and of course they are still with us among barristers, spin-doctors and assorted 'consultants'. How then are they to be combated, and how did Socrates as a teacher differ from those teachers of sophistic skills whose dazzling arrival on the scene brought 'enlightenment' to Greece in the fifth century BCE?

The answer here is not the one often attributed to Plato, or rather to the super-rationalist caricature who often goes by that name. It is not by resorting to the watertight syllogisms of a cleanly unimpeded reason – and thus by renouncing as unworthy the realm of images and feelings – that one resists the lure of sophistry. Here we return once again to the *eros* that must come alive in the soul of the learner. 'Soul' has now an effete ring in English. But 'psyche', the Greek word it translates, is not an ethereal entity, the construct of some vapid 'spirituality'. To the contrary, it is rooted in the depths of a person's nature, in the drives and emotions that give energy to one's living and in the images and symbols (and stories) that influence the direction of this energy. For Plato, human beings are creatures of passion. But true passion for him does not lie in a bundle of drives inwardly propelled to already determined satisfactions. It lies rather in a capacity to be seized and moved by something outside and beyond ourselves. And for Plato there is something that is supremely worthy of being seized and moved by: what he called the beautiful and good *(to kalon kagathon)*. To be sure, we may be deceived – perhaps disastrously – about what the beautiful and good consists of, or wherein it resides. But the task of education, as it is depicted in *Republic* VII, is precisely to turn around the 'eye of the soul' so that, undeceived, one is opened to it.

Perhaps the finest image for this task was given to us, long before Plato, by early ancestors on this island: those who created an opening above the entrance at Newgrange through which, for a brief moment at the winter solstice, a ray of sunlight could penetrate to the inner chamber. Seeing in this building a powerful symbol for the construction of the 'new Europe', Vaclàv Havel is led to ask: 'are at least some of the thousands of designers and builders of this edifice thinking of the opening that would connect it with the great beyond – that would infinitely transcend the project, and yet alone could give it true meaning?' (Havel, 1997, p.246). But perhaps we might see the feat of delicate alignment achieved by those ancient builders as an even more appropriate symbol for educators. The opening which corresponds to the 'eye of the soul' is rightly to be located in the intellect, which must break through illusion and orientate us to the good. But this opening has to connect into that patterning of imagination and emotion without which intellect itself (incapable of anything more than a specious cleverness), and will (as nothing more than a brittle agent of self-control), cannot allow the good to penetrate our lives.

From his reading of Plato Fergal must always have been ruefully aware of just how much of this education of sensibility needs already to have occurred long before a student comes to university. But if his own role as a university teacher was (only!) to enable us to understand the good, he was acutely conscious of how much even this understanding depends on the generation of apt images and feelings. I raised the question earlier of what sustained Fergal in this role, especially at a time when the university milieu was increasingly unconducive to its fulfilment. Part of the answer lay in his practice every summer of bathing his mind, so to speak, in poetry and fiction – in texts that bore no necessary relation to the texts he would be teaching that autumn but which by animating *him* would also, he trusted, animate his teaching. Another, similarly oblique, but perhaps even more important, part of the answer lay in the practices he was engaged in outside the academy. Thirty years ago he founded a hostel for homeless girls in Dublin, which he has guided on an almost daily basis ever since. (For some of us, involved in various voluntary capacities, conversation with Fergal into the small hours around the fireside in the hostel seemed to be our *real* university.) For many years, too, he directed the activities of ALLY, an organisation which – again with enthusiastic co-workers – he founded to support single mothers, and which was able to make itself defunct a few years ago because a change in social attitudes and provisions and, not least, the abolition of 'illegitimacy' as a legal category, had lessened the need for its continued existence. Although in his lectures he seldom if ever spoke overtly about any of these extramural activities, they greatly nourished his teaching. For one thing they freed him from the complacency, born of accustomed privilege, that could so easily become part of the academic persona. And they also provided him with the kind of rich staple of experience that he saw as essential to his role as a theorist. For theory, in his understanding of it, is precisely reflection on experience; and it was the experience he acquired in these settings that gave such 'human truth' to his own theorising, that made it so devoid of pedantry or sentimentality, and that brought such luminous vitality to his reading of philosophical texts.

This kind of lived dialogue between theory and practical social engagement provides a counterpoint to what 'research', formal and published, is for many academics. When a public issue seemed to him to demand it, Fergal wrote incisive pieces for periodicals and newspapers – on prison policy, for instance, or church-state relations. Still, writing never seemed to command his devotion. But this too can be taken as a sign of his fidelity to the Platonic spirit. *Written* words are weak, Plato tells us, because they cannot give 'instruction by question and answer'; 'if you ask them what they mean by anything they simply return the same answer over and over again' and so are 'only a kind of shadow' of the 'living and animate speech of the man with knowledge'. The words that really count are those 'spoken by way of instruction or, to use a truer phrase, *written on the soul* of the hearer to enable him to learn about the right, the beautiful and the good' (Plato, 1973, 275-78). If there is irony in our having these words from Plato's masterly pen, they are of course an entirely unironic allusion to Socrates, whose voice echoes down the centuries, though he himself has left us not a single written word.

The example of a good man

As a great practitioner of the art of dialectical instruction Fergal has surely written on many souls. But have we managed yet to disclose the sources that have sustained him in this task? Fergal's own explanation for whatever gifts might be credited to him has always been easy (and delivered with the customary twinkle): he's a Kerryman. But this answer may be good enough only for others fortunate enough to hail from the Kingdom (though it too might claim endorsement from Socrates, who was sensitive to the spirits of a place, being inspired for example on one of his rare departures from Athens to make his great speech on love by the river Ilissus!) One might speculate here on the influence of a father, grandfather and great-grandfather, all of whom were primary teachers, and on a local love of learning tracing back through the hedge-schools and beyond. Or one might look to the inspiration of Dominican teachers in a wider tradition stretching back to Albert and Aquinas. Or, remembering Socrates' attribution of his own education in the love of beauty to Diotima, a wise woman from Mantinea, one might think of the formative influence of women in Fergal's early life – the source perhaps of what has seemed his exceptional gift for quickening the engagement of women students (something that is entirely absent, of course, from the Socratic dialogues).

In the end, though, the only answer here – whatever the obscure biographical sources – may lie simply in the fact of Fergal's own possession by the good. At the close of the *Symposium*, Alcibiades compares the effect of Socrates' conversation with the spell cast on his listeners by the flute-player, Marsyas: 'the only difference between you and Marsyas is that you need no instruments; you do exactly what he does, but with words alone' (Plato, 1989, 215C-D). And he then describes the exasperating discordance between his thoughts when he is in Socrates' company and his mundane sense of things when he is not. Since the only explanation he can find for Socrates' effect lies in Socrates himself, he goes on to evoke the man in the most vivid and impassioned portrait that we have of the great teacher. One of Socrates' qualities that he highlights is the composure and endurance that he himself had seen him display on the battlefields at Potidaea and at Delium. A similar courage, I believe, is revealed in Fergal's way of facing down such severe arthritis as he has made his way in recent years to the lecture hall in Belfield. And I know no one who could more justly appropriate Socrates' words at his trial:

> I care nothing for what most people care about: money-making, administration of property, generalships, success in public debates, magistracies, coalitions, and political factions … I did not choose that path, but rather the one by which I could do the greatest good to each of you in particular: by trying to persuade each of you to concern himself less about what he has than about what he is, so that he make himself as good and as reasonable as possible (Plato, 1983, 36B).

'Writing on the soul' must not be taken to imply, of course, that the soul is passive, as paper is in receiving marks inscribed on it. No one was less in thrall to the transmission (or, in contemporary jargon, the 'delivery') model of learning than Socrates: 'My dear Agathon … if only wisdom were like water, which always flows from a full vessel into an empty one' (Plato, 1989, 175D) – an early statement of the 'jug and mug' theory of education. The very discrepancy between the student-in-construction-with-the-teacher and the student then left to his own devices, that was so painful to Alcibiades (and has since been so discouraging to generations of teachers), is evidence enough that the teacher's efficacy is not as straightforward as that of the pen. I have already mentioned the kind of gravity exerted in the human world by the force of 'necessity'. And Plato's depiction of the soul in Socrates' great second speech in the *Phaedrus* accords with that image. The soul nourished by beauty, goodness and wisdom grows wings which 'have the power to lift up heavy things and raise them aloft where the gods all dwell' (Plato, 1973, 246D). When one reflects on the experience of many students who have experienced a kind of intellectual liftoff in Fergal's classes which they, like Alcibiades, then find it difficult to articulate or 'retain' in other settings, it does not seem too fanciful to think of Fergal's 'wings' as creating a kind of anti-gravity in which others too can take flight. In this different field of force, the perspectives one entertains, the goals that come into view, and the very questions one finds oneself asking, are freer and more expansive. And this soaring effect of his words is all the more remarkable, of course, in one who has remained so firmly rooted in the ordinary. (How many evenings spent with people in various kinds of distress, how many Saturdays in the hostel fixing door locks, radiators or cisterns with his friend Frank – in whom he finds not only the philosopher but the engineer that he himself, had he chosen another path, would have liked to become?)

I promised at the outset to address the 'issue' of teaching. In concluding, I am conscious of not having abstracted any rules or formulae that might define the essence of this practice. But perhaps we already have enough attempts to do just that, to work out 'strategies' for inculcating 'skills' or 'models' for specifying 'outcomes' – all the better to secure standardisation and thereby, as we suppose, success. I make no claim for Fergal or even for Socrates as paradigms of the teaching art – not, in any case, if that means they must be *imitated* by others who wish to become good teachers. If they are exemplary, as surely they both are, it is because they realise possibilities that are proper both to teaching and to themselves. For those of us who are teachers, then, the challenge of their example is to discover *our* possibilities as teachers. 'Perhaps he shares some of his specific accomplishments with others', Alcibiades says of Socrates, towards the end of his famous encomium. 'But, as a whole', he goes on, 'he is unique; he is like no one else in the past and no one in the present – this is by far the most amazing thing about him' (Plato, 1989, 221C). What is claimed here for Socrates I have wanted to claim also for Fergal. But perhaps education is the space where we must claim that, at least potentially, this 'most amazing thing' holds true for *everyone*. Great teachers surely enter deeply into the minds and hearts of their students; for many of us it is an effect of having been taught by Fergal that, even decades later, there are issues we cannot reflect on without at the same time contending with a Fergal-within – his is still one of the voices in the internal dialogues in which our thinking consists. Still, it was not so that we might become like himself that Fergal taught us so unstintingly and with such élan. It was rather so that we might ourselves be lured into that search which for him was a profession only because it was also an unfeigned reality in his life. Like Socrates, perhaps he did not entertain too many illusions about how inclined most of us are to engage in this search. But by embodying it so powerfully in his own practice – at a time when computers and other machines can be touted for their manifold superiority to mere teachers – can we be grateful enough for what he has shown us about the call of teaching?

References

Havel, Vaclàv. 1997. *The Art of the Impossible.* New York: Knopf.

Kierkegaard, Søren. 1962. *The Point of View for My Work as an Author,* trans. W. Lowrie. New York: Scribners.

Nietzsche, Friedrich. 1984. 'Schopenhauer as Educator', in *Untimely Meditations,* trans. R.J. Hollingdale and J.P. Stern. Cambridge: Cambridge University Press.

Nietzsche, Friedrich. 1986. *Human, All Too Human: A Book for Free Spirits,* trans. R.J. Hollingdale. Cambridge: Cambridge University Press.

MacIntyre, Alasdair. 1984. *After Virtue.* London: Duckworth.

Plato. 1973. *Phaedrus,* trans. W. Hamilton. Harmondsworth: Penguin.

Plato. 1979. *Republic,* trans. D. Lee. Harmondsworth: Penguin.

Plato. 1983. *Apology,* in H. Tredennick, trans. *The Last Days of Socrates,* Harmondsworth: Penguin.

Plato. 1989. *Symposium,* trans. A. Nehamas and P. Woodruff. Indianapolis: Hackett.

Weil, Simone. 1976. *Intimations of Christianity among the Ancient Greeks,* trans. Elizabeth Chase Geissbuhler. London: Routledge and Kegan Paul.

Wittgenstein, Ludwig. 1973. *Philosophical Investigations,* trans. G.E.M. Anscombe. Oxford: Blackwell.

CHAPTER 2

Pluralism and the Liberal Basis of Democracy

Shane O'Neill

Pluralism is best thought of not as a political ideal, but rather as a complex aspect of life in all modern societies. For the citizens of most countries, certainly for those of the North Atlantic, pluralism is, and has for some centuries been, a reality. It is a social fact that has to be dealt with politically. This means that it is not very fruitful, in such a context, either to advocate or to reject pluralism, to be either for or against it. Since pluralism is a social fact, it is simply not for us to determine whether or not we live in a society that is characterised by this phenomenon. Of course we can, and do, evaluate this aspect of modern life in a variety of ways. Some celebrate the diversity that pluralism brings and seek to maximise the extent to which relevant differences among citizens are made manifest. Others lament the fragmentation, and alienation, that has, from their perspective, followed in the wake of a recognition of the fact of pluralism. These two contrasting attitudes can be taken to represent views that might be found towards either pole of a spectrum that is itself a reflection of our pluralist social reality.

Contemporary liberal political theory is, in general, not so concerned with an exploration of the interesting variety of evaluative attitudes towards pluralism, as with the practical task of working out how best to deal politically with this reality. I have two aims here. The first is to give an account of modern pluralism. The second is to outline, briefly, the resources that liberal theory makes available to us in dealing reasonably with this complex aspect of modern political life. I am concerned with theoretical efforts to work out how a moral basis for legitimate politics can be found in a pluralist context. What follows, in the first section, is an account of three dimensions of pluralism that a convincing theory of democratic legitimacy must take seriously. Each modern state is characterised, first, by a plurality of individual conceptions of the good, and second, by a plurality of sociocultural groups which provide an identity-forming context for these individuals. The fact that each modern state is itself rooted in a particular historical and cultural context reflects a third dimension of pluralism; the plurality of ethically unique political communities. In the second section I will present liberalism as a political morality that responds, primarily, to the first dimension of pluralism. I will argue that endorsing the liberal basis of democratic legitimacy is indeed the most reasonable way of dealing with the plurality of individual conceptions of the good. But I will go on to recommend that liberals also respond effectively to the two other dimensions of pluralism that I outline. The aim is not to displace, but rather to fulfill the liberal aspiration of dealing reasonably with all aspects of our pluralist social reality. Not only would this give us a more convincingly democratic conception of legitimacy, but it would also, I suggest, relieve some of the anxieties that are shared by certain critics of those forms of liberalism that seem to respond only to the first dimension of pluralism.

Three dimensions of pluralism

Individual conceptions of the good
Liberals assume that modern societies are characterised by a plurality of irreconcilable conceptions of the good (Berlin, 1969; Dworkin, 1985; Raz, 1986; Cohen, 1992; Rawls, 1993). Individual citizens conceive of a good human life in incommensurable ways. They have differing standards of human value and they have no way of reducing these standards to one scale against which all could be measured and assessed. Furthermore, these conceptions of the good are often in conflict with one another. For some people life has no meaning if it is not directed to do God's will but for others the most valuable life is spent ridding ourselves of the illusion that God exists. Some see no possibility of an enriched life without placing a loving monogamous relationship at its centre while for others any such deep emotional bond of dependence may itself be a sign of human imperfection. Some feel it vital that they give much of

their energy and free time to assisting the needy while others, who think themselves far too busy to contemplate such a commitment, might rather see all basic needs satisfied directly by state officials. Some feel the need to listen to Mahler for sustenance, others turn to Van Morrison, or Oasis, or Kenny Rogers. The issues that are at stake in these examples are all sources of reasonable disagreement. In modern societies the free exercise of reason has led people to differing conclusions about the meaning of life, or of what constitutes the good for human beings. We must accept these differences as a consequence of the fact that our various views are informed by a rich diversity of irreconcilable comprehensive doctrines that shape our conceptions of the meaning of life and the human good. John Rawls (1993, p. 36), the most influential of contemporary liberal theorists, takes such differences to represent the fact of reasonable pluralism.

We might refer to this first aspect of pluralism as the plurality of individual conceptions of the good. In the modern period the idea of a legitimate constitutional democratic state has developed in a way that respects the individual's capacity for critical reasoning and autonomous choice. Liberalism, as a political morality, emerged in the aftermath of the wars of religion that followed the Reformation in Europe. Toleration of differing religious beliefs and a growing respect for freedom of individual conscience was seen to be the only way to secure a moral foundation for political authority in a context where the general endorsement of one comprehensive religious doctrine could no longer be expected. The original basis of liberalism is the idea that political legitimacy could depend only on an acceptance of the fact of religious diversity. Liberals have come to see this neither as a cause for regret or dismay nor as a tragic affliction. They see it rather as a necessary outcome of the free exercise of human reason. So long as our social and political institutions concern themselves with a defence of the most basic individual liberties, such as those that protect our freedom of conscience, then we can expect individual citizens to endorse a wide variety of conceptions of the good. These in turn will be informed by a diversity of reasonable, yet irreconcilable, comprehensive doctrines of religion, philosophy and morality.

Of course individuals do not choose a conception of the good in the same way that they choose a brand of washing powder. A conception of one's good is, as communitarian critics of liberalism have stressed, a question of identity (MacIntyre, 1981, ch. 15; Sandel, 1982; Taylor, 1989). It says something about the kind of person I am if I would rather listen to Mahler than to Oasis or Kenny Rogers. I disclose an important aspect of myself if I declare a belief that a life without love would not be worth living. People learn something significant about the way I want to express my humanity if they find out that I am a vegan, or that I enjoy sadomasochistic sex, or that I have spent a large proportion of my savings in support of Kurdish rebels. We should not think of the commitments, aspirations and ideals involved here as packages that we can consume, or not, at will. It is not as if I could decide over lunch to become a dedicated Mahler listener, or a vegan, or a sadomasochist. These are dimensions of identity, aspects of character, features of one's unique way of being human. They are not plucked from a shelf but rather they emerge from the ongoing quest for self-clarification in which each of us is constantly engaged.

Collective contexts of identity
Our individual identities are formed through interaction with others. I find out who I am as I reflect on the values that were constitutive of the family life in which I was nurtured, or the particular pattern of socialisation that characterised my schooling, or the customs and practices of the social groups with whom I have felt some sense of belonging. Perhaps I affirm some of the values that governed my socialisation, but, after years of critical reflection, I may well have come to reject certain elements of that evaluative framework. In this case I will have experienced a struggle to define myself against the expectations of significant others, typically parents or teachers. The way in which this struggle takes place will depend very much on the new spheres of influence that I have encountered, or the new significant others with whom I have involved myself. The process of identity formation always takes place within a par-ticular context. The context is shaped not only by other individuals but also by the cultural background in which we find ourselves. The doctrines which inform our conceptions of the good, and the commitments and ideals that constitute each of our identities, are always fed through a plurality of sociocultural groups. This is the

second dimension of pluralism that characterises every modern political context.

It could be suggested that the proliferation of different individual life projects, and conceptions of the good, has been driven by the generation, and the regeneration, of a variety of groups that form collective identities. This plurality of sociocultural groups reflects differences among the citizens of every modern society (Phillips, 1993). Differences of religion, gender, social class, ethnicity, sexual preference and orientation, to name but a few, structure the plurality of sociocultural groups that provide the context in which the identities of individuals emerge. These groups engender in individuals a sense of belonging which is constitutive of their personal identity (Benhabib, 1992). If I belong to some particular social group, then I will be personally enriched by any of that group's achievements. Similarly an attempt to undermine or to marginalise the collective identity of that group will be felt by me as a threat or an insult to the integrity of my personal identity. The failure to treat the collective identity with respect involves a failure to treat each individual member of the social group concerned with the dignity to which every human being is entitled (Honneth, 1992). Phenomena such as sexism, sectarianism, nationalistic xenophobia, racism, homophobia and all forms of prejudice against minorities, such as the travelling community in Ireland, represent brutal attempts to deny respect to the full plurality of sociocultural groups. They assert, in different ways, the superiority of one collective identity. These phenomena are mechanisms of subjugation that function as a means of marginalising groups whose needs, aspirations and ideals differ from those of the dominant culture (Young, 1990).

Sociocultural groups provide individuals with an identity-forming context. Most individuals identify, and are identified by others, with a number of groups. Paul is a middle-class, male, heterosexual, Roman Catholic medical doctor. Pauline shares Paul's Roman Catholicism but she is a lesbian factory worker. Michael is gay, Jewish and works as a sales representative for a computer firm. Michelle is heterosexual, Protestant and registered disabled. Each of the listed aspects of these individuals' identities involves a tie with a particular collectivity within their society. We share some aspects of our personal identities with what may be a very large group, in terms of class or gender perhaps, while other aspects may place us in a relatively small minority, possibly in terms of sexual orientation or ethnicity. We may share many aspects of our individual identities in common with certain people, while we may, of course, have virtually nothing in common with others. These collective group identities do not combine to determine the personal identity of the individual. There is much more to each of us than our sharing in the collective identities of various groups. Furthermore, the significance we attach to our membership of any particular social group may vary. Paul's Roman Catholicism could matter a great deal to him while Pauline's may mean little to her. On the other hand Pauline's lesbianism might be of far greater significance to her self-understanding than is Paul's heterosexuality to him. But these groups provide a context in which each individual forms and revises a conception of the good and this context is itself likely to be quite different for each of us.

Just as the individual is constantly engaged in a project of self-clarification, so each sociocultural group forms its collective identity in an ongoing interactive process internally, among its members, and externally, with other groups in society. Group identities are therefore no more static than are personal identities. Nor is the composition of the group static. Membership can fluctuate depending on the social structure, say in terms of class, or some general cultural trends, say in terms of religion. While membership of some particular group may be important at some stage of my life, it might be the case that at a later stage I no longer feel any sense of identification with that group. This kind of disengagement is obviously more likely to occur with groups constituted in terms of religion or class rather than say gender or ethnicity. But collective identities evolve not only as the composition of a group changes. The ideals and aspirations that are constitutive of a group's identity are always evolving as the members engage in an internal dialogue that aims to clarify how that identity is best to flourish in some particular context. This dialogue might well involve some serious efforts to work through tensions and disagreements as to how the group is to develop, and how it is best to present itself to the society in general. These dialogues continue in an informal manner, with a greater or lesser degree of openness and at various levels of organisation, within a wide variety of sociocultural groups in

Ireland. Women wonder about how best to deal with questions of pornography and censorship. Roman Catholics argue about the appropriate role that women should play in the late twentieth century within the hierarchy. Travellers debate among themselves about how their collective identity is best to achieve public recognition and respect in contemporary Ireland. A group's shared identity emerges through an ongoing dialogue that allows such questions to be confronted.

Encounters with other groups in society also help to constitute these collective group identities. Of course most groups are constituted in a necessarily exclusive way. I cannot, for example, be both Roman Catholic and Protestant. Encounters among groups provide a contrast of ideals, aspirations and self-understandings which can deepen and clarify the sense of collective identity among all participating groups. When Protestants and Roman Catholics engage in dialogue with one another, the hope is that they will not only learn something about one another, but that they will also come to a deeper self-understanding through the encounter.

States as unique political communities

So far we have considered two dimensions of pluralism in modern societies; the plurality of individual conceptions of the good and the plurality of sociocultural groups. The third dimension I wish to outline is the plurality of ethically unique political communities, or states. Each state in the modern world is constituted historically and is rooted in a particular cultural context. It is the historical rootedness of each state that marks it as ethically unique in so far as its institutions express a particular political identity. While the constitutions of many modern liberal democratic states may have striking similarities in terms of institutional design or the set of individual rights they protect, each of them also represents the historical achievements of a political community. This may be a relatively homogenous national community, as in the case of say Denmark or the Czech Republic, or a political community that is made up of more than one nation, such as the United Kingdom or Spain. The particularity of the political community is expressed not only in its actual constitution as a state but also in its flags and symbols, its anthem, its celebration of national holidays and even in the performance, and the support, of its representative sports teams.

While each state will have an indeterminate number of socio-cultural groups that provide an identity-forming context for its individual citizens, the institutions of a democratic state should express one collective identity that is shared by all citizens. We can understand many of the most significant of political conflicts as struggles for recognition by particular sociocultural groups who seek to be included as full members and equal citizens of the political community of a particular state (Taylor, 1992; Habermas, 1993; Honneth, 1995). The recent history of most states has been marked by women's struggle to achieve equal status with men. Being on the electoral franchise is an important right of citizenship but it does not amount to equal status. Women continue to confront inequality as they seek to articulate with greater clarity their own particular needs and as they expose with greater force the more subtle effects of patriarchal power that structure the public world in a way that privileges men (Okin, 1989; Rhode, 1989). The demo-cratic politics of modern states has also provided a forum for the ongoing struggle of workers to defend their rights in ways that take seriously the fact that they are, just in the same way as managers, entrepreneurs and politicians, equal citizens. Gays and lesbians, religious and ethnic minorities have also had to engage in political struggles so as to be recognised and respected as being different from the majority yet equal as members of the political community (Young, 1990; Kymlicka, 1995).

This struggle for recognition and inclusion is an important aspect of our collective task of working out what justice requires of us. This task is taken up in each modern state in its own unique way (Walzer, 1983). Since each state is rooted in a particular historical context, it will have its own pattern of sociocultural group mem-bership. In some there will be an important religious minority, in others a large ethnic minority. Some may have a history of accommo-dation between the demands of capital and labour, while others may be starkly divided on class lines. In some the women's movement may be well advanced in its struggle for equality, in others there may be daunting cultural obstacles to women's emancipation, or to the positive recognition of gays and lesbians. What is always at stake in these struggles is the shared political identity of all the state's citizens. When the politics of a state becomes increasingly sensitive to the needs of religious or ethnic minorities, or to women's struggle for equality, or to the rights of gays and lesbians, then this reflects a significant shift in the ongoing formation of the citizens' political identity. This shift becomes part of who 'we' are as citizens of this state; 'we' who are members of this political community that is constituted by this shared culture, these customs, this constitutional history, these hopes and aspirations, this set of pressing problems.

The political identity that is shared by the citizens of each modern state is ethically unique since it is constituted by the ongoing struggle for recognition and inclusion that drives the actual democratic practice of each modern political community. The identity of the Irish citizen, for example, changes as the democratic politics of the Republic of Ireland reflects a growing awareness of the need to take seriously the complex social reality of pluralism. As a recognition of the plurality of individual conceptions of the good continues to feed into ongoing public debates about politics and morality, so a more open and inclusive Irish identity takes root. As minority sociocultural groups are recognised in their difference as equal members of the political community, so the identity of all Irish citizens becomes less constrained by an effort to maintain national purity and more open to a celebration of the diversity of strands that can bind citizens in national solidarity.

Liberalism and democratic legitimacy

The priority of individual autonomy

How can a more or less just and stable democracy operate in the face of these three dimensions of modern pluralism? What is to be the moral source of the state's political authority? How are we to account for the legitimacy of constitutional and legislative politics? Liberal answers to these questions rely on the human capacity to exercise our reason. Liberals acknowledge the fact that democratic authority can no longer be secured within the framework of one generally shared conception of the good that is informed by a particular comprehensive religious, philosophical or moral world-view. In no modern society do all citizens believe in one God. Nor do they affirm the moral views of any particular philosopher or teacher. Furthermore they have good reasons for their disagreements about comprehensive moral and theological claims. Reason leaves open a number of possible answers to many of the most crucial questions regarding the meaning we give to our lives. The social reality of pluralism has come about in the wake of a fragmentation of worldviews that is the consequence of the free exercise of human reason. But liberals do not think of human reason only as the source of this fragmentation of worldviews. They also maintain that we can draw on our capacity for reason in our efforts to find a moral basis for democratic legitimacy in such a pluralist context.

The recognition of a plurality of individual conceptions of the good has motivated the traditional liberal concern to secure for the individual certain liberties and opportunities that facilitate the scope for personal autonomy that we associate with the free exercise of critical human reason. If we are to take the worth of each individual sufficiently seriously in our political morality, then we need to give basic individual rights a certain priority over considerations of the general welfare or particular ideals about what constitutes a good life (Rawls, 1971). This is crucial if we are to treat members of sociocultural minority groups as moral equals (Dworkin, 1977). Individual rights protect these groups, say religious minorities, gays and lesbians or members of the travelling community, from any imposition of a moral ideal that is intolerant of some relevant difference in lifestyle. This ideal may well be adhered to by the majority, typically if they share one set of religious beliefs, but the minority will have good reason to reject this intolerant ideal as a guide to their own way of life. If they are to be treated as equals then they will have to be protected from the political imposition of any such ideal.

By giving some such priority to individual rights we are led to question how a basis of social unity that tolerates a rich diversity of reasonable conceptions of the good is to be found. The political constitution of a legitimate democratic state must be grounded in some reasonable basis of social unity. Since, under conditions of pluralism, we do not share a comprehensive moral ideal, we cannot ground our political constitution in some such particular comprehensive view. We must rather seek common ground in a conception of reasonable politics (Waldron, 1993). If politics is to be reasonable then it will reflect the fact that reason leaves open a number of possible answers to questions regarding the meaning of existence, the highest moral ideals or the best way to live a human life. No particular comprehensive religious, moral or philosophical doctrine can be privileged in the constitution of the state. This is what liberals mean when they suggest that the state should be neutral between competing conceptions of the good (Ackerman, 1980; Dworkin, 1985; Larmore, 1987). There is no way of dealing reasonably with pluralism except by avoiding the political imposition of one moral ideal on citizens who have good reasons not to endorse that ideal. If we take the fact of pluralism seriously then there can be no such legitimate political entity as a Roman Catholic, or a Protestant, state. Nor could there be a legitimate state that facilitates only heterosexually structured families, or vegetarian lifestyles, or the settled way of life.

This means that the political constitution, if it is to be democratic, should affirm principles that all citizens can endorse with good reasons (Rawls, 1993; Habermas, 1996). A constitution that could claim to be liberal will guarantee rights of political participation, including rights to vote and to engage actively in the political process. It will also secure negative liberties, including liberty of conscience, for all individual citizens. Citizens should enjoy the freedom to associate with others and to organise themselves in the pursuit of shared goals. Each citizen should be treated impartially by the institutions and officials of the state and should be protected by the rule of law. Furthermore individual citizens have a right to whatever socioeconomic means are necessary to allow them to make these other basic rights effective. This implies that the state should concern itself, not only with the satisfaction of basic needs, but also with the regulation of the structure of society so that each citizen enjoys a fair distribution of social goods. If these goods, including wealth and power, are not distributed fairly, then the social structure will distort the political process in ways that reinforce the privileges of those who receive more than their fair share. If each citizen is to have an equal voice in political affairs then no citizen should be alienated by poverty. Nor should any be powerful enough to buy the votes of others.

The liberal constitution that is sketched here is grounded in reasons that all citizens can share. It does not privilege one religious ideal nor does it favour a particular way of life. It recognises the fact of reasonable pluralism and it is designed in a way that facilitates the free exercise of human reason through the diversity of conceptions of the good that characterise modern societies. This constitution provides a political framework of co-operation that allows us to live together in a non-violent and mutually enriching way. It avoids the divisiveness, and injustice, of imposing one way of life, or one comprehensive moral ideal, on all citizens. The constitution binds us in social unity by appealing to our shared reason and by encouraging in us the virtues of toleration, fairness and respect for reasonable difference. These are the virtues that can guarantee peace and just social co-operation among citizens who endorse a plurality of irreconcilable conceptions of the good.

In practice then we must choose between liberalism as a politically reasonable way of dealing with pluralism and the imposition of divisive constitutional arrangements that privilege a particular moral ideal. While liberalism recognises the fact of pluralism, the latter project ignores or denies this fact. If reason is to prevail over violence then some political form of liberalism is the only constitutional framework that we can endorse as a basis of social unity. This means that the constitution should respect the reasonable disagreements among citizens regarding theological questions about the existence of God, or philosophical questions about the rights that animals may or may not have, or questions about the moral status of sadomasochistic sexual practices. No answer should be politically privileged and no citizen should suffer because the answer which she or he can defend with reason is rejected by a large majority of fellow citizens.

Let me clarify what the liberalism I present is. It is a political morality that provides a reasonable basis for democratic legitimacy under conditions of modern pluralism. By grounding the principles that inform a liberal constitution in a conception of reasonable politics, this political morality seeks to avoid the imposition of any moral ideal that is not generally shared by the citizens of a particular state. Liberalism is a political morality and not a moral ideal that informs us how best to live a human life. We must all draw on deeper sources than political liberalism if we are to instil meaning into our lives. Liberalism does not privilege atheism over belief. While accepting that atheists and believers appear to hold good reasons that sustain their disagreement, it suggests that we can leave this disagreement aside in providing a moral foundation for our political constitution. Nor does liberalism insist that there are no true moral values. On the contrary liberalism itself makes strong moral claims based on a conception of reasonable politics. It restricts the scope of its moral claim, however, to the political realm and so it leaves more general questions about the nature of morality to the ongoing reasonable disagreements that continue to generate philosophical debate among citizens.

A liberalism not confined to individualism

Some critics of liberalism worry that this reasonable conception of politics is simply too weak as a political response to the fragmentation of moral worldviews that is represented by the fact of pluralism (MacIntyre, 1981; Sandel, 1982). These critics find this liberal response to be premised on an account of human nature that is untenably individualistic. They suggest that modern societies cannot be held together by an appeal to reason alone but that they also need to be grounded in a shared conception of the good. Liberals have often stressed the autonomy of the individual, and the plurality of individual conceptions of the good, to such an extent that they have left themselves open to this charge. While liberalism as a political morality does not insist on any one philosophical conception of human nature, it is important that the intersubjective dimensions of modern political life are given due attention in any adequate theory of democratic legitimacy that responds to the fact of pluralism. What I am suggesting is that liberals can and should pay more attention to the second and third dimensions of pluralism that I outlined above. So far in my account of liberalism as a political morality I have stressed the way in which liberalism seeks to accommodate the plurality of individual conceptions of the good. I will conclude by indicating, very briefly, how a liberal theory of democratic legitimacy should also accommodate both the plurality of sociocultural groups in each modern society and the plurality of ethically unique modern states. In fact it seems to be the case that it is only by taking these dimensions of pluralism seriously that liberalism as a political morality can provide a suitably democratic basis for legitimacy in modern societies.

Democracy is not based only on formal constitutional structures of the political process. While a set of judicially protected individual rights and a fair system of representation, legislation and government are certainly indispensable to the smooth running of any democratic system, they are not sufficient conditions for a democracy. There must also be a critically engaged set of informal public spheres that mobilise citizens and that can provide them with a forum for the articulation of their views on matters of public concern (Fraser, 1992; Habermas, 1996). These spheres breathe life into the more formal constitutional structures of a democracy. They keep these structures open to the opinions of the citizens. If we pay attention to the vital role of these informal public spheres then we begin to see how the plurality of sociocultural groups must be accounted for in any adequate theory of democratic legitimacy. While the strength of liberalism has been the way in which it can offer an account of reasonable politics that facilitates the plurality of individual conceptions of the good, this must be complemented with an account of the role that groups with particular collective identities play in a well-ordered democracy.

As we have seen, groups provide individuals with contexts of identity formation. It is through the self-empowerment of socio-cultural groups within informal public spheres that phenomena such as sexism, sectarianism, nationalistic xenophobia, racism, homophobia and all forms of prejudice are first confronted. Formal political structures only deal with these phenomena, if at all, once they have been identified and resisted within informal public spheres. Groups offer individual members an empowering sense of solidarity that fuels their fight against these forms of oppression and subjugation. If we are to have legitimate democratic politics where each citizen is treated as an equal then the state has to take responsibility to ensure that the empowerment of groups who struggle against such forms of oppression is facilitated. When groups are organised politically they can begin to clarify their own ideals and aspirations and they can articulate the ways in which their particular needs differ from those of other citizens. Groups of women can organise themselves so that they can work out exactly what legislation is needed, regarding say sexual harassment, equal opportunities or child care arrangements, if they are to be treated as equal citizens. Religious minorities can identify changes that might be required of the state education system if they are to be recongised as equal members of the political community. Gays and lesbians can indicate possible ways in which existing family law fails to treat them as equal citizens. If we are to take the plurality of sociocultural groups seriously in our account of legitimacy then we must realise that the ongoing clarification of group identities and aspirations is as indispensable to democratic politics as is the electoral process.

Finally, this emphasis on our second dimension of pluralism must also be complemented by an account of social unity that is more binding than an appeal to reason alone. It is here that the third dimension, the plurality of ethically unique states, comes into play. Citizens of a well-ordered liberal democratic state share more than a commitment to reasonable politics. They also share a political identity. They are citizens of a constitutional state that is rooted historically in a particular cultural context. Each of them is an equal member of a community with a distinctive collective identity. The struggle for recognition of group identities is constitutive of this shared political identity. Because members of particular groups that were marginalised in the past are included, through legislative change, as equal citizens, the shared identity becomes ever more inclusive of the plurality of sociocultural groups. This struggle may also involve a demand for constitutional change, as in Northern Ireland. In this case the Irish nationalist minority insist that they will never be full members of the political community unless there is some meaningful recognition of their group identity at constitutional level. Justice and stability can only ever be secure if they are grounded in a context where no group of citizens feels excluded by the political constitution of the state.

It would appear to be the case then that a liberal conception of reasonable politics provides the proper framework for dealing with the fact of pluralism in modern societies. Liberals should, however, pay greater attention to the second and third dimensions of pluralism if they are to offer a convincing theory of democratic legitimacy. The political constitution of a democratic state defends the rights of individual citizens but it also celebrates the shared identity of the citizens. While liberalism rightly insists that all members of the political community be treated as equals, this requires a greater emphasis on the role of sociocultural groups in the informal public spheres that make demands on the formal political structures of a well-ordered democracy. It also means that liberals should not shy away from the fact that a democratic state cannot but celebrate a particular political identity. If the state is to be liberal, as well as democratic, then this identity will have to be inclusive of every sociocultural group in the society.

References

Ackerman, B. 1980. *Social Justice in the Liberal State*, New Haven: Yale University Press.

Benhabib, S. 1992. *Situating the Self.* Cambridge, UK: Polity Press.

Berlin, I. 1969. *Four Essays on Liberty.* Oxford: Oxford University Press

Cohen, J. 1993. 'Moral Pluralism and Political Consensus', in D. Copp, J. Hampton and J. Roemer (eds), *The Idea of Democracy.* Cambridge, UK: Cambridge University Press.

Dworkin, R. 1977. *Taking Rights Seriously.* London: Duckworth.

Dworkin, R. 1985. 'Liberalism', in *A Matter of Principle.* Cambridge, Ma: Harvard University Press.

Fraser, N. 1992. 'Rethinking the Public Sphere: a Contribution to the Critique of Actually Existing Democracy', in C. Calhoun (ed.), *Habermas and the Public Sphere.* Cambridge, Ma: MIT Press.

Habermas, J. 1993. 'Struggles for Recognition in Constitutional States', *European Journal of Philosophy* 1, 128-155.

Habermas, J. 1996. *Between Facts and Norms: Contributions to a Discourse Theory of Law and Democracy*, trans. W. Rehg, Cambridge, UK: Polity Press.

Honneth, A. 1992. 'Integrity and Disrespect: Principles of a Conception of Morality Based on a Theory of Recognition', *Political Theory* 20, 187-201.

Honneth, A. 1995. *The Struggle for Recognition*, trans. J. Anderson, Cambridge, UK: Polity Press.

Kymlicka, W. 1995. *Multicultural Citizenship: A Liberal Theory of Minority Rights*, Oxford: Clarendon Press.

Larmore, C. 1987. *Patterns of Moral Complexity.* Cambridge, UK: Cambridge University Press.

MacIntyre, A. 1981. *After Virtue.* London: Duckworth.

Okin, S. M. 1989. *Justice, Gender and the Family.* New York: Basic Books.

Phillips, A. 1993. *Democracy and Difference.* Cambridge, UK: Polity Press.

Rawls, J. 1971. *A Theory of Justice.* Oxford: Oxford University Press.

Rawls, J. 1993. *Political Liberalism.* New York: Columbia University Press.

Raz, J. 1986. *The Morality of Freedom.* Oxford: Clarendon Press.

Rhode, D. 1989. *Justice and Gender.* Cambridge, Ma: Harvard University Press.

Sandel, M. 1982. *Liberalism and the Limits of Justice.* Cambridge, UK: Cambridge University Press.

Taylor, C. 1989. 'Cross-Purposes: The Liberal-Communitarian Debate', in N. Rosenblum (ed.), *Liberalism and the Moral Life.* Cambridge, Ma: Harvard University Press.

Taylor, C. 1992. 'The Politics of Recognition', in A. Gutmann (ed.), *Multiculturalism and 'The Politics of Recognition'.* Princeton: Princeton University Press.

Waldron, J. 1993. 'Theoretical Foundations of Liberalism', in *Liberal Rights: Collected Papers, 1981-1991.* Cambridge, UK: Cambridge University Press.

Walzer, M. 1983. *Spheres of Justice: A Defence of Pluralism and Equality.* Oxford: Blackwell.

Young, I.M. 1990. *Justice and the Politics of Difference,* Princeton: Princeton University Press.

CHAPTER 3

The Once and Future European Nation-State

Attracta Ingram

There is a common, but perhaps mistaken, belief that we Europeans finally hit on the best format for collective political action – the sovereign nation-state. In its ideal form this is a political actor vested with sovereign political power – power that admits of no superior power or higher authority. It spans a territory occupied by a homogeneous cultural community, or, at the least, a dominant majority culture. Some supporters were taken with the nation-state as a matter of divine design. Thus the Italian nationalist, Giuseppi Mazzini, offered the following political theology: 'God divided Humanity into distinct groups upon the face of our globe and thus planted the seeds of nations. Bad governments have disfigured the design of God' (Mazzini, 1907, p. 52).

Éamon de Valera was a believer in natural boundaries also. In 1939 he cited with appreciation a speech of Mussolini:

> There is something about the boundaries that seem to be drawn by the hand of the Almighty which is very different from the boundaries that are drawn by ink upon a map: frontiers traced by inks on other inks can be modified. It is quite another thing when the frontiers were traced by Providence (Quoted in Bowman, 1982, p. 30, and in Whyte 1990, p. 131).

The nation-state format proved superior, in terms of global repetition and the spread of citizenship, to the earlier city states or empires. It emerged in post-revolutionary France at the end of the eighteenth century and was paralleled by the moral claim of nationalism – the boundaries of state and nation should coincide – by the latter half of the nineteenth century. In this nationalist form the nation-state idea continues to challenge existing state boundaries in many multinational states. Since the early 1990s several multinational states have fallen apart on national lines – most strikingly the Soviet Union, Czechoslovakia and Yugoslavia. There are continuing struggles in Northern Ireland, Quebec, Flanders, Catalonia, the Basque country, Kashmir and Punjab, the Kurdish regions of Turkey and Iraq, to list only some of the more widely reported cases. Most nation-states are neither fully sovereign nor fully national in the sense of encompassing a single ethnocultural nation. But the idea that nations have a collective right to self-determination remains a powerful justification for claims about boundaries and the conduct of nationalist politics in newly independent nation-states.

Ireland views itself as a sovereign nation-state. That is the message of Articles 1 and 5 of the *Constitution of Ireland* and the view was endorsed recently in the *Report of the Constitution Review Group* (1996) which recommends no change in these articles. Indeed, the Review Group not only endorses the nation-state format but also the nationalist logic that runs from the premise of the nation in Article 1, through an alleged national right of self-determination – which the Group boldly asserts as a principle of 'universal validity' – to the conclusion of the state, 'sovereign, independent, democratic' in Article 5. The Review Group acknowledges that the scope of the phrase 'The Irish Nation' has been questioned, but does not see any reason for amending this article (1996, p. 9). Of course recent events, especially the electoral endorsement North and South of the Good Friday Agreement, have made national self-determination subject to the wishes of the unionist people of Northern Ireland, a reversal of the precedence de Valera gave to national territorial unity over unionist wishes. Thus, the national right of self-determination can no longer be interpreted in Ireland as an unconditional right, unless one adheres to the views of some tiny terrorist splinter groups.

The Report also endorses the constitutional pillar of popular sovereignty stated in Article 6. The appeal of this idea is to the democratic principle that all political and legal power rests on the will and consent of those over whom power is exercised. These comprise the democratic legal subject we call 'the people', but that does not have the same extension as 'the nation', for 'nation' carries the sense of a pre-political community sharing a particular history and culture or form of life. This is why in the 'pluralist society' referred to in the chairman's introduction to the Report there is good reason to raise the question about the scope of 'The Irish Nation'.

Nation-states are of course sovereign according to the standard view. The constitution wobbles over where exactly sovereignty resides, but ensures that it is plentiful. It is an attribute of the nation (Article 1), of the state (Article 5), and of the people (Article 6). This raises an awkward question about how the sovereignty of the nation over its right of self-determination is related to the sovereignty of the people over its form of government and issues of fundamental national policy. Can the people (sovereign in Article 6) alienate the sovereignty of the nation (inalienable and indefeasible in Article 1)? On this turns the possibility of our trading/pooling some of the sovereignty of the state for more substantive European citizenship. More generally, the fate of democracy turns on whether the word of the people as a *demos* has priority over the presumed interest in political self-determination of the nation as a pre-political *ethnos*. Indeed the report of the Review Group seems blind to the radical implications of our EU membership for the sovereign nation-state format. Nor does it reflect the common agreement that the sovereign nation-state as political actor is impotent to solve the new problems of the dying century – military, economic, and ecological problems that observe no boundaries; internal cultural and political problems that are imposing severe strain on the political capacities of the nation-state complex.

Fortunately the constitution's traditional image of the nation-state is not the only one available to us. There is another belief about the sovereign nation-state. This is that it is no more than the passing phenomenon of a few centuries, a product of a particular process of state-building in European history, not the prototype of a desirable political master-plan for all humanity. This is a complex belief. It may be about the passing of the *sovereign* state, something that is happening before our eyes as we witness the erosion of nation-state sovereignty, at least in the European Union. It may also be about the passing of the *nation*-state, something that is happening to homogeneous ethnocultural national identities with the increasing interpenetration of national cultures.

According to this second belief our received ideal of a world of fully sovereign, homogenous nation-states was never a plausible global option. Not for India, not for much of Asia, not for Africa, not even for the UK and the USA. And if it was once a model that applied in some European states, it has few examples now.

Some people leap from observation of the decreasing cultural homogeneity and political powers of actual nation-states to the conclusion that the nation-state is over as a political unit – if not yet dead, then certainly mortally wounded by the pressures for dispersal of power to supranational and regional levels of organisation. I believe that this judgment is hasty. The nation-state, understood as a bounded political community whose members recognise each other as belonging together politically, will survive in the immediate future, on Auguste Comte's principle – that one can only destroy what one can replace. As yet we have no alternative collective political actors with the legitimacy, power, and experience of nation-states. For now, neither small-scale utopias nor global villages are possible or desirable political actors to replace the existing state system. So the question is not: what is to replace the nation-state? But rather: how can we adapt it? Can we construct a new model of the nation-state – one that frees it from the talons of ethnocultural nationalism and the trappings of full undivided sovereignty? I believe that we can and must if we are to preserve democratic citizenship in circumstances of internal pluralism and globalisation.

I make my case in four steps. The first explains why the nation-state as a political unit will survive in the immediate future. The second step shows that the elements of the nation-state complex have a functional empirical, not a conceptual, connection and this is why they admit of recombination. The modern state offers citizens a new form of social integration as a civic nation of legally empowered citizens that is logically distinct from nationalist integration and can, in principle, dispense with it. The third step argues that the modern state has now reached a plateau of self-conscious citizenship that makes it feasible to cast aside the national idea and this enables us to face the challenges of internal pluralism and global interaction. Finally, I defend the citizenship state idea against some prominent objections.

Why does the nation-state survive?

The modern nation-state sets itself up as the agency that delivers civil order, economic management and social justice, that deals with environmental protection, cultural and moral erosion, and all the disasters that befall the nation. The state is plainly incapable of delivering most of these services in anything like the amount needed by all its members. Even more obvious is the fact that the nation-state cannot address the drastic new dangers to its members posed by global economic rationalisation, nuclear might, and environmental peril. How is it then that the nation-state seems set to survive its obvious incapacity for effective agency? There are four main reasons.

First, we are disinclined to blame the state for its internal inefficacy, because its powers of action are inherently restricted by the form of limited government and checks on power that we believe in. There are limits to what a government can do to remove crime or terrorism, or improve the economy, or redistribute welfare, limits set by us in the interests of personal liberty. We think it better to spancel the state, even at some cost in reduced security and uneven prosperity, than to give it more powers. Fear of a high concentration of state power also predisposes us to think that it is better to have a world of states rather than a single world state. And since we already have a world of states, reasons of international order and security then enter to favour conservatism about existing state borders. Respect for the integrity of existing borders is one of the basic agreed principles of international law. So while we may try to hold the state to a better standard of efficiency within its powers, we have little motivation to dismantle the current state system, though we may want to adjust borders or make them more permeable from time to time.

Second, the global scale of the new hazards to human life, security and prosperity tells against the nation-state as the theatre of political action in these areas. But the size and urgency of the problems also demand that we use the nation-states, which are the only established political actors we have, in the international arena, to establish common powers and to collectively decide on their use.

Third, the nation-state is the only channel we have for national sentiment, that sense of partiality for one's own people that John Stuart Mill observed 'is more worthy of savages than of civilized beings' (Mill, 1975, p. 383). National sentiment has not everywhere pre-existed the states that fostered it, often fanned into chauvinism, for their own ends. But, as Mill also observed, as long as national sentiment exists 'nationality is practically of the very first importance'. Mill's political point is repeated more than a century later by Isaiah Berlin who writes that 'no political movement today . . . seems likely to succeed unless it allies itself to national sentiment' (Berlin, 1981, p. 355).

If Mill and Berlin are still right the political project of European integration depends on working through structures that accommodate a sense of national identity. These are likely to remain the nation-states because European integration cannot rely on the creation of a European nation or identity. It cannot then provide for the identity-needs of people – for self-confidence and self-esteem – that a healthy national sentiment provides. Those needs must continue to be the responsibility of the existing nation-states because we have so far no higher loyalty, nothing that supersedes the nation-state as a legitimate source of social identity.

Fourth, the nation-state by its very existence generates a message that sustains a core idea of modern life, the idea of standardisation. The message is that the merely local and idiosyncratic is backward and shuts people out from social and economic advancement which is open only to those who master certain abstract, standardised, formally transmitted, styles of communication and conduct. Historically the nation-state is the cultural space for the creation of an impersonal society of mutually substitutable individuals knocked into shape by standardised education. National societies project themselves as communities, even organic or natural communities, but in every nation-state the fact of the matter has been different. An artificial common culture has been created in the pursuit of common literacy and communication, sold as the national identity, and transmitted by state controlled education, aided by the 'national' mass media of the time. To be a citizen of a national state was to be able to comprehend its political culture and manipulate its symbols.

It is a kind of self-deception to think that current academic preoccupations with difference and cultural pluralism signal any diminution of demand for standardised and abstract systems of communication and social relationships, or that this demand can be met at sub-national level. The demand is an imperative of modern economic conditions and communities which fail to meet it cannot thrive and may die. For now, in Europe at least, nation-states are the only agents with the experience and authority to engage in the generalised diffusion of the culture and technological mastery people need to survive.

In sum we are not done with the nation-state, despite its obvious limitations. So it will survive a while yet. But if the nation-state itself is not at stake, the received view of it is. The sovereign, relatively homogeneous nation-state hinders moves beyond the political world of Mazzini or Mill or Woodrow Wilson, a world of co-operating 'nations' which retain their native sovereignty no matter what collective decision-making organs outside themselves they create. Some people think this a good thing. It gives a picture of Europe as a common agent of a group of sovereigns which leaves our sense of independent sovereign power intact and counteracts the bogeyman fear that our state is a mere delegate in a new Euro-sovereign superstate.

Others think that the received model is no longer an accurate representation of the realities of the nation-states of Europe. And they think that a good thing. They believe that the sovereign nation-state is a proven recipe for war, and a licence for historical majority cultures to oppress minorities and deviants. They also think that it is a mistake to suppose that either the organs of the EU are the creatures of the member states or the member states are the creatures of the EU. Instead they believe that the EU constitutes a new political and legal order co-ordinate with that of the member states. If they are right, the EU is the site of an evolutionary transformation of the nation-state. The latter will survive, but with diminished external sovereignty, and it will likely have much increased internal pluralism and need to base its unity on shared political values, not national identity.

So the nation-state that is projected to survive is a political nation. The thought is of a self-standing legal order of citizens that can now detach itself from the unitary cultural nation that facilitated the modern state's main achievement, namely mass democracy. To understand this idea of a political nation it may be useful to remember that the fusion of state and nation that we find so 'natural' is merely the product of processes of modernisation that occurred in the last two hundred years.

What is the nation? What is the state?

The European nation-state is a union of two very different ideas and modes of integration. A nation consists of those who, for one or more reasons (a common ethnic origin, a common language, a common and distinctive history, a common culture), feel that they belong together in one community. Nations feel linked by bonds that transcend time and space, bonds that held forebears together in the midst of suffering and triumph, and that suffice in the present to sustain the desire to go on as one community into the future. Nations, at least those which want states of their own, have a territorial basis, a land they call their own, which provides the material substance of existence for those at home and a sure refuge in times of trouble for those abroad. Since Ernest Renan's famous description of the nation as an 'everyday plebiscite' it has been common to think of nations as constituted by recognition, that is a mutual belief among people that they belong together and are willing to continue their national life (Ernest Renan 'Qu'est-ce qu'une natien?', in Hutchinson and Smith, 1994, p. 17)

This idea reinforces the role of the nation as the primary secular object of social identification and allegiance. Nations also carve up the wider social world into them and us, strangers and friends, aliens and kin. Nations can evoke love and self-sacrifice as well as xenophobia, chauvinism and racism. As ethnocultural communities nations offer unconditional belonging to their members.

The modern idea of the state takes it to consist of those who are subject to their own common legal authority. The state is a voluntary association, established and held together by the will of the people. In the social contract tradition that flows from Hobbes, Locke, Rousseau and Kant the modern state is held together by the willing subscription of citizens to a set of universally valid ideas about human rights and democracy, ideas which start from the proposition that people are born free and equal, and are rightly subject to no political authority other than one they establish themselves. These ideas are translated by different states into their own political vernacular as that is shaped by their different history and circumstances.

Still the concept of citizen is of a cosmopolitan being. What it takes to be a citizen is simply a certain universal aptitude for sharing in ruling and being ruled. The world of the state is a universal world. To be a member of this state rather than that takes only being willing to abide by its particular version of universal rules. States can be associations of strangers.

It is quite otherwise with nations. Nations are nothing if not particular. Their emotional appeal as objects of love and identification comes from the belief in their unique individuality and distinct and valuable identity. To be a member of this or that nation is to be different, to have a particular identity, shared with some but not all others, to be something that is concrete and particular rather than abstract and universal.

A pure nation-state therefore would consist only of those who belonged to the ethnocultural nation and were subject to its legal authority. Evidently the real world does not shape up in this way, unless made to do so by horrific programmes of ethnic cleansing. And it is hard to see that there would be any moral or practical merit in having such a world. So what we call the sovereign nation-state exists in its pure form only in our imagination. But there are lots and lots of nation-states even if they do not quite match up to the pure form.

The nation-state is a union of these two different ways of thinking. The compound phrase refers to a political unit in which the abstract legal integration of the state rests on the social integration of the nation.

The nation-state merger

The nation-state has been the most successful basis in European history for political integration under the rule of law. How was this merger of such different ideas possible? And why was it necessary? Jürgen Habermas has traced a conceptual history that shows that these concepts could be merged because the modern term 'nation' inherited its meaning from a history in which nation came to have a political as well as a cultural meaning.

In the ancient Roman usage which contrasted *natio* with *civitas,* Habermas writes, nations are composed of people of common descent who are not yet organised into the political form of a state but hold together by geographical proximity, common language, religion and customs. This idea of the nation as a concept of origin stretches through the Middle Ages into modern times where it is joined by a new political concept of the nation as a party to a contract with the King or Emperor. Initially the political nation is confined to the aristocracy. But sustained political assault on received views of political legitimacy eventually bears political fruit in three great revolutions – in England, France and America. In turn these lead to the democratic transformation of the previously restricted political nation into an inclusive political nation of the people (Habermas, 1991).

The new political or civic nation is first of all conceived as a purely artificial union freely made by individuals for certain limited purposes, usually security of life, liberty and property. It is thought of as an enlightening idea that frees people from the inequality and deprivation and ignorance they suffer under an increasingly corrupt and inefficient Old Guard, the *Ancien Regime* in France and its equivalents everywhere (Audard, 1996, p. 168). Unfortunately it proves hard to mobilise people for this abstract idea of the state and of their part in it. People have to be persuaded to relinquish familiar concrete relationships and corporate ties for a wider, more abstract and unproved civic identity. But there is an enormous mental and emotional gap between traditional communities and the abstract juridical community offered by the emerging modern state.

The process that mediates the transition is the development of the cultural nation. This becomes the tool of civic integration by providing a new kind of connection between people who are otherwise strangers to each other.

The cultural nation is first of all a work of imagination – the imagined nation as a completed project unified by a common culture. The cultural nation trades on the descriptive sense of *natio*, which in the classical usage picked out really existing communities and ways of life, in order to recruit adherents to a largely invented tradition. This is usually called a revival, as in the Celtic revival, and vested with ethical significance to make up for its factual deficit. The work of invention is carried forward by poets and essayists, by historians and linguists, by journalists and archaeologists and ethnologists, by musicians and architects and painters. The project is to cultivate common tastes and sensibility, to foster sentiments of sympathy and union, that will glue people together in the new and wider legal order of citizenship. Many of the paradigm nation-states in Europe followed this pattern of developing nations within existing states. France is the classic example of a nation-state that developed a cultural nation within the existing framework of the nation-state.

The process of nation-state-building sometimes went the other way with an emergent modern cultural nation building a state of its own. This was the case in Germany and Italy, and later Israel. Ireland might be said to have built a modern nation within an existing state in order to jettison that state for one of its own. Of course the contours of the state follow those of the nation when the process is from nation to state. Furthermore the purpose of the state is determined extra-politically by the nation. The nationalist project is always to capture the state as the instrument of the nation (in conflict, ironically for Ireland, with the republican project which is to develop the state as a realm of civic freedom conceived as an intrinsic good, and which may instrumentalise the nation, as was the case in post-revolutionary France). The partition of Ireland in 1921 was necessary if the nationalist project was to go forward at that time. A state that is designed to reflect and sustain one ethno-cultural nation cannot command the allegiance of those who do not share the national identity. At least this is so given modern democratic assumptions about equal citizenship and the role of consent in justifying political authority.

Still there is a regime of democratic citizenship in Ireland and this may be due in no small measure to the fact that the state could use the nation as a source of legitimation in order to bypass the difficult point that it had no mandate for partition from the people of the island as a whole. On the contrary the last all-Ireland election in 1918 had seen a substantial majority for parties dedicated to all-Ireland independence. If stability and legitimacy were in fact established in this way by getting a rough congruence between the borders of state and nation, the project of state-building in Ireland followed a pattern already established in the mainstream history of the modern European state. That is a history in which political modernity had to reach for and develop an idea of the nation in order to solve two pressing problems, one of legitimacy, the other of social integration.

The political legitimacy problem arose in the aftermath of the wars of religion in Europe. The principle of toleration was developed to allow accommodation of religious pluralism. But religious pluralism destroyed the divine right basis for the political authority of monarchs. And toleration in the end is seen to require a secular state. Political authority requires a new basis of legitimation. The new theory of political authority rested it on the consent of its subjects. Henceforth the only basis of legitimate political power is the people. (In the Preamble to the Irish Constitution the residue of a divine right theory is retained to fortify the people's claim to author political power.)

Initially the new mode of legitimation is purely theoretical. The state is legitimate in so far as the consent of its subjects can be conceived or imagined. It is the merely 'hypothetical consent' that Immanuel Kant in the eighteenth century advocates as the test that rulers should apply to their ordinances. It took a long time for legitimation by consent to achieve actual form in real processes of democracy. This is not merely a problem of the people having to wrest political power from the hands of an exclusionary ruling class. It is first and foremost a matter of converting minds and hearts. For people to be related in the mode of democratic citizenship they have to be converted from a consciousness of themselves as mere private subjects of law to one in which as citizens they are also authors of law and responsible for each other. Popular sovereignty presupposes a *demos*. Historically there could not be a *demos* that matched the territorial ambitions of the state until the population had unified as a people. This social unity is just what is lacking in the fragmented society that falls out of the outworn forms of social integration that the modern state wanted to replace.

The second problem is social integration. The modern state offers people a new form of legal relationship and an abstract new civic identity in place of the traditional relationships and social forms that the processes of early modernisation destroy. But the gap between traditional concrete identities and the new abstract civic identity is too great. People losing their familiar sources of identity have urgent need of a substitute source of identification, one that fits their experience of communal connection at the same time as broadening its base.

The nation is a response to both these problems. By offering people a way of conceiving themselves as part of the same whole it broadens the base of people prepared to take responsibility for each other. Only in this way can people used to narrow communities be prepared for responsibilities to the wider world of strangers that the territorial ambitions of the state bring together.

The nation is an idea that captures the imagination of the masses in a way that abstract civic legal order cannot. Its principle of unity is identity – the thought that we are one because we are the same. Similarity is achieved through common culture, consciously produced and transmitted for the purpose of customising people so that they are willing to live together politically. Thus the nation supplies the people who are destined to be the *demos*, which alone can legitimate political power according to the principle of popular sovereignty.

The same process of national acculturation offers a form of social integration that bridges the gap between the early modern world and the new master community of the abstract civil society. The nation offers emotional connection between strangers by making them sufficiently alike to identify with each other as kin. And it also stitches them one on one into the juridical state, ready to melt away when civic ties have grown and hardened.

This way of viewing the modern nation sees it as essentially a mobilising force for the state. In this role it first created a body of legal subjects to which the state is accountable. Second, by providing an assured common national status, it empowered people to demand democratic participation rights and established civic freedom alongside personal liberty.

This is the positive picture of the historical role of the nation. There is a negative picture too. The integrative force of the nation which initially supported the democratic state of free and equal citizens may make a rival claim on the citizen's highest allegiance. The fate of liberal democracy hangs on which claim succeeds. If the nation dominates the state then national sentiment may be mobilised for missions of national self-assertion. The nation may uphold itself against enemies within – deviants and minorities. It may also call on its patriots to fight enemies beyond state borders, people said to belong to inferior races or occupying 'our' ancestral land. The potentiality for xenophobia and racism is an aspect of the inherent instability of the nation-state mix. This is because the ambiguous 'nation' holds in tension two different ideas of community

– the universalistic voluntary nation of citizens, which authors democratic legitimation, and the particularistic unchosen nation of those who find themselves already socially formed by an inherited way of life and a common history. The voluntary nation is a universally repeatable community of legal equals ordered by principles of basic freedom and democratic rights. The inherited nation is projected as a unique historical growth, a natural organism, animated by its own particular mind or personality, or self-understanding.

These two ideas can be harmonised only if the universal nation of citizens frames and subordinates the pre-political cultural nation. The basic liberties and democratic rights that structure the civic nation can then regulate the form of life of the pre-political nation according to a universal code of conduct.

When the reverse ordering occurs and the pre-political cultural nation dominates, both personal liberty and democracy are in danger. The inherited roles and relationships of the natural nation give rise to a burden of unchosen obligations that inevitably trump personal liberty. When the natural nation dominates the state, democracy too is subordinated, usually by being reduced to a technique for discovering the collective will or common good – what we really want in light of the received values embedded in our national identity. Majority rule then becomes a way of discovering the common good. National majorities are thereby licensed by democracy itself, it seems, to subordinate all competing rights to their view of the common good. So democracy as self-rule, an idea that flows from the independence and equality of people as individuals, is hijacked as a group right of the national majority while minorities are treated as unequal subnationals whose part in democratic processes is entirely ineffective and irrelevant to national life.

The nation-state break-up

Modern states have to address the challenges that arise from two facts of contemporary political life: the fact of pluralism in civil society; and the trend towards globalisation in economic, military, and environmental matters.

Pluralism

Today, most of us live in societies that display a diversity of cultural forms of life, religions, moral and philosophical views. In these circumstances our received image of the ideally homogeneous nation-state will no longer wash. We can no longer defend the historical prerogative of the majority culture (the nation) to define the constitutional terms on which all citizens are to live together in one political community. A constitution for pluralism has to provide for interaction and coexistence of different groups on equal terms. If this is to happen the ethnocultural nation has to be uncoupled from the state. The tier of public political culture which is to be shared by all citizens has to be separated from the tier of subcultures and pre-political identities, including a majority national identity. These domesticated identities may then be accorded equal protection, recognition, or even given positive support, depending on each state's own history of pluralism and the kinds of accommodation between different groups that are possible and desirable within it.

The uncoupling strategy is meant to accommodate diversity within the unity provided by a common constitutional order. The same universal principles of human rights and democracy are particularised in each national constitution from the standpoint of its own historical experience and traditions. This constitutional base is to become the focus of unity and the object of allegiance. Thus, the patriotism of the nation is to be transformed into what may be called the patriotism of the constitution.

Our earlier discussion of the historical role of the nation shows that it is possible in principle to uncouple state from nation, for there is not a conceptual, only an empirical, tie between the two notions. The original function of the nation, of providing a more emotionally satisfying basis of social identification than the thin juridical bonds of citizenship, might now be said to be fulfilled. Citizens, at least those in the original European nation-states, can see citizenship as the very substance of their social unity and mutual responsibility. They can appreciate the interdependence of personal and political liberties, in supporting and bettering the conditions of the lives they want for themselves. They realise that they can only obtain a fair regulation of personal liberty by actually participating in citizenship, and that they are empowered to participate only in so far as there is a social basis for personal independence. The welfare states of postwar Europe all moved their citizens on to this citizenship plateau. As a result their citizens have developed the capacity to substitute ethical relationship for ethnocultural relationship as the basis for political unity.

But the institutional expression of a post-national consciousness is not yet well developed. In the case of Ireland an overly long and detailed written constitution not only picks the nation as the source of citizenship, but tries to maintain a certain shape for Irish identity for all time. The Constitution Review Group left intact the existing constitutional ordering of nation and state as well as the religious references that provide a large part of the normative core of Irish national identity in one phase of history. In Europe and elsewhere there is a great deal of talk about the basis of integration in pluralist and multicultural societies, but as yet there are no constitutions for pluralism.

One main reason for the institutional lag is that the economic basis of a constitution for pluralism is no longer in the full control of national governments. It has long been recognised that civil and political rights must be supplemented by economic and social rights if citizenship is to be a successful mode of social integration. Democratic citizenship can bind strangers if it is the very means by which they can have the legal and material supports for control over their own lives. The original citizenship arguments for social welfare may have been politically successful because they were made in homogeneous societies such as post-second world war Britain. But if civic integration is to be successful in multicultural societies, something like the same deal must be made. Members of the variety of groups must be able to find in common citizenship the basis of their mutual acceptance and survival. In addition to civil and political rights, they must enjoy social and cultural rights.

Unfortunately for this new phase of civic integration the welfare state is on the retreat all over Europe. So at the very time when more equality is needed to meet demands for mutual recognition between mobilised self-differentiated groups, the basis on which states might meet those demands is eroding. We already see the effects of the declining welfare state in the emergence of an underclass in our cities and towns everywhere. This is composed of people who are not able to participate in the new tiger economies, because they lack relevant skills, aptitudes, education and, more generally, fair equality of opportunity. In the absence of appropriate welfare provision these people cannot improve their lot in life and, unless they can somehow raise themselves by their own efforts, they become cordoned off from the main society. But society cannot cordon off more and more socially redundant groups without repercussion. We already see these in the growth of the drug business everywhere in Europe, but with astonishing speed in Ireland; in the growth of attendant crime and the consequent costs of policing and prisons; and in growing indifference to the plight of the homeless and destitute.

More alarming for the fate of democratic politics itself is the cordoning off of cultural minorities who are thereby deprived of their own voice and effective political participation. In such conditions formally equal civil and political rights may become devalued as worthless and the procedures and institutions of democratic politics may be undermined as mere instruments of ruling majority cultures.

In Ireland we have seen the cost to Northern Catholic nationalists of political and social marginalisation and the cost of that for the whole society in civic disintegration and political deformation. Marginalised cultural groups may struggle for civic integration. But everywhere the evidence is that such groups may harbour members who repudiate such a struggle and work instead with the bullet and the bomb for brute supremacy over the rejecting society.

The consequences of social marginalisation are so bleak that some people think we should halt the erosion of the nation-state and try to rebuild communities focused on shared identities. The trouble is we cannot go back. The problems that now beset nation-states stem from their inability to act politically for their own citizens. The main reason for this defect in political agency is the trend towards globalisation.

Globalisation
We now live in societies which are more or less globally related. We talk of global networks and systems in relation to production, markets, employment and communication. We are all familiar with the fact that decisions taken far away can affect local lives and

livelihoods, and vice versa. Worldwide relations of production and movements of capital and labour mean that investment decisions are made on the basis of global prices. National governments are increasingly exposed as incapable of the level of political action needed to deal with the attendant risks of globalisation, risks with consequences for us all – to the environment, to human rights, to the balance of world power, to national economic wellbeing. Here we hit the limits of the national state and the main reason it must join with others forming supranational regimes capable of responding to global systems.

The EU is one such political formula. It is our best shot at creating capacities for political action that match the scale of the problems we have to address.

Facing the future

The argument for uncoupling citizenship from national identity is not meant to cast national identities into the trash bin of history. The move is to make the democratic people guardian of the plurality of ethnocultural identities that the state contains. There are a number of ways in which the guardianship of identities can be given institutional form – through the provision of polyethnic and special representation rights, for example in addition to forms and degrees of self-determination appropriate to the circumstances and needs of different groups. While I cannot discuss these efforts to institutionalise multicultural citizenship here, one observation about them seems worth making. As strategies for civic inclusion they heed the warnings of Mill and Berlin against ignoring national identities. In Europe, where these identities continue to be strong, the citizenship state is not subtended by the cosmopolitan melting pot of an immigrant culture such as the United States. Instead what we can expect is a mosaic of identities, perhaps less diverse than the Canadian one, and more insistent on common citizenship rights.

Nevertheless the projected political nation is open to a number of objections. I deal briefly with two of the most important. The first is a worry about whether constitutional patriotism, unsupported by the ties of a unitary nation, is a thick enough bond to hold complex societies together. States need anchoring in nations, it is said, because the modern state cannot engender the spirit of self-sacrifice on which depends collective action for necessary or desirable social goals – welfare provision for the needy, or provision for the future, or national security. This is an empirical claim for which no well-considered evidence has yet been produced. Nevertheless there is enough evidence to suggest that the fragmentation of some modern societies into self-consciously different identity groups is accompanied by increased unwillingness on the part of better off groups to shoulder the burdens of common citizenship with other, worse off, groups.

But the solution to this problem is surely not the attempt to impose a dominant ethnocultural identity on all in the name of common nationality. That is the nationalist solution that the politics of difference has emerged to combat. Nor is the solution one that encourages political fragmentation by dissolution of the citizenry into self-determining groups, each pursuing its own common good, presumably behind fortified fences.

What is needed instead is a kind of cosmopolitan education for unitary citizenship among respected differences. For, first, it seems likely that constitutions for pluralism in western-style democracies can gain their force for integration between different identities only in so far as they are repositories of universal political values that can be reconciled with the internal values of each identity. For a large range of the identities we encounter in the nation-states of Europe for example, commitment to the values of human rights, the rule of law, and democracy, is consistent with, or entailed by, the internal values of those identities.

Second, it seems plausible that civic identification is strengthened when constitutions can be seen as the very means by which various groups can secure legal and material support for their own identities. This need not entail the creation of ethnic or cultural enclaves insulated from processes of cultural interchange. Few groups want to live the way their ancestors lived, or to close themselves off from worthwhile aspects of other cultures. What they want is to preserve their existence as a culturally distinct group, able to transform and adapt their identities without the pressure to abandon their group life altogether. What an open and pluralistic society needs is legal and social space in which mutual recognition of identity is seen as the basis for the security and flourishing of different groups. That, and not new communitarian fortresses, can provide the security from civil strife that individuals and groups, even the well off, need from the modern state.

Third, it is worth remembering that the building of constitutional patriotism is not some completely new political venture. It pre-supposes the continuity of the nation-state unit, but on a model that gives primacy to the political values that sustain coexistence. Citizenship is developed as a mode of integration for a historical 'we' that knows itself as a historical subject spun like a yarn from many overlapping and discontinuous threads. 'We' who are the contemporary part of one of these historical subjects have made a distinct constitutional history, something that evokes loyalty not just because of its character, but also because it is the result of our own efforts to address the problems that have arisen in our historical situation.

A good example of the successful implementation of universal values in particular circumstances is the building of a democratic state in Ireland after the Treaty. Ireland is almost alone is sustaining a democracy on the basis of such fragile beginnings – incomplete independence, an immediate civil war, a continuing political dis-agreement about the partition of the island, internal terrorism, and external threats to sovereignty during World War II (Garvin, 1996, ch. 6). This is the kind of effort to instal and maintain universal political values in particular contexts that patriotism of the con-stitution is about. We can think of ourselves with pride as the people who built a democratic path in inauspicious circumstances. We may be able to continue our distinctive thread of historical agency as the people who overcame nationalism on this island.

The second major objection to the political nation is that it conflicts with national self-determination. There are, it may be claimed, good arguments to suggest that nationality may properly belong to a person's sense of identity and value in the world. Further it is sometimes right for nationality to be the basis for political self-determination, to degrees and particular kinds of independence, if not to a fully sovereign state. The citizenship state appears to conflict with this case for national self-determination, because of the priority it gives to civic over national identity.

But the appearance of conflict here rests on a misunderstanding of the role of the state in relation to nations or identities, the same type of mistake that occurs when the state is seen as the strong arm of religion. This is to think of the state as a purposive association with ends or goals that may be advanced through the use of coercive force, rather than as a framework of rules and conditions that provides the social order within which individuals and groups may pursue their own purposes. The state is neither a voluntary association nor a community, but an inescapable domain of coercive force. That is why it cannot have its own purposes, for these belong to individuals as free agents. To think that the coercive power of the state may be used not only to defend identities or religions, but to promote them and guarantee their continuity, is also a misunderstanding of the character of these identities. Nations like religions survive because of their abilities to attract the willing adherence of their members, including the willingness to continue them. And these identities are what they are in so far as they are believed in as a matter of an internal endorsement rather than external compulsion.

Rightly understood then, a claim to *national* self-determination is a claim exercised in the face of some injury to the self-esteem or dignity of people of a particular identity, an injury that can best be rectified by their having a state of their own or some lesser degree of self-determination. The point about having a national state is to have the free space in the world to assert that identity, not for the state to do it, but to be the social space within which it can happen without interference by others.

Conclusion

Where do we stand? I began this essay by suggesting that our conventional views about the character of the European nation-state can no longer stand up to the realities of diminished state sovereignty, and to the decline of cultural homogeneity within the nation-states of Europe. I proposed that we rethink our ideas about how nations and states fit together (a job that the Constitution Review Group conspicuously chose not to tackle). I argued that we need to uncouple state and nation, not with the idea of disposing of nations, for they will continue as long as people want them, but with a view to reordering their relationship, giving priority to the civic/political over the cultural nation. I argued that the new ordering would make possible new forms of political relationship that allowed many national identities to share a common citizenship; that the possibility of a juridical order of citizens across nationalities is the basic step we need to take to deal with internal pluralism and to join with others in the bigger political units we need in order to tackle the problems of globalisation. I proposed that we face the problem of political motivation as something to be solved rather than as a reason for paralysing us in the outworn nation-state format, and I suggested that it may not be that big a problem anyway. Finally, I argued that this new way of thinking – the political nation – does not conflict with a belief in national self-determination.

References

Audard, C. 1996. 'Political Liberalism, Secular Republicanism: two answers to the challenges of pluralism', in D. Archard (ed.), *Philosophy and Pluralism*. Cambridge: Cambridge University Press.

Berlin, I. 1981. *Against the Current*. Oxford: Clarendon Press.

Bowman, J. 1982. *De Valera and the Ulster Question: 1917-1973*. Oxford: Clarendon Press.

Constitution Review Group. 1996. *Report of the Constitution Review Group*. Dublin: The Stationary Office.

Garvin, T. 1996. *1922: The Birth of Irish Democracy*. Dublin: Gill and Macmillan.

Habermas, J. 1991. 'Citizenship and National Identity: Some Reflections on the Future of Europe', *Praxis International* 12.1, 1-19.

Mazzini, G. 1907. *The Duties of Man*. London: Everyman.

Mill, J. S. 1975. 'Considerations on Representative Government (1861)', in John Stuart Mill, *Three Essays*. Oxford: Oxford University Press.

Renan, E. 1994. 'Qu'est-ce qu'une natien?', in J. Hutchinson and A. Smith (eds), *Nationalism*. Oxford: Oxford University Press.

Whyte, J. 1990. *Interpreting Northern Ireland*. Oxford: Clarendon Press.

CHAPTER 4

The Common Good and the Politics of Community

Iseult Honohan

Introduction

In the last twenty years in Ireland we have witnessed debates – notably about abortion and divorce – which featured not only radically opposed viewpoints but also significantly different vocabularies. Many advocates of divorce legislation, for example, spoke of the individual's right to remarry, focused on individual freedom as the most important value at stake, and opposed state intervention in matters perceived to be of personal morality. Their opponents spoke of the common good and the fabric of society, and argued that the state should support social institutions that embody the values of the community. At least at the polarised extremes of this debate, inhabited by so-called 'fundamentalist liberals' and 'authoritarian conservatives', the protagonists often seemed to talk different languages, built respectively around 'individual freedom' and 'the common good'.

The trends underlying successive referendums seem to suggest that the language of individual freedom has become marginally more persuasive to the electorate. In the wider political context, however, there has recently been a widespread revival of talk of community values, notably in the US and Britain, suggesting that claims of rights have become too extensive and need to be balanced by recognising duties and responsibilities. This has been taken up with some enthusiasm by quite a range of political actors including Tony Blair and Bill Clinton, and has also received some attention in Irish political circles.

In some respects at least, these practical debates mirror the wider theoretical debate between liberals and communitarians which dominated the field of political theory for a number of years. Liberals argued broadly that individual autonomy is the primary value and that the state, although it may need to make provisions to reduce inequality, should be more or less neutral on the sort of lives individuals should lead: a just political society is one that, subject to some quite general rules of distribution, allows all its members to define and pursue their own life plans. Communitarians, on the other hand, argued that individuals are fundamentally defined by the communities in which they are born and grow and cannot fulfil themselves except as members of communities; they rejected the liberal view of the autonomous self as a false description and an undesirable aim; hence, they argued, the state must help to promote the communal settings in which individuals reach their fullest development.

In the course of this debate many issues were clarified, causing theorists on both sides to modify their arguments significantly; while major differences still prevail, much more subtle positions are now maintained. For example liberals have taken on board some communitarian points, often holding that liberalism never denied these. However, liberals steadfastly resist the idea of what is called a 'politics of the common good' largely on the grounds that there is no common good (at least in the sense of a shared view of human good or destiny) in modern pluralistic societies.[1]

In this paper I argue that the liberal dismissal of the notion of the common good is too sweeping. I am also concerned here to address some issues that have arisen in practical politics where, it must be said, less nuanced positions predominate. While some of what I argue may not apply to the most considered expressions of liberal and communitarian thought, I believe it has a bearing on popular ideas currently in circulation. Sometimes political life gets stuck in the grooves of earlier theoretical debates. We might say, to paraphrase Keynes, that every self-styled 'practical' person is the victim of some defunct political theorist. My aim is not to take up the cudgels against liberals or communitarians as such; part of my point is that things are much more complex than extremists on either side suggest.

---

[1] The evolution of this debate is well covered in Kymlicka (1990) and Mulhall and Swift (1996).

I should state at the outset that there are at least two sets of issues connected with the notion of the common good – those concerning just distribution in society and shared values respectively.[2] While the first raises very important and related issues, it is on the question of shared values that I wish to focus here.

My concern is that the notion of the common good may be either too sweepingly dismissed or too unreflectively embraced. There is a traditional argument for the common good which has been used to justify authoritarian politics, but this is not the only way of approaching the issue. By considering a range of meanings of common good I examine what is involved in a more complex and less widely recognised sense. I introduce this in the context of examples from current debates about the environment, culture and morality, and specifically about the contentious status of marriage and the family. I suggest that the notion of shared goods is important to politics, and does not imply the oppressive government that some liberals fear. Without a concept of common good only quantifiable benefits distributable among discrete individuals can be considered part of a human good. But human life involves complex layers of existence and social interdependence. To fail to acknowledge this would be to miss much of what matters most to people and contributes to their development as individuals. While human good cannot be simply determined by reference to a fixed, universal nature, neither is it radically individual. Even in a world where we are conscious of the variety of fundamental goals and cultural values that people may embrace, we need to make provision for recognising some common, shared goods. I do not attempt here to affirm what specific measures are and are not common goods, but rather what structures may best allow their identification and realisation. This leads to the further question of whether the state can have any function in promoting the common good, an issue which is one of the fundamental sticking points between liberals and communitarians. I argue that the state inevitably embodies some perception of common good, that this should be conscious on our part rather than unconscious, though it should not generally take the form of

---

[2] For a variety of views about the common good and distributive justice, see Jordan (1989), Riordan (1991), Taylor (1995), Novak (1989) and Williams and Houck (1987).

constitutional or legislative coercion or prohibition, and that it should be a matter of public deliberation. Rather than carrying the authoritarian and conservative entailments which have rendered the term suspect to many in Ireland today, this notion of the common good has radically democratic implications.

Three conceptions of the common good

In what follows I want to separate out three ways in which the discourse of the common good is used. I will call these *teleological*, *individual-instrumental* and *intersubjective-practical* approaches respectively. In the first, common goods are seen as predetermined human purposes, in the second as conditions of individual fulfilment, and in the third as products of human interaction, which relate participants through certain kinds of practices. Teleological conceptions have been dominant in ancient and early modern societies, but the individual-instrumental usage has become increasingly prevalent; it has the advantage of being analytically very clear, and hence fits easily into the influential modern discourses of economics and law. The third, intersubjective-practical sense of shared goods, however, resonates strongly with people's experience, particularly in the areas of the environment, culture and morality.

First, *teleological* conceptions identify the common good with specific human ends or purposes common to people because of their similar nature – for example rational philosophical contemplation in Aristotle, union with God in Aquinas, harmony with a wider nature in some native and ecological philosophies – an approach to the good which though differently specified in different cultures and at different times has carried considerable weight, and still has power mainly in relatively homogeneous societies. The conception of the common good most familiar to us (and embodied in the Irish Constitution) comes broadly into this category, derived as it is from early twentieth-century Catholic social thinking. It is grounded in an Aristotelian view of humans as essentially social animals, who not only live together but, in order to develop themselves fully, need to be members of a political community. In this tradition the state is not merely an instrument to provide public order or to protect individual rights, but is concerned with the moral formation of citizens. Catholic social thinking builds on

Aristotle's idea that human wellbeing depends on a number of objective needs; this means that the good for human beings is predetermined in general by their natural ends or purposes. This theory was specified in more detail in the work of Thomas Aquinas, who put the notion of the human good in a theological framework, expanded it to apply universally to all humans, and developed a very complex hierarchy of levels of the good up to the supreme common good. In the natural law tradition of Thomism which has been carried on up to the present the state has a major role to play in promoting the common good; as determined by the understanding of nature it is to be embodied in law: 'the idea of the common good implies the request to describe exactly the good or complex of goods which ought to constitute the final aim of power' (d'Entrèves, 1967, 226). This, however, is only one understanding of the common good and its political status. Here the common good is that of human beings in a political framework 'united under God' in a society designed to realise human needs and values as universally defined by natural law, an approach based on assumptions that are not unproblematically accepted today, when we recognise that there are many different accounts of what are *the* purposes of human living.[3]

In the second, *individual-instrumental* approach the common good is identified as the ensemble of conditions for individual fulfilment, or the *aggregate of individual goods*. This is how those liberal theorists who do not reject the idea of a common good out of hand tend to define it. The common good is initially understood as whatever benefits all. 'The common good I think of as certain general conditions that are in an appropriate sense equally to everyone's advantage' (Rawls, 1971, 246). In the first place this

---

[3] A recent expression of this strand of common good thinking may be found in Dougherty (1984); rather different emphases will be found in MacIntyre (1991) and Novak (1989). Note, however, that natural law theorist Finnis (1980) adopts a version of the common good closer to the second, individual-instrumental approach. The combination of rights and common good discourse goes back at least to Maritain (1966). The recent *Catechism of the Catholic Church* (1994, ch. 2 II, 'The Common Good') combines elements of several different approaches. Two interesting accounts of the evolution of Catholic thinking on the common good are given by Langan in Douglass, Mara and Richardson (1990), and by Curran in Williams and Houck (1987).

requires a basic framework making civilised life possible. Further political measures can be justified as being in the common good if they benefit all equally; the laws which ensure the basic peace and security of society, public order, and measures promoting public health, traffic regulation and so forth are generally seen in this light. From this perspective all measures are considered in the light of their impact on individuals, though in many cases the benefits of some will have to be balanced against the benefits of others; in these cases the notion of the common good contributes nothing to the discussion.[4]

It is understood that benefits are to everyone's advantage in the sense that they are *distributable* among separate individuals. We may all benefit from peace or the improvement of traffic flows, but it is as separate individuals with our own priorities and purposes that we do so. While this is a valuable use of the term common good, it is too narrow and restrictive if it is considered as the *only* legitimate sense. This use does not entail the recognition of shared goods, and indeed often involves the denial of their possibility. As Margaret Thatcher might have said, there is no such thing as the common good, only the good of individuals, families and so on. I will argue that we need to consider wider senses of common good to grasp adequately what is at issue here.

It should be mentioned here that the concept of 'public goods' described by economists is completely consistent with this sense of the common good. It simply refers to benefits from which, if provided, it is not possible to exclude people, such as fresh air, streetlighting and, classically, lighthouses. But the enjoyment of these goods is taken to accrue to individuals separately.

This sense of the common good is often stretched to mean the good of the overwhelming majority in society as distinct from that of a small section or faction. In this sense, the term 'the public interest' emerged in the seventeenth century to signify the interest of the people in contrast to the private interest of the monarch, and has since become a notion used to limit the power of sectional groups in society. Thus the common good is invoked in debates

---

[4] This approach to the common good is expressed clearly by Rawls (1971 and 1993). Various aspects are discussed critically in Douglass, Mara and Richardson (1990).

about salmon farming in the west or goldmining on Croagh Patrick[5] to convey the interest of the wider society as opposed to the interest of individuals or companies who own property. But the term 'public interest' significantly implies or connotes an aggregate of individual interests, usually of a material kind (Barry, 1965, chs X-XIII).[6]

This understanding of the common good leads us, however, towards a third sense of the common good that is not so easily resolved into the benefit of individuals, what I have called the *intersubjective-practical.* The common good which may be achieved in preserving an area of natural beauty, religious significance, cultural heritage or ecological importance is not exactly comparable to the benefit which individual shareholders receive from the dividends of their mining or salmon farming companies. It is much *less tangible* and quantifiable; how do I measure my benefit from the preservation of Croagh Patrick? It may never be distributed: I may never climb Croagh Patrick, but I still derive some value from its being there as a possibility open to me. Some argue that in all such cases the benefit is merely switched from a small number of shareholders to a slightly larger or more vociferous number of religious traditionalists or nature lovers, but others rightly think it too narrow to say this. There is a real social benefit to a wider group; the wider benefit is *not easily distributable* or assignable across individuals; even identifying the beneficiaries in question may be difficult because they may not yet be born. The urgency of environmental and heritage issues derives from the danger that certain options may be shut off for ever for future members of our society. The common good in this sense is no longer that of equal benefit to all individuals tangibly enjoyed (and measurable in a balancing exercise of the good of different individuals). Conversely for public harm to be

---

[5] Croagh Patrick is an interesting example because of the multiple meanings it conveys – as an example of spectacular scenery, a distinctively Irish landscape, and a place of pilgrimage and religious devotion with associations that go back beyond modern Catholicism, and indeed Christianity itself, as the late July pilgrimage may hark back to the feast of Lughnasa (Harbison, 1991, 67-70).

[6] It is interesting to note that it is in terms of the 'public interest' and 'social justice' rather than 'the common good' that the justification for limiting property rights is expressed in the *Report of the Constitution Review Group* (1996, p. 361).

experienced it is not necessary that each member of society suffer a specific harm or loss, but that positive possibilities are shut off, and negative ones become more likely. For example some feminists argue that the harm to women done by pornography or sexual harassment cannot easily be understood by focusing on individual cases. Rather it 'inheres in social practices which are not susceptible of analysis in terms of an accumulation of individual discriminatory acts' (Frazer and Lacey, 1993, 82).

I am arguing then that we should recognise a third sense of the common good as *shared goods*; this is based on the belief that there are some goods that can be realised by individuals only in interaction with others, through certain cultural and social practices. The first level of these practices includes such things as the game of tennis, symphony orchestras, and most occupations – from computer programming to practising medicine. At this level we are just saying that these activities need a social framework to be possible at all. However, much of the benefit enjoyed by their practitioners might still be at an individual level – the satisfaction of winning, playing well, solving a problem or curing a patient. But at a second level there are goods which involve the experience of sharing. A simple example is the conviviality experienced at a good party. This is different from individual enjoyment of the food, wine or music. It is not just that individuals converge on enjoying some aspect of the party, but that they recognise that part of what they appreciate is the communal enjoyment, a notion captured by the colloquial term *craic*. 'In cases like these, the individual experiences are unintelligible apart from their reference to the enjoyments of others' (Waldron, 1993, 355).[7]

Shared goods are valued at least in part because they are shared, and not individually assignable or enjoyed. More substantial examples may include being a member of a language or religious community, sharing a common natural or cultural heritage, and other collective endeavours. Some part of our appreciation of the

---

[7] If true, the fact that most people watched the England-Germany match in the 1996 European Cup at home, whereas they watched Ireland play in the World Cup in the communal setting of the pub, may reflect the difference between the individual enjoyment of a match and the shared enjoyment of what was perceived as a communal endeavour.

Burren or Croagh Patrick may be that we share it as part of our common culture. In contrast we might want to save the tropical rainforest for strictly ecological reasons such as maintaining biodiversity.[8] Self-expression through a common culture is often held to be one of the central common goods. It is not just a matter of speaking one's own language, knowing one's own history, holding one's own religious beliefs, but living among people and within institutions that recognise these. It is not reducible to realising individual preferences – a fact which seems borne out by the difference between the number of people who actually speak Irish as their language and those who declare their support for its preservation as part of our common culture. It must be said that language, culture and natural heritage are shared in different ways. While a language literally is shared by all its speakers, often unreflectively, without any explicit endorsement of particular beliefs, people participate in other forms of cultural heritage less immediately and more abstractly, and may interpret and evaluate these differently. But all contribute to the relatively immediate communication between members that is one feature of a community.

I would argue that shared goods are not incidental but central to individual fulfilment. 'A person's wellbeing depends to a large extent on success in socially defined and determined pursuits and activities' (Raz, 1986, 309). For individuals to realise their most deeply held values there must be social practices that embody these values. At a simple level we can see that an Irish speaking family trying to bring children up in their culture will face major obstacles if schools, newspapers, television and government services through Irish are not available. At a more complex level there are certain options that lack real significance without social practices that recognise their value. The significance of individual behaviour depends on the existence of social forms. You cannot be a monogamist in a polygamist society, you are just someone with one wife so far (Raz, 1986, 162). Committing your life to Third World development means something in modern western society it could not have meant in Ancient Athens, where there was no notion of the universal dignity of human beings and no socially established practice of

---

[8] Though here too we might think in terms of the heritage of the whole human race.

humanitarian aid. Social institutions not only create the possibility of certain kinds of life, but also confirm their value.

This move from individual goods to shared goods entails a more complex understanding of human beings. Instead of seeing them as wholly separate entities we have to recognise how they are interconnected, and the good of one often dependent on the good of others. People are intrinsically social as well as significantly separate. Membership of a community is itself part of living a worthwhile life. In the light of our recognition that there are common goods as well as purely individual ones, we may say that, *contra* Mrs Thatcher, there *is* such a thing as community, which exists through these communal activities and enjoyments, which is not reducible to individually distributed benefits, though its point is the good of individuals. This view does not entail that there is a macro-entity, be it society, the nation or the earth, which is valued over and above the human beings who live within them.

This notion of the common good emphasises the importance to individual autonomy and identity of what are variously described as cultural identity, shared understandings, or common meanings. It diverges from the teleological natural law interpretation which derives from a single determinate account of human nature a hierarchy of human goods culminating in *the* common good. Thus it may be more appropriate to talk of 'common goods' rather than *the* common good. What is in the common good will vary with the specific circumstances in every case. The cultural interpretation of the common good is sometimes seen as just as rigid and oppressive as the teleological, even if it imposes *our* way of life rather than *the* good way of life. But it is not that an 'Irish way of life' or 'Unionist traditions' have any mystical claim to realisation, but that there are particular ways in which the people who live in Ireland, building on their historical situation, can most fully realise their possibilities now and in the future. Here, unlike in teleological approaches, it is acknowledged that cultures grow and change, and the forms and relative importance of various elements such as language, customs, settlement patterns, expressions of beliefs, and relations with smaller-scale and larger communities change over time. We may need to recognise the value of our communal practices, but that does not mean that a particular interpretation of the Irish 'way of life' and the practices that compose it be set in stone. There will clearly be different levels of community nested in one another, from the local to the national and beyond, and the nature and boundaries of these potential communities depends on specific circumstances. In any case it is clear that in this way people may have multiple identities, as members of several communities. Some common goods will be more local, others more wide-ranging. We may, for instance, be at the point of constructing a community with substantive shared goods at the European level, where up to now there has been just an association for mutual benefit.

Communities and their interpretations of the common good will not always be in harmony with one another. Deeply held values may come in conflict. The dynamic notion of culture I have outlined admits the possibility not only of common goods, but also of arguments about the nature and direction of the common good. To connect these theoretical considerations with a particular case: one very familiar disagreement in current politics centres on the role of marriage and the family in social life. Are we or are we not to conclude that marriage is essential to the social fabric, and what political implications should we draw?

My answer would be something like this: we may believe that family structures and continuing relationships are an important part of the social matrix of our community. Those who claimed that they could not make a lifelong commitment in a society tolerating divorce may have been exaggerating, but nonetheless glimpsed the way in which some personal goals depend on established social practices. As Raz puts it, 'monogamy requires a culture which recognises it, and which supports it through the public's attitude and through its formal institutions' (Raz, 1986, 162). My relatively communitarian sense of the common good does not, however, presuppose a single account of the role or form of the family that is a common good. Nor does it assume that the primary function of the family is to act as a kind of social cement, as distinct from its enabling individual development. Indeed there has been a number of shifts in the shared meaning of the family in modern times – for example from a relationship concerned primarily with reproduction to one of shared affection and joint projects, and from a strong commitment to an extended family to a more intense commitment to a nuclear family. Thus the meaning of the family may not be as simple and clear-cut as some of the opponents of divorce like to suggest. The core of the family may be relatively permanent relationships of affection and concern, or as Finnis puts it:

> a common stock – of uncalculated affection, physical and psychological rapport, of shelter and means of support and material bases for new projects, of memories and experience, of symbols, signs, and gestures to bear moods and meanings, of knowledge of each other's strengths and weakness, loves and detestations and of formal and informal but reliable commitment and devotion (Finnis, 1980, 145).

Yet the common meaning of the family and what it requires may develop over time, as all but the most dyed-in-the-wool conservatives recognise in the practice of their own day-to-day lives. This can be seen in the growing intolerance of domestic violence and child abuse, and in the readier acceptance of young unmarried mothers by their families. Some contributors to the Constitution Review Group which reported in 1996 suggested that 'the family' should still be incorporated as the 'primary and fundamental unit of society' in the constitution while including a wider range of relationships than formal marriage, relationships in which people live in continuing close association out of mutual love and intergenerational concern.[9] It remains a matter of reflection and debate just how wide this definition should be, and what institutional framework it requires. Since this raises the question of the role of the state in realising the common good, it is to this I will now turn. I will return to the treatment of the family in the context of discussing what the political response to our understanding of the common good should be.

The state and the common good

What role if any should the state play in promoting the common good? Some liberal thinkers have argued that while communal practices are valuable, they must be left to smaller communities to develop below the political level and must be oppressive to indi-

---

[9] In fact the group retained a more traditional notion of the family as based on marriage, while outlining arguments for and against a looser definition. (*Report of the Constitution Review Group,* pp. 319-337).

viduals and dissenting minorities if expressed through the state (Simpson, 1994). In their theoretical debates it became clear that the best exponents of liberal and communitarian thought, as Kymlicka puts it, 'disagree not over the social thesis, but over the proper role of the state, not over the individual's dependence on society, but over society's dependence on the state' (Kymlicka, 1990, 230).

The classical liberal position is that, given the diversity of goods which reasonable people may adopt as their goals, the state should be neutral about questions of the good life. But in practice liberal societies can survive only because the liberal state *does* promote certain values of trust, tolerance, mutual respect and so forth, and embodies a particular view of the common good. If the principles of state neutrality were to be rigorously applied, many of the things liberals value would not be preserved. Even the market requires state support to function efficiently. Neither the market nor lower-level institutions can guarantee the preservation for future generations of valued heritage or common culture. Markets are structured by individual preferences, not common values. Few communities can match the muscle of multinational corporations and states. If the precepts of the *Economist* were literally applied we might live in a world in which you could buy only *The Sun*. Even if we are all more enlightened than we think, our individual appreciation of the Aran Islands or the Burren does not guarantee that they will be available for future generations. However, a liberal might grant all that I have just said, and agree that the state cannot be wholly neutral, while still claiming that the state should not favour any more substantive idea of the good life, or any particular culture.

But the state cannot be wholly neutral in this sense either; whatever its form it exerts enormous influence for better or worse on the possibilities and values endorsed in society. It is not only a power mechanism or redistributive agent, but ineluctably a source of moral authority. For example, more severe penalties against drunken driving appear to be altering moral views on a practice that was hitherto widely condoned in Ireland. What we think of as private is often the subject of extensive state intervention. In the case of marriage for example, the state determines what constitutes a marriage: 'Who can marry whom, who is legally the child of whom and whether both spouses or only one must consent to their dissolution, are all directly determined by legislation' (Okin, 1989, 130). The laws and policies the state implements do not just tolerate social actions, but are bound to legitimate certain practices; it structures the social practices within which we act. Recognising a right to divorce *does* legitimate the practice. Not having strong provisions to deal with domestic violence *did* tacitly endorse men's right to act in certain ways. The relationship of marriage hitherto available was not strictly natural or God-given, but a relationship that had been heavily shaped by the state over time through the effect of laws (or their absence) on the legal existence of married women, their role in the home, adoption, domestic violence and rape within marriage, and the availability of contraception, as well as by policies on taxation, social welfare, education, health admin- istration and child-care provision.[10] Any modern state is so involved in the provision and regulation of goods and services that decisions about the good life and what is central to culture are pervasive.

So the state shapes our possibilities and embodies social practices for better or for worse. We need to admit this and construct institutions so that its impact can be conscious rather than unconscious. Communitarians (and some liberals) may argue, like MacIntyre, that 'the modern state is indeed unfitted to act as the moral educator of any community' (MacIntyre, 1984,195). They may claim that we need communities embodying shared values *below*, but not at, the level of the state, which they see as a power mechanism which at best minimises conflict and protects individual interests. But it seems naive to think that such communities alone can resist countervailing forces, whether of the market or of the state itself. Better that we should be able consciously to determine how the state shapes social practices and constructs the common good than have it constructed behind our backs.

Deliberative politics and the common good

The view that the common good is shaped by the citizens through politics recalls the tradition of civic republican thought. This shares with the Aristotelian tradition the beliefs that the common good is

---

[10] It has been suggested that the declining numbers of those entering marriage may itself be partly the effect of the absolute prohibition on divorce.

central, and that human fulfilment requires a political community. In the civic republican community, however, the emphasis is on the shared values developed in an historically evolving community. This communality derives not from the purposes laid down by a common human nature, or even by a common race or language, but from membership of the same political community, on which depends many of the possibilities of individual fulfilment. The shared values of politics are not just the implementation of values that are pre-political, but may themselves be constructed through politics. Citizens are united by joint membership and commitment to maintaining the institutions of their political community. The classic interpreter of this tradition was Machiavelli, who broke with the Aristotelian notion of a single determinate human good (Berlin, 1979; Skinner, 1990) and emphasised the importance of active citizenship in guaranteeing personal liberty and fulfilment. While classical republicanism was less sensitive to the potential dangers of oppression and exclusion even of a politically defined community, its modern representatives emphasise personal freedom and active deliberation as the heart of civic republicanism.[11]

This idea of the political community and the politically defined common good need not be as oppressive as some liberals fear. In the first place not all the actions of the state need be coercive, and in the second the formulation of the common good is open to discussion and, once formulated, is open to critique.

The use of coercive and prohibiting legislation has preoccupied both conservative and liberal movements in Ireland. (Should we or should we not legislate for personal morality?) However, while some element of coercion seems essential to guarantee public order and to limit oppression within society, it may not be appropriate in moral and cultural concerns. Here there is great room for disagreement, and it is almost impossible to express nuances of interpretation within the constraints of coercive law – as we discovered in the first abortion amendment, which turned out on judicial examination not to exclude all possibility of legal abortion in Ireland. Given the power of the state, the cost to citizens if the state endorses an interpretation which does not reflect their deep beliefs is very great

---

[11] See Arendt (1973) and (1959), Skinner (1990) and Sunstein (1988) for approaches that emphasise the centrality of freedom to civic republican thought.

– in the case of abortion for example, life and personal integrity may be at stake; if abortion becomes an entrenched right, the law creates difficulties for health workers who on conscience grounds do not wish to participate; if abortion is totally prohibited, the law creates other victims, as we saw in the *X* case. In addition the exercise of such power is a double-edged sword which may have effects other than those intended. For example legislation against pornography supported by feminists in Canada was used by others to restrict genuine women's self-help health books. Thus many feminists are opposed to dealing with the real harm they perceive to be done to women by pornography through censorship or prohibition; instead they stress other methods of minimising it, such as public identification and boycotting of mainstream distributors and retailers who deal in hard core pornography, and restrictions on its display and sale. That the state should exercise direct coercion and prohibition is not then the immediate conclusion we should draw from the desirability or undesirability or certain social practices.[12]

The state can influence its citizens in at least three ways, by legal coercion and prohibition, and also by economic subsidisation and taxation, and by symbolic endorsement or condemnation. These other means are not insignificant. Though most people believe the Irish language should be supported, they reject the compulsory requirement of Irish at every level in education and the public service, and it is now widely agreed that the coercive approach to the revival of Irish was counterproductive. In contrast, far more people are prepared to endorse the subsidisation of *Telefís na Gaeilge*. The role of President Mary Robinson was often to use the less tangible symbolic power of the state to cultivate certain shared values, such as the equal status of women in Irish society, to emphasise the richness and variety of our traditions, and to shift the expression of Irish identity from irredentist longing to collective pride in achievements. To take another example, recognising the

---

[12] There may be circumstances in which moral and cultural values should be supported by coercive legislation; it is suggested, for example, that minority cultures should be allowed to enforce language requirements. This is a matter of considerable debate. My concern here is not to rule out coercive legislation absolutely, but to point out that it is not the only way in which the state shapes society.

value of a community's religious beliefs no longer means outlawing minority faiths and need not mean establishing a state church, or funding specific churches. The state can act quite strongly to endorse shared values without applying coercive legislation. Thus it may also introduce measures which support not only the practices of the wider community, but also the varying needs of lesser communities – linguistic, cultural, etc – on which individual fulfilment depends. While endorsing particular cultures, it need not do so in an exclusionary manner.

As an example of the sort of relationship between the state and community values I am outlining, let us return to the case of marriage and the family. That we understand the family as a common value does not mean that marriage should necessarily be compulsory or even permanent for every person who enters it. We may live in a world where circumstances such as the power of market forces, the strain of urban life, the growth of social mobility or other factors, make permanent commitments more vulnerable than before; demanding that people should be bound to destructive relationships may be to demand the wrong thing in certain cases. Aquinas recognised that it is not possible, and is counterproductive, to demand from people virtue beyond a certain level, and was not as rigorist in his proposals as some of his successors. The widely shared values of compassion and individual dignity now make us more reluctant to enforce long-term suffering on people in unhappy marriages. While issues as complex as this cannot be resolved in a few sentences, we may suggest that the state can recognise marriage without making it compulsory or binding for life in every case; it can allow divorce without endorsing polygamy or even creating a 'divorce culture'. Different circumstances can be dealt with differently, in provisions that recognise the impact on all, including children, affected by marital breakdown. Support for the family can also be embodied in very different ways, such as assistance for those with young children or caring for aged parents, statutory parental leave, and more effective provision for people in situations like long-term unemployment that put strain upon families. What is required to support the good of family life needs much more complex attention than simple universal legislative prohibition or admission of divorce.

The role envisaged for the state in promoting the common good should not then be seen as essentially coercive. Moreover, from this perspective, because of the complexity of the common good and the need for interpretation, the direction in which the influence of the state works and the specification of the common good should be open to reflection and deliberation by those who are affected by it. The common good cannot be simply read off from a static account of human nature or natural law, nor can the right to define the common good be exclusively claimed by any particular set of people, expert or lay, who claim either to know definitively what is natural or to read the mind of the nation. Since the common good evolves historically, and varies with circumstances, it cannot be identified with the status quo, or existing expressions of shared understandings or culture; as cultures develop and change, and social practices evolve, every expression of the common good must be tentative and provisional. This is not an endorsement of moral relativism, as is often asserted, but of moral *fallibilism.* Cultures and social practices are provisional embodiments of what is good for those who live within them, but some cultures and practices achieve this better than others, and all are open to improvement.

Since the state is bound to express some version of the common good, it is most important that the public formulation of the common good should be just that. This requires that there be substantial public discussion of issues that concern the common good, and institutional provision for a public space for such discussion.

This is a point which popular communitarians are in danger of overlooking; in the rush to maintain social values and re-emphasise individual duties and responsibility, the specific requirements of the common good and community are too hastily assumed, and not enough emphasis is laid on its interpretation and on enabling all members of society to participate in deliberation about what the common good and responsibility requires in particular contexts.[13] Ascertaining what is in the common good is not a matter of a simple aggregation of preferences or unreflective opinions; it requires serious deliberation and judgment (Sunstein, 1988, 1991). It may be said that decisions have to be made in politics, that there

---

[13] The communitarian most widely cited in newspaper and magazine reports, though not particularly prominent in the earlier theoretical debates, is Amitai Etzioni. See Etzioni (1993).

is no acid test to distinguish conclusively unreflective preferences from serious deliberation, and that in many cases reflective agreement will not be reached. Thus decisions may often have to be made by a process that seems to involve a simple aggregation of preferences. Nonetheless decisions should be preceded by as much and as open debate as possible, and the laws or policies to which they lead should not be placed beyond discussion, critique and possible future change. Thus issues which divide a society deeply, like divorce, should not be the subject of constitutional entrenchment.

Some liberals have argued that debates on public issues should be based only on values and beliefs that are shared between the participants, and that individuals and groups should not attempt to influence policy by citing their own particular religious, moral or cultural beliefs. This takes fundamental moral disputes off the political agenda. Thus, for example, in the divorce referendum debate, some anti-divorce campaigners and some churchmen framed their opposition not in religious terms, but in secular terms of damage to the social fabric. But it is not clear to me that this is the standard towards which we should aim. Reasonable people who have fundamentally different ideas about when human life begins, or whether capital punishment is ever justified, may find it impossible to talk to one another if they have to exclude their deep-seated beliefs from the discussion. If the 'public reason' in terms of which they are constrained to speak must be stripped of reference to their particular values, they may never really come to understand one another's positions, their differences, or the genuine feeling that underlies them. In such circumstances they may mutually appear more irrational and remote, and they may lack motivation to continue talking. Given the centrality of moral beliefs, and the difficulty of disentangling private and public matters, such a politics would truncate the political process of discussion, and would not eliminate moral conflict from politics. Therefore I suggest that political debate should allow people to advance arguments drawn from their deep-seated moral convictions, while requiring them to recognise that not everyone may share these convictions. Where it can be achieved, the common good of politics lies in joint deliberation about what our substantive goods may be – in discussion where we can bring arguments from our 'comprehensive doctrines,' our cultural or religious beliefs to the table, not to stonewall the political process but to have a deeper understanding of what is at issue. It would involve reflection on rather than bracketing of our fundamental beliefs. For many this is what actually was going on in the 1995 divorce referendum debate, rather than a decision to set aside their fundamental beliefs in a political context. In the light of experience and the arguments advanced, people reflected on what their moral views entailed and came to their decisions on that basis. Thus the Taoiseach at the time, John Bruton, could say afterwards that the result was not a victory for any side, as the divisions were experienced within as much as between citizens.

This perspective does not assume that consensus will always be reached; there will be situations where people will continue to disagree fundamentally. Politics has very tangible limits. At least it may be said that this form of political community is potentially less exclusive than racially or culturally defined political communities, and less oppressive than pre-political communities without institutionalised space for discussion and critique.[14]

It could still be argued that contemporary societies contain such widely divergent perspectives that any substantial embodiment of the common good must privilege the values of one group over others. There are two possible answers to this; one is that beneath the much cited moral diversity in modern societies there lies a deeper framework of common values than we recognise; the other is that whatever our differences we are driven together by the fact that we face a common future in an increasingly interdependent world and a threatened natural environment. I cannot argue either of these in detail here, but these are points which must be taken seriously. In the present Irish political context too, we may already have common goods we underestimate, and are in danger of eroding. In addition, where there *are* different cultural and moral values, we may create through politics further common meanings which allow us to reflect on and understand the differences between our most deeply held values.

In this paper I have argued for an understanding of the common good as shared goods that arise between people engaged in prac-

---

[14] Writings that are closest to the view defended here are to be found in Taylor (1985), Gutmann and Thompson (1990) and Sunstein (1988).

tices. These goods are a crucial aspect of human fulfilment, and need political expression and protection. But we should be critical in our approach to popular communitarians who derive over-hasty conclusions from this. Questions of the good should not be excluded from politics, but formulations of the good should not be too hastily embedded in constitutional and legislative measures. Indeed, rather than excluding the question of substantive goods from politics, we should recognise that any definitions of the good are provisional and open to improvement, and that one of the most important institutions required for the common good is a public space in which people may not just seek accommodation with those who have different values, but deliberate over what is the good for all significant parties. In the public space of politics common meanings are developed, not just reaffirmed.

References

Arendt, H. 1959. *The Human Condition*. New York: Doubleday Anchor.
Arendt, H. 1973. *On Revolution*. Harmondsworth: Penguin.
Barry, B. 1965. *Political Argument*. London: Routledge and Kegan Paul.
Berlin, I. 1979. 'The Originality of Machiavelli', in *Against the Current*. Harmondsworth: Penguin.
Catechism of the Catholic Church. 1994. Dublin: Veritas.
d'Entrèves, A.P. 1967. *The Notion of the State*. London: Oxford University Press.
Dougherty, J. 1984. 'Keeping the Common Good in Mind', in L.J. Elders and K. Hedwig (eds), *Studi Tomistici*. Vatican City: Liberia Editrice Vaticana.
Douglass, R., Mara, G. and Richardson H. (eds). 1990. *Liberalism and the Good*. London: Routledge.
Etzioni, A. 1993. *The Spirit of Community*. London: Fontana.
Etzioni, A. (ed.). 1995. *New Communitarian Thinking*. Charlottesville: University Press of Virginia.
Finnis, J. 1980. *Natural Law and Natural Rights*. Oxford: Oxford University Press.
Frazer, E. and Lacey, L. 1993. *The Politics of Community*. London: Harvester Wheatsheaf.
Gutmann, A. and Thompson, D. 1990. 'Moral Conflict and Political Consensus', in R. B. Douglass, G. Mara, and H. S. Richardson (eds), *Liberalism and the Good*. London: Routledge.
Harbison, P. 1991. *Pilgrimage in Ireland*. London: Barrie and Jenkins.
Jordan, B. 1989. *The Common Good*. Oxford: Blackwell.

Kymlicka, W. 1990. *Contemporary Political Philosophy: An Introduction*. Oxford: Clarendon Press.

MacIntyre, A. 1984. *After Virtue* (2nd edn). Notre Dame: University of Notre Dame Press.

MacIntyre, A. 1991. 'The Privatization of Good', *Review of Politics* 52, 344-361.

Maritain, J. 1966. *The Person and the Common Good*. Notre Dame: University of Notre Dame Press.

Mulhall, S. and Swift, A. 1996. *Liberals and Communitarians* (2nd edn). Oxford: Blackwell.

Novak, M. 1989. *Free Persons and the Common Good*. New York: Madison.

Okin, S. 1989. *Justice, Gender and the Family*. New York: Basic Books.

Rawls, J. 1971. *A Theory of Justice*. Oxford: Oxford University Press.

Rawls, J. 1993. *Political Liberalism*. New York: Columbia University Press.

Raz, J. 1986. *The Morality of Freedom*. Oxford: Clarendon Press.

Report of the Constitution Review Group. 1996. Dublin: Stationery Office.

Riordan, P. 1991. 'The Plausibility of Arguments from the Common Good', *Milltown Studies* 28, 78-101.

Riordan, P. 1996. *The Politics of the Common Good*. Dublin: IPA.

Simpson, P. 1994. 'Liberalism, State and Community', *Critical Review* 8, 159-173.

Skinner, Q. 1990. 'The Republican Ideal of Liberty', in G. Bock, Q. Skinner and M. Viroli (eds), *Machiavelli and Republicanism*. Cambridge: Cambridge University Press.

Sullivan, W. 1990. 'Bringing the Good Back In', in R. B. Douglass, G. Mara and H.S. Richardson (eds), *Liberalism and the Good*. London: Routledge.

Sunstein, C. 1988. 'Beyond the Republican Revival', *Yale Law Journal* 97, 1539-1590.

Sunstein, C. 1991. 'Preferences and Politics', *Philosophy and Public Affairs* 20, 3-34.

Taylor, C. 1985. 'Atomism', 'Interpretation and the Sciences of Man', and 'The Diversity of Goods', in *Philosophical Papers* Volume 2: *Philosophy and the Human Sciences*. Cambridge: Cambridge University Press.

Taylor, C. 1995. 'Irreducibly Social Goods', in *Philosophical Arguments*, 127-145. Cambridge: Harvard University Press. .

Waldron, J. 1993. *Liberal Rights*. Cambridge: Cambridge University Press.

Williams, O. and Houck, J. (eds). 1987. *The Common Good and U.S. Capitalism*. Lanham: University Press of America.

CHAPTER 5

Fergal O'Connor's Plato: The Family, Private Property and the State

Denys Turner

I

It was in 1961, as one of two lay undergraduates in a second year Philosophy class of some one hundred clerical students, that I first encountered Fergal O'Connor. I think it was the first lecture he gave at UCD. For us – at any rate, for me – it was a revelation. It does no discredit to his colleagues in the Faculty of Philosophy if I say that whereas until then we had been taught by many a *soi-disant* 'Thomist' and by at least one genuine Aristotelian, Fergal succeeded in coming across to us with a distinctively Socratic impact. Intellectually, he was pure midwife. He told us nothing by way of solutions, except, perhaps, where to look for them. He posed questions, not in that bullying manner – in fact little more than a defensive mannerism – which demands to know 'what do you mean by ...?' (you clearly do *not* know); nor because he even remotely appeared to entertain the thought that, absurdly, questions matter more than answers; but because he knew that answers are answers to *questions* and are dependent on them: from bad questions only bad answers come.

I suppose we found this refreshing because much of what we had experienced until that time had consisted in answers, the questions they were answers to being largely undisclosed: so that the recommendations that came with the answers seemed to depend not on their adequacy as responses to the questions so much as on a rather more extrinsic authority – that of Vatican regulations concerning the philosophical doctrines appropriately to be taught to clerical students. Later when I became a postgraduate student Fergal persuaded me to read Thomas Aquinas himself, which I was then able to do with an appreciation of the sort Wittgenstein is reported to have had for Thomas, that while he did not think a lot of his answers, his questions seemed right. But already Fergal had got me reading Plato, as an undergraduate, and there can scarcely be a thought I have had since, or a word I have written, which does not reveal some form of reaction – whether of puzzlement or of exasperation or (quite often enough) of simple awe – to Plato's thought.

I left UCD at the end of 1976, then as a junior colleague of his in the Department of Ethics and Politics, and I do not know much about Fergal's teaching since. But unless his practice changed a great deal subsequently he has now taught many generations of undergraduate how to read Plato, but more particularly *why* they should. And it may very well be asked why the undergraduate teaching of Plato by a Dominican friar in the UCD of the 1960s should be worth a comment in a volume largely devoted to issues of contemporary Irish society and politics. I hope to answer that question in the course of this essay; in the meantime it is worth noting that Fergal's Plato was distinctive for its time: in the sixties and seventies it was necessary to do some radical restorative work on the picture which Plato presented, very especially in view of the patina of misrepresentation smeared over his political philosophy by the likes of Karl Popper and Von Hayeck, for whom *Republic* was little more than a proto-fascist, or alternatively a proto-Stalinist, tract – which, absurdly, for Von Hayeck and Popper seemed to amount to much the same thing.

So why Plato? We may ask that question all the more particularly since a deeply Catholic culture, or at any rate that intellectual version of it formed by the theological instincts of the second Vatican Council, is bound to be hostile to Plato's abstract idealism, to his apparent contempt for the empirical, contingent and material, to the 'dualism' of body and soul which underpins that contempt for the body, and to the spiritual eroticism which aspires so passionately to 'beauty as such' at the price of distrusting any particular beautiful thing. And, as I understood his own intellectual and theological commitments, Fergal the Thomist had every reason for rejecting that much of what Plato stood for. Yet for all these evident intellectual antipathies, it was Fergal's Plato which we students found most memorable about his teaching, above all Plato the theorist of politics and education, Plato the theorist of the politics *of* education.

For of course it was less the programmatic educational strategies recommended in *Republic* V – the censorship of poetry and classical myth, the elitism, the eugenic breeding policies – that seemed important, so much as the 'spirituality' (as one might call it) of education which Plato recounted narratively in the story of Socrates' trial and death and embeds metaphorically in the famous 'Allegory of the Cave' at the beginning of *Republic* VII.

The narrative is simple enough and well known. Socrates had been arraigned by the Athenian ruling elites on charges of corrupting the youth of Athens, but in his unsympathetic eyes the democratic ruling party had merely acted on self-interested motives to suppress his exposure of the corruptions of conventional politics, education and morals. In his defence Socrates explains why it was that his method of relentlessly questioning all conventions was laid upon him as a divine charge. He had sought wisdom from the experts but had found none there, for they could not answer the simplest questions; they did not know, Socrates concluded, though they thought they did; he on the other hand knew at least that he did not know. In despair of finding a master to follow among Athenians, Socrates consulted the divine oracle at Delphi as to who was the wisest of humans and received the unhelpful reply, 'Socrates'. One and only one thing could follow, in Socrates' view, from the indisputable truth of the divine utterance: if he, Socrates, was the wisest of men, then this could be only *because* he knew that he knew nothing, whereas the experts knew less even than he, less even than nothing; because in addition to knowing nothing they did not know that they knew nothing. The knowledge of the experts he had proved to be ignorance. But his knowledge of his own ignorance was the only true knowledge to be had.

It was this story which Plato retold in the Allegory of the Cave in *Republic* VII. Picture men, Socrates asks, who are imprisoned deep in a cave facing its back wall, unable to move their heads or any other parts of their bodies; imagine that, above and behind them, there is a low wall, behind which again is a fire casting the shadows of puppets representing all kinds of objects upon the back wall which the prisoners face. The prisoners are able to see no more than the shadows of these puppets and hear nothing but the echoes of their operators' voices and, significantly, they cannot see even themselves but only their own shadows, for they cannot turn their faces to each other or to their own bodies. Would not such prisoners, Socrates asks, 'deem reality to be nothing else than the shadows of the artificial objects?' (*Republic,* 515c, trans. P. Shorey; Cambridge Mass, 1956).

Suppose further that one of the prisoners is released and turned to face the light which throws the shadows: will he not 'feel pain and because of the dazzle and glitter of the light' be 'unable to discern the objects whose shadows he formerly saw?' (515c). Disorientated, his conversion has gained for him the worst of both worlds, for dazzled by the excess of light he derives no profit from that, and worse, as a result he is unable to see even in his former twilight world, to whose undemanding security he pines to return.

The prisoner, then, will not willingly proceed further 'up the ascent', for it is 'rough and steep' (515e); and so he will have to be dragged forcibly out of the cave into the light of the sun, where 'his eyes will be filled with its beams, so that he would not be able to see even one of the things which we call real' (516a).

Once again the excess of light is distress to the eyes which for a second time are plunged into darkness, now even deeper than the first. Gradually however, as his eyes become stronger and more used to the new light, the prisoner feebly glimpses first in shadows and in reflections in pools the objects outside the cave, and then the things themselves: 'and from these he would go on to contemplate the appearances in the heavens and heaven itself, more easily by night, looking at the light of the stars and the moon, than by day the sun and the sun's light' (516a-b).

Finally, his eyes being at last fully habituated to the light, the prisoner will, Socrates says, 'be able to look upon the sun itself and see its true nature, not by reflections in water or phantasms of it in an alien setting, but in and by itself in its own place' (516b). And in contemplating the sun the emancipated prisoner sees not only the highest and most luminous of all things, but also that which is 'the cause of all these things that they had seen' (516b-c).

Now the philosopher will pity his one-time fellow prisoners who, he realises, at best compete with one another in an absurd game of precedence in the perception of shadows and appearances, mistaking them for reality, trapped in a world of lived unreality. Having seen it for what it is, the philosopher 'would choose to endure anything rather than such a life' (516e), and in his pity he returns to the cave with the hope of persuading his former fellow-inmates to turn away from their world of unreality and to turn, as he had done, towards the contemplation of the true light he has seen for himself.

But the shock of the contrast between the light he inhabits and the gloom of the cave casts his eyes yet again into darkness as he descends. There he debates with the prisoners and is ridiculed for his account of his own ascent, for they complain that his adventures have but ruined his eyesight. The prisoners resent his claims to a better vision of things and they will kill him if they can. And of course, in the person of Socrates, they did.

II

It is, perhaps, easiest for a contemporary western reader to respond to this allegory in a highly individualistic fashion as the story of the individual's search for truth through humane and liberal values of enquiry. Yet, given that reading of the allegory, the contemporary reader is left with a puzzle as to how it can be reconciled with the evidently political context in which it is set within the argument of *Republic* as a whole. Nor is the contemporary secular liberal alone in offering an individualistic reading, for the allegory was for centuries read, within the Christian medieval West, as the story of the individual soul's search for God, a search which was described very largely through Plato's imagery, of progression from the twilight of half-ignorance, which is all that can be obtained by the soul trapped in the cave of carnality, contingency and temporality, through stages of ascent to increasing measures of light until the soul is confronted by the full light of divine reality, a light so excessive as to be experienced only as 'a dazzling darkness', a 'knowing un-knowing'. Nor is there any doubt that there is a partial legitimacy to both historical readings. For what the medieval 'mystical' reading took up from the allegory was Plato's profound sense of the contrast between 'illusion' and 'reality'; and the contemporary secular liberal reading rightly takes up Plato's instinct that the transition from the one to the other is progressive and dialectical – that is to say is a progression whose strategy is that of debate, questioning, openness. But both the contemporary secular and the medieval Christian readings of this allegory omit much that is essential to what Plato intended his allegory to illustrate. While the Christian reading was happy to carry with it from Plato his casting of the contrast between illusion and reality in terms of that between the temporal, material, contingent world and the eternity, immateriality and necessity of 'Ideas', the contemporary response is almost wholly suspicious of such notions and on the whole will have nothing of them. What neither reading of Plato in any way captures is Plato's sense that this whole movement from 'illusion' to 'reality' is essentially a political process, one which is not just in some way *dependent upon* certain political conditions obtaining, but one whose dynamics are themselves social and political. The dialectics of knowledge-acquisition in Plato are principally the dialectics of politics and society.

For the prisoners trapped in the cave are not just deluded individuals in need of a decent education: they represent a society, a construct of social relations, founded in and reproductive of 'illusion'. It is not difficult after all to imagine contemporary analogates on a smaller scale: marriages settled into patterns of mutual engagement and response which serve principally to sustain and reinforce mutual dishonesty, self-ignorance and ignorance of each other; fantastical public images of gender or of body promoted as ideal, yet profoundly untruthful, media of human interaction between the sexes; the systematic promotion of unrealistic satisfactions designed to induce in consumers the perception of appropriately idealised desires. All these commonplace phenomena describe, intuitively and anecdotally, what Plato understands by the condition of the prisoners in the cave: that of a society which lives by illusions, a society whose structures can function only on the condition of illusion, hence a society which can survive only in so far as it sustains the illusions it lives by. The condition of those imprisoned in such a society is that of a 'lived unreality'. For they do not have any reality to live by other than their illusions. Unreality *is* their reality.

There is an element of deliberate paradox in this description: yet this is unsurprising, since what Plato's theory of knowledge seeks to respond to is a highly complex and self-sustaining paraphernalia of illusion. The social world of Plato's day seemed to him to exist by means of the conjunction of apparently contradictory elements. On the one hand it seemed to him that that society was, in some way, 'unreal'; on the other hand it was that society and only that society, with all its structures and processes productive of illusion and unreality, which actually existed. It was in and through their *illusions* that people lived out their *real* relations with each other, for it was by, for, and in that 'unreal' reality that people desired and satisfied themselves, competed, won, lost, married, had children, sought happiness, knowledge and the good life. It was an 'illusory' society in that deeply structural way in which any pattern of social relations can be structurally 'false', even if and when its members consciously live by beliefs they *know* the falsehood of. Yet 'false' as it is, its members know of no contrasting, alternative truth which is the measure of its falsehood: the falsehood is all they have, is all there is. (By way of a partial illustration of this complex possibility I think of the XVII Congress of the Czech Communist party in 1969, in the year following the Soviet suppression of the 'Prague Spring'. At that Congress, the General Secretary of the Soviet Communist party, Leonid Brezhnev, declared that the invasion of Czechoslovakia by Warsaw Pact troops in August 1968 had been in response to the popular demand of the Czech people. Brezhnev knew this was a lie. The delegates to the Congress knew this was a lie. Brezhnev knew that the delegates knew he was lying and the delegates knew that Brezhnev knew that he knew he was lying. In short, the whole panoply of falsehood was entirely transparent; but it did not, for all that, in any way fail to 'structure' the assembly, nor was the structural efficacy of the lying diminished by its transparent falsehood.)

It was by no means Plato's view that these social structures of 'unreality' could be corrected, or even significantly ameliorated, by means of education itself. On the contrary the experiences equally of Socrates' life and of his death were for Plato decisive evidence that 'education' was quite capable of its own betrayals of its own and society's truths, of serving in its own way the purpose of sustaining social illusions. For throughout his life Socrates had struggled against those educators – Plato ironically called them 'Sophists' or 'wise men' – who took the view that to educate was to instruct rich young men in the arts and crafts of serving a society's ends, without questioning the values which those ends embodied. The sophists were relativists, or, as they thought, 'realists' and 'modernisers'. For they saw themselves as responding to drastic changes in the society of their day: they at least perceived and apparently welcomed the transitions from a traditional form of society in which values were determined by the exigencies of fixed and stable roles and relationships, to one in which those roles and relationships had been thrown into disarray internally and into competition internationally, through war and commerce; and they happily espoused the consequence (as they saw it) that in such a world there could be no values, whether of goodness or truth, other than those of particular societies, hence no 'absolute' standards of comparison by means of which to evaluate those societies. As we would put it today, what the sophists perceived and witnessed to was the collapse of the traditional moral, cognitive or social 'meta-narratives', the overarching stories or 'myths' of truth, goodness or reality in terms of which to read the particular narratives of particular social formations.

Consequently, for the sophists there was nothing to be taught except a training in the abstract, subjective meta-skills required for social success in any society, whatever its goals or goods or 'realities'. The sophists were 'nowhere' people who taught you how to be 'anywhere'. In short, and this was what Plato principally objected to, the sophists detached education from its critical, practical role in relation to society, with a view to its serving better the indeterminate purposes of an abstract 'utility', or worse, of personal worldly success, without regard to the social values or goods of the society in question. What is more, Plato believed that Socrates' hostility to this abstract relativism about justice and truth, and to the sophists' role as morally neutral educators into it, was the chief motive for his execution at the hands of the democratic regime in power in Athens in 399 BCE. For Plato the one significant attempt to 'educate' a society out of its fantasies, Socrates', had proved a tragic failure.

Plato therefore had learned the lesson of Socrates' failure. 'Socratic' though the Allegory of the Cave certainly is in its advocacy of a dialectical account of the ascent from ignorance to knowledge, above any lessons it may incidentally contain for individual learning processes it was for Plato principally an allegory of social and political transformation; in particular that allegory is a lesson in what it takes to achieve the transition from a society dominated by the fantasies of an individualist relativism to one which socialises it citizens in the pursuit of truth. But it is also an allegory of hard lessons learned from Socrates' own personal fate, above all the lesson that those who settle for an education in the relativism of an abstract social utility, for whom only the relative is real, can expect to be subvented by those political masters whose power and interest such sophistry flatters. Contrariwise, neither such educators nor their political masters can seriously be expected to tolerate those for whom education is the search for those values in terms of which to criticise those utilitarian social goals. For the prisoners, Plato notes, will reject any account of things, or any promotion of one, which allows for a reality beyond the prison of their illusions. It is of course not hard to re-identify the same repressive instincts in our own times, when it is increasingly evident that the ever diminishing state funding for education will be forthcoming for the production, no doubt, of servile sophistry, but hardly for an annual output of Socratic critique. When, as that supreme sophist Humpty Dumpty observed, words can mean anything you choose to mean by them, the only question that remains is who has the power to determine their meaning – or for that matter, their market rate.

The Plato to whom Fergal introduced us in UCD was, therefore, Plato the philosopher, more specifically Plato the educator, as social critic. This was no 'idealist' Plato, the conservative philosopher of abstract, eternal 'Ideas', resisting social change, despising the body, sex, and the material world, advocate of neofascist collectivism and of intellectual elitism: it was a Plato critical of the illusions of a society, of a society organised so intimately in and through its illusions that its fantasies and its realities had become inseparable from one another. It was for this theoretical reason, but also for the more practical one that it was impossible for us, hearing him, to ignore the obvious relevance to our own Irish society, that Fergal's Plato had a profound effect of politicisation upon his students. Not that Fergal himself could ever be induced into offering a party-political view of his own: he insisted, as Socrates himself had argued, that good midwives must themselves be barren; hence, in matters political, educators induce their students into political birth only on the condition of their own abstention. But the politicising effect was there, and it was deliberate and conscious in his reading of Plato, for whom, as he correctly saw, questions of knowledge could not be detached from questions of power, questions of truth from questions of good, values from facts, or philosophy from the study of society – more particularly from the study of one's own society.

Which is why, as a result of our exposure to Fergal's Plato, not a few of us began to read Marx. Of course in the universities of the mid- to late 1960s so did everyone else, but Fergal's reaction to the modishness of Marx, Marcuse and Mao was just that: reaction. For there were those whose reading of Marx was so uncritical and 'idealist' as to amount to a betrayal of the Marx they were claiming to appeal to: the student Marx of 1969 was read as the author of eternal truths, proclaiming a materialism of method as if it were a self-justifying and self-confirming dogma. And in response to those, the Maoist and Trotskyist entryists into the so-called 'student revolution' of the late 1960s, Fergal simply insisted that Marx's 'materialism of history' had to be turned back on Marx himself: if the political, legal, moral, religious and philosophical ideas of an epoch had to be understood as in some way a product of the economic forms of life characteristic of that age, then so too did Marxism itself. If Marxism was in essence a 'deconstruction' of a society and of its thought, then that same deconstruction had to be recursive, turned back upon the Marxism which proclaimed it.

III

Yet it was not Marx but another 'economic determinist' who was, after Plato, the subject of Fergal's most influential teaching: the English political theorist of the seventeenth century, Thomas Hobbes, perhaps the most stereotypically 'modern' thinker in the English political tradition. Whereas Marx, at least as represented by the standard textbooks of the time, had appeared as the prophet of the 'social' and 'collective', these being the determinants equally of how 'the individual' was to be understood conceptually and of the conditions under which real individuals could conduct their lives, Hobbes stood as Marx's mirror image. For Hobbes 'society' was simply the product of the interaction of individuals acting out their most fundamental, and in principle egoistic, desires. It was another English politician of the late twentieth century, Margaret Thatcher, who concluded, somewhat inconsistently from the standpoint of the Hobbesian political psychology which she espoused, that 'there is no such thing as society, only individuals and their families': inconsistently, because Hobbesian individualism is perhaps the political theory least of all friendly to 'the family' or to any other of those spontaneous forms of non-state association which we call today 'civil society'. For Hobbes society was properly to be conceived of as a construct – he called it 'compact' – of adult males who, as he imagines them, apparently had neither had any childhood nor have any children of their own. Hobbes understood society as a system of contractual deals done between consenting males under conditions of individual autonomy and freedom. 'Society', therefore, has no reality except in so far as it can be construed as resulting from such deals between equals: which is why women and children, understood by Hobbes to exist in relations of intrinsic dependence on men, could have no place as political agents, nor any in the determination of society. Consequently, for Hobbes, families no more exist than does society.

It could not therefore but soon become apparent why, after Plato, Fergal's second enthusiasm was for Hobbes. There were of course superficial parallels. If in Book I of *Republic* Socrates had been got to debate with a sophist called Thrasymachus, it was not hard for us students to make the leap from the extreme individualism which characterised the 'sophist' view of society to that of Hobbes. Nor was it beyond our ability as undergraduates to perceive the common lines of inference with which the Greek sophist and the English philosopher traced out the consequences of that individualism: that if all that moves society is the egoistic desires of individuals, the social mechanism which they move can only be that of the incessant competition for power; and that 'justice' in such a society can consist in nothing but the will of those who win out in that struggle.

For a political psychology so rampantly individualistic as Hobbes's – or Thatcher's – is inevitably afflicted by the threat of its inherent centrifugality: because unconstrained by other forces a society so constructed can have no natural equilibrium and is bound to fly apart under the pressure of its egoistic components unless held together by some other glue. The contradiction in Thatcher's position was that she sought that countervailing force of social solidarity in the one civil association which her own economic individualism at the same time most put at risk, the family; nor, on the evidence of recent British history, is there much doubt concerning which was the more powerful force, the centrifugality of the economics, or the cohesive power of 'family values'. Nonetheless, the thrust of Thatcher's propaganda was to persuade us to perceive of a radically individualistic polity as if it were the bearer of family and civic values which that polity simultaneously undermined: a paradigm, or almost a parody, of the Platonic 'illusory society' which lives out its realities in the medium of its illusions.

For a contradiction central to the neo-liberal project is that between the 'traditionalism' of its morality and the modernising tendencies of its political economy. They need each other as they subvert what they need. Like a cancerous growth, the market individualism feeds off the organism it destroys. It is in the conceptualisation of such complex relations between the morality and the economics of the neo-liberal project that one needs something like the Platonic analysis of society as being a *structure* of illusion, as being a society which can live out its own reality only in and through an *un*reality. The significance of Margaret Thatcher's rhetoric always lay in its ability to reflect transparently the contradictions within her own political philosophy, and those contradictions achieved this transparency nowhere more strikingly than in the incoherences of her thinking about 'Victorian values' and 'the family'. For she praised the 'traditional family' as the bedrock of those Victorian values while at the same time effecting economic and political programmes which subverted when they did not directly crush out all forms of 'mediating' civil association which might have sustained those values: above all the very 'family' which she espoused.

For which reason it is once again instructive to compare her view of the family with Plato's. The neo-liberal idealises the family because it is only in and through its values of low-level co-operation and communitarianism that the naked competitive individualism of the market can be tolerably lived. Plato on the contrary had no illusions about the family and in *Republic* recommended its abolition as an essential ingredient in the training and lifestyle of rulers. Plato's reason for abolishing the family was the opposite of the neo-liberal's reason for idealising it; for he believed that the family did little but sustain and promote the hegemony of the property motive and the acquisitiveness which he saw to be corrosive of a truly just society. For him then it was only the family, as agent and bearer of the property relationship, which was consistent with the individualism and egoism of the market and there could be nothing but contradiction and illusion in the notion of a society finding its values of solidarity and community in the family when it has abandoned those values in the political and economic spheres.

But there is another, more fundamental, paradox, this time one which Thatcherism and the politics of the neo-right genuinely shared with its Hobbesian inspiration: all profess an economic liberalism in conjunction with political and moral state authoritarianism. For Hobbes there was no contradiction in this conjunction, for he was well aware of the inherent instabilities of a society whose economic transactions were governed by nothing but the ideas and practices of the market. Even if sustained by the perception that 'rational' egoists will spontaneously prefer, as being in their long-term interests as egoists, to consent to market outcomes whatever they are, he recognised that those outcomes will inevitably result in opportunities, and so temptations, for powerful individuals to 'buck' the market. I have only to fear, he thought, that some would do so, and it ceases to be entirely rational for me to consent to market rules. Hence if it is demonstrably *more* 'rational' for market agents to consent to market rules than to the alternative of pure anarchy, Hobbes saw perfectly well what Plato had seen centuries earlier, that for pure egoists, the *most* 'rational' option must be that *everyone else* should consent unconditionally to the rules of the game, but that *I* should do so only when it is in my interest. But since this is the most rational option for me, necessarily it is the most rational option for everyone else too. That being the case, Hobbes concluded, it follows that consent to the rules of the market is in no one's interest, unless that consent is given in the first place, unconditionally and absolutely, to the enforcement by the state of everyone's absolute and unconditional consent to market individualism. The free-market economy, Hobbes calculated, is possible only on the basis of the politics of the absolute state. The logic of this vicious circle is unbreakable, given its starting point in the egoistic individualism of Hobbes's, and for that matter Thatcher's, psychological theory. Hence again the inconsistency in Thatcher's nostrum: in a properly regulated market society, there is room for only two sources of social power, the centrifugal force of the market and the countervailing centripetal force of the state, all bound together by the self-interest of self-regarding 'individuals'. Once again there is simply no place for, because no relevance to, the family.

Now quite apart from the theoretical interest of these issues, they had an obvious relevance in the Ireland of the 1960s. For that decade saw the initiation (in the first instance under the government of Sean Lemass), and a rapid development under a succession of Fianna Fáil administrations, of the bourgeoisification and 'modernisation' of Irish society, but more particularly of the economy. And these developments represented very fundamental, long-term upheavals in the relations between the family, private property and the state which were consequent upon the bourgeoisification of society, culture and politics.

It was unsurprising that among the institutions placed under particular stress and scrutiny then, and its seems with considerably enhanced intensity in more recent decades, was the family, both in itself and as the bearer of so-called 'family values'. And it was wholly unsurprising that this should have been so. For given that the processes of bourgeoisification almost inevitably crush out and marginalise the non-state associations of citizens between the millstone of 'the market individual' and 'the political state', it is to be expected that the family, as a primary association of 'civil society', should experience most fully the strain of those pressures. No doubt there were, and still are, many other factors at play here, but not all of them operated with complete independence of the modernising effects of the transition to a bourgeois form of economy and polity: for example if the Church in the 1960s began to stand somewhat less unambiguously united over family issues and issues of sexual morality, this was at least in part because the principal effect of the Vatican Council on the Churches of the North was that of their bourgeoisification or, as it was called, their 'modernisation' – so that the modernising forces already at play in Irish society were reinforced. Be that as it may, it was in that decade that the family first began to seem part of a problem of modernisation, the problem having at least partially economic roots in the transformation of forms of property ownership, their relation to traditional family structures, and the state.

It was against such a background that Fergal's interventions on the family, marriage and sex acquired their impact – at that time as much, as it seemed to us, in the media as in the classroom. What was perceived then was his radicalism, which consisted, one might reflect by hindsight, mainly in the fact that he was prepared to discuss these issues openly at a time when their discussion, certainly in public *fora*, was taboo. It is scarcely to the point to recount the story of those weekly appearances on Gay Byrne's 'Late Late Show', except to note the seriousness with which the issues he raised were treated on what was, after all, a 'chat show', and to contrast that seriousness with the dismissiveness and irony with which the interventions of academic philosophers are treated within the British media. The contrast between the intellectual seriousness of Irish public life and the philistinism of the British is among the more obviously noticeable differences in culture (perhaps particularly to a British resident, as I was); that greater openness to intellectual debate provided Fergal with the forum in which to practise the theory in public, neatly dovetailing his theorising of the practice in the university.

Which brings me back to that other site of crisis inevitably visited by the destructive pressures of modernisation, the one identified by Plato in the society of his own day: education. A society effecting the transition, economically and politically, from a traditional structure of inherited role and relationship to the free-flowing interchangeabilities of the market will question, under the pressure of a liberal-pluralist ethic, not only the absoluteness of its moral categories but even its own character as a community. And, as Plato saw, that unleashing of the energies of relativism and pluralism, whether of thought or morals, is bound to shake confidence in what there is to be taught, what values there are to pass on from one generation to another. Fergal's Plato diagnosed two indications in a body politic of this kind. The first is that such a society, under the guise of its relativism, masks deep illusions about itself, illusions which are rooted in its insecurities. For a society whose solidarities consist in little more than an agreement on the rules by which competing and irreconcilable interest-groups regulate their mutual incommensurability can live *as if* by the ideologies of freedom and mutual tolerance. But such febrile tissues of social interaction can never bind a people into a community of belief and conviction nor achieve any common perception of shared goods. The second is that a society thus sustained by no common values, except the perception that it possesses none, must model the pursuit of knowledge upon a corresponding relativism which wrenches apart the nexus between intellectual and moral values, between theory and practice, between 'the good' and 'the true'.

But, as Fergal used to say, 'justice is the common good'. A society therefore which lacks a perception of the goods which are genuinely common to *all* its members, a society for which 'justice' consists in nothing but 'fairness' in its relations of exchange between market individuals, is a society which has broken free from the roots of its own solidarities. For those sources of a society's communality lie deeper in the nature of human persons than at the level at which self-interest is perceived. What Plato taught is that we do not and cannot know ourselves – our desires and needs – in so far as we perceive ourselves and our relations with one another as refracted through the prism of a possessive individualism – or, as today, through the prism of those analogous market relations into which a bourgeois society inserts us. And though the nomenclature is more recent than was available to Fergal in my time as his student, there is not much new in that contemporary myth of 'postmodernity', according to which there can be no ultimate ethical 'meta-narrative', no account of the 'the good' which transcends the particularity of individual desire, no 'foundational reality' in which to root an alternative ethic. For Fergal's Plato retains the capacity still to teach us how little there is in this myth that was not already in Hobbes and criticised by Marx. For the 'foundationless' relativism of the postmodernist yields an individualism of desire in motivationless 'free play' which is parodically Hobbesian. Can that radical individualism of the postmodernist itself be more than the apotheosis of a society in ultimate bad faith with itself, terminally ignorant of its own 'truth', invincibly sustained by the self-contradictoriness of its illusions? At any rate that will be so if, as one might suppose with the Marxist, the self-proclaimed 'foundationlessness' of postmodernity is itself rooted and founded in the 'reality' of capitalism as its natural and spontaneous mode of thought. In short the illusion of post-modernity consists in the fact that its denials of 'foundations' are themselves 'founded', derivable as they are from the 'reality' of late capitalism, derivable as *bourgeois necessities of thought*. Naturally a society so deluded will get only the education that it deserves.

CHAPTER 6

The Challenge of Irish Inequality

John Baker

No one can walk through Dublin without being struck by many contrasts. Outside the fashionable shops of Grafton Street, children beg for loose change. Near the gleaming financial services centre stand desolate blocks of housing. Rotund executives driving away from expensive restaurants in their BMWs pass women selling fruit from old prams. People with elegant houses in leafy suburbs use burglar alarms and a harsh prison system to protect themselves from drug addicts chasing the price of their next fix. Women, working class people, disabled people and Travellers are conspicuously absent from stories and pictures about people with power and status, while the very idea that there are people with power and status is taken entirely for granted. Inequality is as obvious as the pubs and Georgian streetscapes. It is a striking part of the background of our lives.

This inequality is not inevitable. Like Dublin's buildings it is a human creation, shaped by law and custom, by history and fashion, by powerful elites at home and abroad. And just like architecture, inequality varies from one society to another. Even among the relatively similar societies of western Europe, Ireland is one of the most unequal (Atkinson, Rainwater and Smeeding, 1995). Inequality is not a fact of nature.

Can we imagine an Ireland without inequality? What would the social landscape look like in an egalitarian society? In this paper I set out a radically egalitarian perspective under five main headings, defining what might be called 'equality of condition' or 'full equality'. I also discuss some intermediate principles representing steps or stages to full equality. I do not try to argue for this perspective (for which see Baker, 1987), but only to provide an alternative vision worth arguing for. The five headings are need, respect, economic equality, political equality, and group-based equality. I close by commenting on some of the problems we face in bringing such a vision into reality.

Need

As complicated social creatures human beings have a wide range of needs. Of course we need water, food and air just to survive. We also need love, self-respect, a sense of purpose and many other things. But our needs are not limitless. Most of us do not really need cars, VCRs, foreign holidays, designer clothes or many other commodities, though they make life more pleasant or convenient. So we can surely imagine an Ireland in which everyone's needs are met, or at least in which every reasonable effort has been made to meet them. Everyone would be able to live in decent housing conditions, could afford a healthy diet, would have access to an education which not only equipped them for a useful, productive life but broadened their horizons and stimulated their imaginations, and so on. Different people have different needs, due to their different circumstances and abilities, so catering for everyone's needs would involve appreciating and respecting differences between them: differences between Travellers and settled people, between people with physical impairments and the able-bodied, between people with different religions and those with no religious beliefs. Equality does not mean uniformity.

Satisfying needs is not an all-or-nothing affair. It would be a real step forward if we could say even that we had taken care of everyone's most urgent needs, for basic subsistence and security, and beyond that if we could say that we had eliminated poverty. This has led some people to think in terms of a 'hierarchy of needs' ranging from the most basic to the most advanced. I wonder how useful it is to compartmentalise needs in this way. For example the quality and character of people's education has a tremendous effect both on their individual economic prospects and on their collective ability to achieve political changes, so it isn't very helpful to think that we should worry about poverty now and education later. To take another example, we can't address the issue of adequate and appropriate shelter for Travellers without tackling the issue of everyone's need for social acceptance and respect. So even though it is true that some needs are more urgent than others, it may not be possible to satisfy those needs without thinking in a more holistic way.

Another important issue around needs is who defines them. It has always been possible for privileged people to define their own needs, while the needs of others are defined, according to their circumstances, by teachers, social workers, doctors and bureaucrats. This form of the power of professionals represents one of the ways in which the welfare state, even though it is based on the idea of need, can be an oppressive force in the lives of those whom it is supposed to be helping (Fraser, 1989). In an egalitarian society we could no longer subject ourselves to that kind of power. It would be up to us as citizens to define our own needs in a process of democratic deliberation.

Respect

As human beings and fellow citizens we need and deserve each other's respect. No society is truly egalitarian if it treats some of its members as superior or inferior to others. In Ireland we sometimes pride ourselves on being egalitarian in this sense and contrast ourselves with class-ridden England. But we have many very similar gradations of status, ranging from the outright contempt and hatred shown to Travellers to the subtler snobbery of middle-class people towards working-class people, of the urban towards the rural, of men towards women, of straight people towards lesbians and gays. Imagine how refreshing it would be to put all of that behind us, and for people to appreciate and value these differences instead of using them to prop up their own threatened egos. That would be a pluralistic society worthy of our allegiance.

As with need, respect has various levels. At the most basic level of respect for human dignity it coincides with the rejection of torture, slavery, degrading treatment and religious persecution, and more generally with the promotion of fundamental human rights. At a higher level it involves toleration for people who seem different because of their physical impairments, skin colour, culture, sexuality, religion or class. But toleration still implies a kind of grudging acceptance of difference. A yet higher level of equal respect occurs when people appreciate and value diversity, for its variety, vitality and testimony to human freedom. It is only when we reach that higher level of respect that minorities feel really secure. So, as with need, we should not make too strong a contrast between different levels of respect.

Economic equality

Imagine for a moment that we really took seriously the needs and equal status of everyone in Ireland. We couldn't possibly go on to endorse a distribution of income in which some people are expected to live on £3,822 a year (the current [1999] long-term social welfare unemployment assistance rate) while others had incomes tens or hundreds of times that amount. We might well agree to income differentials which reflected differences in need or differences in working hours, but that would hardly produce inequality on the scale we have at the moment. Perhaps we would end up with no one having more than twice the average income or less than two-thirds of it, so that the richest person was only three times richer than the poorest. That degree of equality would do wonders for the general morale and sense of community in Irish society.

Economic equality isn't just about income. It is also about the nature of work and the provision of opportunities. As things stand there are striking divisions between people whose work is autonomous, satisfying and empowering and people who tediously carry out the orders of others, between people in secure employment and those in short-term or casual jobs, between people who are paid for their work and people who do unpaid work at home. One of the obvious injustices in our society is that women are predominantly at the raw end of all these divisions of labour. But isn't it even more unjust for these divisions to exist in the first place? Why not imagine an Ireland in which workplaces are organised democratically, in which everyone has access to satisfying work, in which everyone is protected against the ravages of the labour market, in which all do their share of tedious work and of unpaid work in the household?

That question is very closely related to the idea of equal opportunity. We are used to thinking of equal opportunity in terms of a fair competition for attractive jobs and for the education they require – as an equal opportunity to become unequal. In an unequal society that kind of equal opportunity matters a lot, and it is perfectly reasonable for egalitarians to complain about the lack of opportunity experienced by the long-term unemployed, disabled people, women or Travellers. But in an egalitarian society equal opportunity would mean much more: it would mean the real opportunity for each person to develop their talents in a satisfying and fulfilling way. That idea of equal opportunity would change the educational system from a competition for Leaving Certificate points to a system which truly valued and developed each pupil's potential. It would reshape our ideas about the division of labour and about the value of different ways of living.

As before, these ideas about the distribution of income and wealth, economic democracy, the division of labour and equal opportunity can be used to define more limited goals, such as a guaranteed minimum income, worker consultation, job enrichment, family-friendly work practices for fathers, mothers and other carers, affirmative action and so on. Irish governments have already legislated on some of these issues and others are on the horizon. Even these reforms encounter stiff opposition, which shows that they're worth fighting for. But I would like to suggest that many of the strains and contradictions that such reforms create are symptoms of their attempt to promote particular equalities in a context of severe general inequality. Worker participation looks fragile and hollow if ultimate power remains with management and share-holders. Households find it difficult to choose equality in unpaid work if one partner can earn much more than the other in paid employment. Equal opportunity and affirmative action policies are harder to implement and have much higher stakes when the payoffs for winners and losers are very unequal. To these problems of equality the solution is more equality.

Political equality

Political equality is much easier to assert than to analyse. At its most minimal it involves the protection of basic political rights such as freedom of expression, freedom of assembly, freedom of association and the right to vote, all of which are guaranteed by our constitution (*Constitution of Ireland*, Articles 16.1, 40.6). But political equality can mean much more, namely the real sharing of power through popular participation in decision-making. That would mean, first of all, looking at all those relations of power in our society which avoid even the semblance of democratic control, most notably in the economy, which highlights one way in which economic and political equality overlap. We are passionate defenders of our rights to democratic government, but most of us accept that we have no such rights in our places of work and in the broader management of economic affairs. In an egalitarian society, that would have to change.

Political equality also means finding new ways of involving citizens in decisions which affect them. An interesting recent example of extending participation is the National Economic and Social Forum (NESF), which for the first time gave a formal role to representatives of 'groups traditionally outside the consultative process including women, the unemployed, the disadvantaged, people with a disability, youth, the elderly and environmental interests' (NESF 1996, p. 59). Of course the NESF is only a consultative body, with significant influence but no formal powers. If we are serious about political equality we have to look at how traditionally marginalised groups can gain real power both to govern their own affairs and to influence broader social and political issues. That might involve formal political group representation, formal protection of certain group rights, or group vetoes over certain types of issues. These options are a matter of considerable contemporary debate inter-nationally but so far have barely made it onto the agenda in Ireland.

Political participation is also about new ways of relating to each other politically. The standard party-political contest typical of parliamentary politics has its place, but it is hardly an appropriate image for the self-government of local communities, workplaces, group-based organisations and other forms of small-scale association. Many marginalised social groups have themselves developed inclusive and participatory procedures which could serve as models of participation for others. Key principles are equal respect for all and the search for consensus, so that everyone feels that their point of view has been heard and respected and that they can accept the group's decision (Mansbridge, 1983). This model of democratic participation is not necessarily appropriate in every context, but where it is it provides a stronger basis for political equality than more traditional models.

Another area of democratic practice that needs development is the role of various forms of mass communication. One issue is how the mass media, and particularly TV and radio, can help to promote political equality and effective democratic discourse (see McCaffery, 1992). Another is how modern forms of communication, ranging from the postal service to interactive computer networks, can be used to enhance citizen participation. The two issues are clearly related, since political equality requires a well-informed and thoughtful public.

One of the biggest risks of expanding participation in an unequal society is that it could simply reinforce existing inequalities. Many countries, including Ireland, have limited financial contributions to political parties and candidates. But even if we had stronger rules about political finance we could not do away with other ways in which economic privilege translates into political power. Effective participation takes time and energy as well as organisational and communicative skills, and to get one's message across to fellow citizens one needs material resources like desktop publishing facilities and media training. The privileged members of Irish society are better resourced in all these ways than the unprivileged. If we are serious about political equality we need to promote economic equality as well.

Group equality

Inequality in Irish society has clear patterns. Some groups – Travellers, disabled people, lesbians and gays, women and working-class people, among others – are dominated and oppressed, while other groups are privileged. This oppression takes many forms, including exploitation, marginalisation, powerlessness, cultural imperialism, and violence (Young, 1990). Equality is not about eliminating the differences between these overlapping groups, but about undoing the relations of dominance and oppression between them. What we need is the full participation and inclusion of all social groups in Irish society. That ideal is implicit in the ideas I have discussed, but thinking in terms of groups helps to ensure that those ideas are truly inclusive and not biased against the weak and marginalised.

I have already mentioned group difference in distinguishing levels of respect, from human dignity to toleration to valuing diversity. A focus on group equality can also help our thinking about levels of material equality. The following discussion draws on collaborative work done by the UCD Equality Studies Centre (Equality Studies Centre, 1995).

At its most basic level, material group equality consists of the protection of formal rights and opportunities, so that for example it is illegal for employers to hire people because of their sex or religion. This kind of anti-discrimination legislation already exists in Ireland for some groups. Closely allied to formal rights and opportunities is equal access to major social institutions, so that for example there are no insurmountable physical or legal barriers to the participation of women or disabled people in education or politics or family life.

A step beyond equal access is equal participation, the goal of ensuring that different social groups have equal rates of participation in education, employment, politics, the arts, and so on. Equal participation requires not just the right to participate, but the resources and encouragement to be able to participate. This idea is closely related to need, because one way of defining what people need is to say what they require for participating fully in society.

Even if all groups are participating in society there is no guarantee that they will all do equally well. This idea of equality of outcome is a strong principle which requires equality between social groups in educational attainment, average income, occupational status, political power, cultural recognition, and other indicators of social success. As things stand many people are likely to react to such a radical principle with disbelief, as though it is simply unthinkable that the different groups in Irish society are capable of doing equally well. That shows how deeply engrained these inequalities are in our way of looking at the world. It doesn't show that the world cannot be changed.

Equality of outcome still presumes that there will be major inequalities in Irish society and that our objective should be to ensure that one group is no better or worse off on average than others. In a thoroughly egalitarian Ireland, based not just on group equality but on all the other principles I have mentioned and which together constitute equality of condition, there would be equality within social groups as well as between them.

What is the relation between these four levels of material equality and the levels of respect I mentioned earlier? Although there is no neat correspondence, it seems obvious that we could not hope to achieve the stronger forms of material equality without higher levels of respect, and that these higher levels of respect would themselves be empty if not matched by strong material equality. That is just another illustration of the interconnections among egalitarian ideas.

The global context of Irish equality

I have concentrated on Ireland in this paper, but it is impossible to think about radical equality in one country without thinking of how that project relates to the rest of the world. The first major issue has to do with the obstacles facing any radical political project in a small country. Radical egalitarianism challenges the power and privilege of the people in charge of transnational corporations. It is not just that they can move operations elsewhere, but that they have huge resources for opposing radical local initiatives. Confronting this power requires international co-operation. That is one reason why it is important for egalitarians to find ways of engaging in and developing supranational structures like the European Union and the United Nations in spite of their shortcomings.

Another major issue is that we cannot pursue equality in rich countries like Ireland without thinking about global justice. The rest of the world's people also have needs and deserve respect. They are as entitled to economic, political and group equality as Irish people are. The principles of global justice are not essentially different from those in Ireland. Of course, the scale of the problem of achieving global justice is daunting. But if we really want to imagine an egalitarian future, our imaginations have to stretch beyond the boundaries of our own country to embrace the rest of the world as well: a world at peace, in which everyone's needs are satisfied, in which differences are respected and valued, in which resources and power are equally shared, in which no group dominates or oppresses another.

Putting it into practice

The contrast between the pervasive inequality I discussed at the beginning of this paper and the global equality I have just been imagining can make the egalitarian project seem utopian. How can we possibly presume that we can end thousands of years of inequality and oppression? We can look at the world in an optimistic vein, and take some encouragement in the genuine progress that human beings have made in struggles against slavery and for human rights, sexual equality and democracy. But we can also see the world in a pessimistic light if we think of the Holocaust, of Rwanda and Bosnia, of Tiananmen Square and East Timor. The struggle for human progress has often seemed hopeless in the past and yet progress has been made. Somehow it always seems that the privileged believe in the inevitability of oppression more than the oppressed do. Doesn't that tell us something about what's possible?

Promoting equality can occur in many contexts. At the core of the egalitarian project in Ireland are groups of women, disabled people, Travellers, gays and lesbians, unemployed people, political activists and many other groups who are acting together to promote social change. At their best these groups operate according to egalitarian standards of mutual acceptance, consensual decision-making and co-operative action. In a number of areas, such as the NESF, Local Area Partnerships, and various government-sponsored commissions and task forces, these groups have a role in formal political structures. How to build on these developments and to find more effective ways of empowering marginalised and oppressed groups is a continuing challenge. Speaking impressionistically, there seems to be little interaction between these progressive groups and political parties, even though equality is an explicit value of at least the parties of the 'left'. Instead there seems to be a pattern of direct contact with government ministers and agencies. Is this because people no longer see political parties as effective agents of change? Are political parties irrelevant to the struggle for equality? It is hard to believe that major changes in the structure of Irish society can be brought about without their involvement. We need to do more work and reflect more on developing a political model of progressive social change.

The struggle for a democratic, egalitarian society depends on the development and sharing of skills and knowledge among egalitarians. So there must be a role for the educational system in promoting equality. The major long-term challenge is to create an educational system which truly values all our citizens in all their diversity. The question is how to get there from a system which for the most part reproduces Irish inequality. Fortunately many committed teachers, parents and students in all educational sectors are working hard to redress inequality. Some policies are being developed, although all too modestly, to widen educational opportunities for disadvantaged groups. Various third-level programmes, of which Equality Studies at UCD is the clearest example, are designed particularly to focus attention on equality and to provide intellectual support for egalitarians. As always, it is important to try to structure these educational developments in an egalitarian way. That means, among other things, trying to find ways of working in partnership with marginalised and oppressed groups. It also means developing a new way of conducting equality-related research which supports and gives a voice to marginalised groups rather than treating them simply as 'subjects' (Lynch and O'Neill, 1994).

Politics and education are two key arenas for promoting equality, but other areas are also very important. In the economy some trade unions and employers have recognised that egalitarian reforms are not just fair but can also make firms more efficient and productive. In the area of religion many voices have supported egalitarian aims ranging from the protection of human rights to the case for a guaranteed basic income (e.g. Reynolds and Healy, 1995). In Irish families there have been major changes in ideas about relations between men, women and children, although changes in people's behaviour have sometimes been slow to follow. Equality is not the business of any one group of people in one area of life. It is the business of us all.

Conclusion

In this paper I have tried to contrast the pervasive inequality of Irish society with a vision of a radically egalitarian alternative. I have set out that vision under the headings of need, respect, economic equality, political equality and group equality, but I hope that it has become clear that these are only rough and ready headings and that the principles of equality are strongly interconnected. I have also tried to show that the path to full equality can involve many steps, starting with provision for people's most urgent needs and the protection of their most basic rights, and including at various stages such objectives as the toleration of difference, a guaranteed minimum income, worker participation, extensions of democracy, formal protections against discrimination, and so on. There are degrees of equality, and Ireland could be a much more equal society long before it became a fully equal one. At the same time I have suggested that it is not always a good idea to separate apparently long-term from short-term goals, because of the way these goals interact.

I have pointed to the relation between the challenge of Irish inequality and the broader challenge of global inequality, for the sake of both justice and strategy, and I have touched upon how we can develop a stronger movement for equality in Ireland. I am acutely aware that these remarks are sketchy and open-ended and I wish I knew the answers to the questions I have raised. But I take heart in the thought that the challenge of Irish inequality is indeed a challenge for collective, co-operative action, and that together we can meet it.

References

Atkinson, A. B., Rainwater, L. and Smeeding, T. 1995. 'Income Distribution in European Countries', DAE Working Paper Number MU 9506, The Microsimulation Unit, Cambridge University.

Baker, John. 1987. *Arguing for Equality.* London: Verso.

The Constitution of Ireland [*Bunreacht na hÉireann*]. Dublin: Government Publications Office.

Equality Studies Centre. 1995. 'A Framework for Equality Proofing', Paper prepared for the National Economic and Social Forum.

Fraser, Nancy. 1989. *Unruly Practices: Power, Discourse and Gender in Contemporary Social Theory.* Oxford: Polity Press.

Lynch, Kathleen and O'Neill, Cathleen. 1994. 'The Colonisation of Social Class in Education', *British Journal of Sociology of Education,* 15

Mansbridge, Jane J. 1983. *Beyond Adversary Democracy* (2nd edn). Chicago, Il: University of Chicago Press.

McCaffery, Colum. 1992. *Political Communication and Broadcasting: Theory, Practice and Reform.* PhD thesis, University College Dublin.

NESF (National Economic and Social Forum). 1996. *Equality Proofing Issues. Forum Report No. 10.* Dublin: NESF.

Reynolds, Brigid and Healy, Sean (eds). 1995. *An Adequate Income Guarantee for All.* Dublin: Conference of Religious of Ireland.

Young, Iris Marion. 1990. *Justice and the Politics of Difference.* Princeton, NJ: Princeton University Press.

CHAPTER 7

Feminism and Justice

Maeve Cooke

F eminist critique since the early 1980s has directed a thorough-going attack on modern (post-Enlightenment) traditions of moral and political theory. The language and concepts of modern moral and political theory are claimed to contain a 'masculine' bias and to have been guilty of excluding systematically the experience of women. More specifically it is argued that the ideals of impartiality and universality – ideals at the centre of moral and political thinking since the Enlightenment – are suspect to the extent that they are inherently gendered.

It may be noted here that the terms 'masculine' and 'feminine' are used not to refer to innate and immutable characteristics of given categories of human beings but rather to specify dispositions and values that, for historical and sociological reasons, have come to be associated with certain such categories. In order to emphasise this point, feminist theorists often appeal to the distinction between 'sex' and 'gender': the category of 'sex' is taken to refer to *the fact* of biological difference among human beings, the category of 'gender' refers to the *construction* of certain kinds of difference among human beings as a result of various social and historical processes. It is claimed that although sexual difference has traditionally been used as a basis for the construction of gender difference, no internal relationship exists between the two. To be sure, as other feminist theorists such as Judith Butler (1987) have pointed out, the distinction between 'sex' and 'gender' is itself problematic for it implies the possibility of identifying a body that pre-exists its cultural interpretation. Butler and others insist that even categories of anatomical difference are social and historical constructions. Although this debate raises many interesting questions about notions of human identity, the important point for our present purposes is that the predicates 'masculine' and 'feminine' do not refer to innate and immutable properties or predispositions.

Care versus justice and rights

A seminal contribution to contemporary feminist debates within moral and political theory has been the work of Carol Gilligan. Gilligan's sociological investigations, of which the best known is probably *In a Different Voice: Psychological Theory and Women's Development* (Gilligan, 1982), suggest that the dominant tradition of moral theory excludes and devalues women's more particular and affective experience of moral life. Broadly speaking, Gilligan believes that this is true of mainstream post-Enlightenment moral theory to the extent that it has followed Kant in holding that questions of right and justice – and not questions of the good and self-realisation – are its proper concern. Such a perspective can be termed deontological, for it focuses on moral duty and obligation as opposed to virtue and happiness as the central concern of moral theory.

Although Gilligans's insights have since been used to criticise the very notion of a deontological ethics, Gilligan herself was specifically concerned with the developmental moral psychology of Laurence Kohlberg. Working within the tradition of Jean Piaget, Kohlberg proposed a schema to account for the various stages of moral consciousness through which, in the passage from childhood to adolescence, all human beings are said to move. Kohlberg suggested six stages: the child moves from the *preconventional level* (stages one and two) through the *conventional level* (stages three and four) to the *postconventional, autonomous or principled* level (stages five and six) (Kohlberg, 1981). Kohlberg's theory is universalist in scope: it asserts that its claims hold good for all human beings irrespective of sex/gender, racial, cultural or social background. Gilligan's findings query the universal validity of Kohlberg's schema for they imply that it has an inherent sex/gender bias. Gilligan used empirical studies to show that the moral development of adolescent girls differs from that of adolescent boys in several important respects. Her findings suggested that, speaking generally, boys learn to think in terms of rights, abstraction and autonomy as their moral skills develop; against this, girls learn to focus on responsibility, contextuality and connection. These differences in learning patterns are reflected in differences between the moral judgment of men and women and the respective notions of self that inform this. Whereas men tend to think of moral agents as essentially independent subjects of rights who must be protected from interference by others, morality for many women arises from the experience of connection and is informed by demands of nurturance, responsibility and care.

Thus there is some evidence to suggest that the developmental pattern identified by Kohlberg is tailored to the development of males. Clearly, if this is so, there is a danger that it may prejudice any account of female moral development. For if male socialisation patterns are taken as the norm, an orientation towards responsibility for others and an emphasis on the specific features of the case at hand may be regarded as signs of moral immaturity. Gilligan argued against such a conclusion, claiming that women's tendency to be more contextual in matters of moral judgment, to be more immersed in the details of relationships and narratives and to be more adept at developing feelings of empathy and sympathy represents an important alternative to those capacities identified by Kohlberg as the highest stage of moral development. At the very least this argument suggests the need for a reassessment of the importance of the capacity to abstract from actual situations and to think impartially and universally.

Generalised and concrete others

Gilligan's book sparked off a lively debate as to the relative merits of a contextual ethics of care and concern over an abstract ethics of justice and rights. This debate also became known as one about the relative merits of two standpoints: on the one hand the standpoint of the generalised other, corresponding to an ethics of rights and justice; on the other the standpoint of the concrete other, corresponding to an ethics of care and concern.[1] Seyla Benhabib (1986, 340-341) defines the difference as follows:

[1] The term 'generalised other' was borrowed from the social theorist George Herbert Mead but it took on its own distinctive meaning in the context of the feminist debate. Since even the feminists concerned admit that their definition of the term differs significantly from Mead's, there is some disquiet about this appropriation. However, although the choice of terms may not be perfectly felicitous, the distinction between the two standpoints has been a useful one.

> The standpoint of the 'generalised other' requires us to view each
> and every individual as a rational being entitled to the same rights
> and duties we would want to ascribe to ourselves. In assuming
> this perspective, we abstract from the individuality and concrete
> identity of the other. We assume that the other, like ourselves, is
> a being who has concrete needs, desires, and affects but that
> what constitutes his or her moral dignity is not what differentiates
> us from each other, but rather what we, as speaking and rational
> agents, have in common.

The moral categories corresponding to the standpoint of the
generalised other are those of rights, obligation and entitlement
while the corresponding moral feelings are respect, duty, worthiness
and dignity. The standpoint of the generalised other is linked with
a vision of community based on rights and entitlements.

Benhabib (1986, 341) defines the contrasting position as follows:

> ... the standpoint of the 'concrete other' requires us to view each
> and every rational being as an individual with a concrete history,
> identity and affective-emotional constitution. In assuming this
> standpoint, we abstract from what constitutes our commonality
> and seek to understand the distinctiveness of the other. We seek
> to comprehend the needs of the other, their motivations, what
> they search for, and what they desire.

From the standpoint of the concrete other, the norms of our interactions are usually private, non-institutional ones: norms of friendship, love and care. The relevant moral categories are responsibility,
bonding and sharing. The corresponding moral feelings are love,
care, sympathy and solidarity. This perspective is linked with a
vision of community that is based on needs and fraternity.

Whereas some feminist theorists such as Iris Marion Young (1987)
have rejected the standpoint of the generalised other out of hand
as repressive, others maintain that attention to the concrete other
should be complemented by considerations of impartiality and
universality. This is particularly true of those who are concerned
with feminist political theory and with working out a feminist theory
of justice. For one thing, the standpoint of the concrete other, drawn
as it is from the sphere of intimate relationships, may not be adequate
in its initial formulation for political contexts in which relationships
are not intimate. Moreover many feminists acknowledge that in
modern complex societies a theory of rights should be an essential

component of any feminist theory of justice – not least because women themselves have had to struggle for rights over the centuries. Nancy Fraser (1986) suggests a distinction between the standpoint of the 'individualised concrete other' and that of the 'collective concrete other' to take account of this difficulty. In the latter case the emphasis is not on confirmation of the specificity of an individual but on that of a collectivity; that is, on the particularity of groups with culturally specific identities, solidarities and forms of life. The appropriate moral feelings are not, as in Benhabib's conception, love, care and friendship but fraternity and *solidarity*.

Fraser's contribution usefully draws attention to the fact that what it means to take account of the concrete other varies according to the context of moral deliberation. It means something different in context-specific everyday processes of moral deliberation than in political contexts of moral deliberation in which, for example, rights are formulated and justified. Furthermore Fraser's notion of the collective concrete other raises the difficult question of implementation. It raises the question of *how precisely* a feminist theory of justice can combine affirmation of the importance of rights (and associated values such as equality or impartiality) with sensitivity to difference and context. One of the central debates within what has become known as 'second wave' (i.e. roughly post 1960) feminist theory concerns the tension between equality and difference.[2] There are many strands to this complex debate, which has clear connections with the debate about the two standpoints and which overlaps in interesting ways with other contemporary debates (for instance, on multiculturalism or on the politics of recognition). From the point of view of political theory one important aspect has to do with the question of whether the struggle to overcome women's oppression should emphasise women's fundamental commonality with men and aim for equal opportunities, entitlements and rights; or whether, alternatively, it should focus on women's distinctiveness, as it arises from a distinctively feminine 'experience' or 'nature', and aim for political recognition of feminine difference. For some time there appeared to be a deep-seated divergence between, on the one side, feminists

---

[2] For a discussion of the equality-difference debate see, for example, Evans, 1995.

who reject out of hand universalist values such as equality and impartiality and, on the other, those who affirm these values while calling for recognition of the particular, distinctive needs and value-orientations of oppressed and disadvantaged groups. Now, outright rejection of universalist values is less common.[3] However, although in principle it may seem to make sense to aspire towards a reconciliation of the demands of equality and difference or, more generally, of the two standpoints, it is far from easy to say what this would actually entail in concrete contexts of political deliberation and action. Many contemporary societies are characterised by value pluralism and the absence of any overarching standard that could generally be accepted as determining what is right and good. In such societies it is by no means easy to specify just how political deliberation could be conducted impartially without considerable abstraction from particular needs and value-orientations; or how in actual situations of political deliberation, groups with widely diverging needs and value-orientations could at one and the same time be treated equally and afforded recognition of their distinctiveness.[4]

Contours of a feminist theory

The task of spelling out what it would mean to combine commitment to rights and universalist values with attention to particular needs and conceptions of the good in the concrete contexts of actual political life is central to the project of a feminist theory of justice. As soon as we begin to outline the contours of a feminist theory of justice we find that the problem of how to reconcile the demands of universality and particularity emerges as a pressing – and extremely difficult – one.

What would a feminist theory of justice look like in outline? I want to suggest some conditions that such a theory would have to

---

[3] When reviewing recent writings on feminism for the purposes of this essay, it seemed to me possible to identify a general increase in sympathy for universalist values such as equality and impartiality, even for a new, improved humanism (see, for example, Grant, 1993).

[4] For a discussion of some very different possible interpretations of the demand for recognition of difference, see Cooke, 1997a.

satisfy. I shall do so through reference to certain aspects of the work of Jürgen Habermas – a contemporary thinker whose views on matters relating to justice are often seen by feminists as compatible with their own concerns, and as potentially useful for feminist theory (see, for example, Benhabib, 1992; Waugh, 1992; and Meehen (ed.), 1995).

Habermas proposes a communicative ethics which, although neo-Kantian in its emphasis on duty and obligation, is seen by a number of feminist writers as having the potential for moving beyond a rigidly procedural universalism to take account of considerations of care and context. However, Habermas's ethics has also been accused of not living up to its inherent potential. In sketching the outline of a feminist theory of justice I shall take a look at some strengths and weaknesses of Habermas's theory of justice as well as at a recent attempt to modify it constructively.[5]

To begin with, a feminist theory of justice that affirms universalist values while taking account of the perspective of the concrete other would have to start from a *relational* conception of the self. Several feminist critics have drawn attention to the way in which a conception of the self as disembedded and unencumbered underlies both the deontological tradition of moral theory and the contractarian tradition of political theory (see, for example, Moller Okin, 1989). To use Benhabib's term, the self is regarded as a mushroom – as though it had sprung up overnight – without history and without connection to other persons. Such a conception of the self is unacceptable to a feminist theory of justice on at least two grounds. First of all it denies women's experience of the self as a being immersed in a network of relationships with others. In addition, when combined with the idea of self-identity as self-ownership, it

---

[5] Discussion of Habermas's communicative ethics is complicated by the fact that, in his most recent writings, Habermas has modified both his theory of discourse and his theory of law and politics in several important respects without, however, acknowledging the implications of his modifications for the *content* (as opposed to the status) of his theory of justice (for the main modifications, see Habermas (1996) esp. ch. 3 and ch. 4). Although I hold the view that Habermas's theory of justice is in fact substantially affected by developments in his most recent work, I cannot show this within the scope of our present discussion. In the following I shall thus rely on his theory of justice as he develops it up to *Between Facts and Norms.*

links up easily with the politics of the minimal state, which is alleged to be destructive of community and the caring values that are important to many women. Habermas's moral and political theory is built on a quite different conception of the self. The self is conceived primarily in terms of its relationships with others. More specifically, Habermas (1992) gives an account of the process of development of the individual human subject in terms of mutual recognition.

Drawing on the insights of Hegel and George Herbert Mead he argues that we develop as autonomous human subjects through being recognised by others as accountable for the validity of what we say and do. Similarly we develop our identities as subjects capable of self-realisation within a framework of recognition by others of our claims to uniqueness, authenticity and the continuity of our life histories. Thus, in contrast to those theorists who conceive the human individual as radically independent of its relationships with others, Habermas secures the connection between subjectivity and intersubjectivity and underscores the social constitution of the self.

A second, connected – but more tentative – condition that would have to be met by a feminist theory of justice is that it operate with a *dialogical* conception of reason. It seems plausible that a theory of justice that starts from a relational conception of the self would operate with a model of moral judgment and insight that conceives of this as dependent on moral deliberation in dialogue with others. To be sure, the step from a relational conception of the self to a dialogical conception of (moral) reason is not a necessary one. A further argument that propels us in this direction, has to do with the apparent absence of any ahistorical metaphysical standard that would enable us to determine what is right or good *without* consulting others. Most feminist theorists are 'postmetaphysical' in this sense – although there seems to be nothing specifically feminist about this position. This may be one of the reasons why Habermas's theory is congenial to feminists. Habermas's theory of justice draws on a conception of rationality that attempts to move beyond metaphysics while retaining the notion of a critical standard for the assessment of claims to truth or moral validity (see Cooke, 1994, especially chs 2 and 5). Habermas rejects as metaphysical the notion that justice can be determined independently of dialogue with others, conceiving it instead as the outcome of a *discourse* between all concerned. His theory of moral deliberation is thus not only congenial to feminists who reject metaphysical notions of reason or validity; it has a further attraction in that it places central importance on a dimension of identity that many feminists want to highlight: the constitution of the subject (and especially its moral development) through interaction with others.

A third condition that would have to be met by a feminist theory of justice is that it start from an *embodied* conception of the self. The standpoint of the concrete other reminds us that the rationality of the individual human being is tied up with its affective, emotional, sexual and physical constitution. All rational agents are embodied agents and, as such, have desires and material needs on which they are capable of reflecting and that influence their thinking on matters of the right and good. A feminist theory of justice would have to acknowledge and attempt to accommodate this dimension of rational agency. Admittedly the question of how the affective-emotional-sexual-physical dimensions of rational agency can be accommodated in actual deliberation on justice is far from easy, especially where these deliberations are political ones. It is one thing to acknowledge that rational agency is intimately bound up with needs and desires, it is another to show that particular needs and desires should – *and can in fact* – play a central role in our deliberations on matters of justice, especially where these form part of processes of legislation and decision-making in contemporary pluralist societies. For even if we were *in principle* convinced by the argument that needs and desires, as crucial elements of human identity, should play a central role in a theory of justice, its force would be considerably weakened by the demonstration that this is not in practice possible.

It could be argued that, under conditions of contemporary value-pluralism, it would be impossible to make decisions on matters of justice – especially in the contexts of political life – unless those concerned were prepared (temporarily) to abstract from their particular needs and desires. That this difficulty goes to the heart of the debate on the two standpoints is evident in feminist reactions to Habermas's theory of justice. Much of feminist critique of Habermas's communicative ethics has challenged his insistence that participants in dialogically structured processes of moral deliberation (moral discourse) must abstract from their particular motivations (see Habermas, 1990b). Iris Marion Young is just one of those who maintain that Habermas reneges on his promise to define normative reason contextually because of his commitment to an impartial point of view (Young, 1987, 69). For Habermas defines just norms and principles as *generalisable* ones: he regards only those norms and principles as morally valid (just) that could be agreed by all participants in a moral discourse as equally in the interest of all concerned (Habermas, 1990a, 61). Generalisability requires impartiality (see Habermas, 1993, especially 48-54). Impartiality implies some abstraction from empirically existing, individual and group needs and value-orientations. In the face of Habermas's requirement that participants in moral discourses abstract from their particular needs and desires, Young responds that a more thoroughly pragmatic interpretation of dialogic reason would not have to suppose that participants must abstract from their particular motivations in aiming to reach agreement.

But how would this be possible in practice? Habermas insists that his theory does not require that participants in processes of moral deliberation suppress their needs and desires – they merely adopt a 'hypothethical attitude' towards them for the duration of the discussion, relativising them in light of the needs and desires of others. Otherwise – and especially in modern complex societies in which there are deep-seated divergences as to conceptions of the good life – no agreement could be reached that would be acceptable to everyone (Habermas, 1982, 255).

However, Habermas's insistence that his theory of justice does not require suppression of particular needs and desires seems somewhat disingenuous. On the one hand he suggests that the abstraction required by participants in moral discourse amounts to no more than the adoption of a critically reflective attitude to one's particular motivations; on the other hand he presents the aim of moral discourse as a consensus among those participating that a given norm or principle is equally in the interest of everyone. Under conditions of value-pluralism, consensus as to the general acceptability of a norm or principle can be achieved only at a high level of abstraction. Examples that Habermas himself suggests of norms that could be agreed to by all in a moral discourse are: 'you should not kill', 'you should not lie', or 'you should keep your promises' (Habermas, 1993, 60-69). But norms such as these, precisely because they are abstract enough to be acceptable to everyone, take no account of particular needs and desires in concrete situations.[6] Indeed Habermas now acknowledges that the plurality and irreconcilability of value standards in contemporary societies means that the norms and principles on which it is actually possible to reach agreement in discourse become increasingly abstract and the set of questions that can be answered rationally from the moral point of view becomes smaller and smaller (Habermas, 1993, 90-91). However plausible we might find Habermas's position in this regard, it seems clear that his theory of justice, in requiring general agreement on the validity of norms, affirms universality at *the expense of* particularity. It thus seems problematic from the point of view of the feminist commitment to the standpoint of the concrete other. It is not clear, however, what alternatives are available.

Interactive universalism

It could be argued that the problem with Habermas's theory of justice is not his emphasis on dialogue but his insistence on an internal connection between justice and consensus (see Cooke, 1993). If this is the case, one obvious way of rescuing particularity would be to sever the connection. This is the path chosen subsequently by Benhabib. In what can be seen as a response to the task of reconciling the universalist standpoint with that of the concrete other, Benhabib proposes a model of 'interactive universalism' (Benhabib, 1992). This is a theory of justice which, though it takes Habermas's communicative ethics as its starting point, diverges from it in several significant respects. Benhabib attempts to reformulate Habermas's discourse theory of justice by making it more sensitive to differences of identity, needs and modes of reasoning, and by fitting together principled, universalist morality and context-sensitive moral judgment. However, while the foregoing discussion has helped us to see why this attempt is important, I do not believe that is altogether successful. Benhabib presents a theory of justice that avoids the abstract universalism of Habermas's consensus model. But she pays a price for this.

---

[6] Such general norms require interpretation and application in particular contexts of moral judgment before they can do so. Habermas himself recognises this (see Habermas, 1993, 35-39).

As we shall now see, the interactive universalism proposed by Benhabib rectifies Habermas's denial of the particular at the cost of giving up one vital ingredient of Habermas's theory of justice. Benhabib puts forward a dialogical but nonconsensual theory of justice that shifts the emphasis from the *result* of the process of moral judgment to the *process* itself. Whereas Habermas focuses on the outcome of moral deliberation (consensus), Benhabib emphasises the process of generation of reasonable agreement about moral principles via an open-ended moral conversation. She regards it as less important that we discover the general interest and more important that collective decisions are reached through procedures which are radically open and fair to everyone. Benhabib insists on the universalist thrust of her theory for, as we have seen, she holds that the standpoint of the generalised other is indispensable in modern complex societies. However, in doing so, she obscures the crucial difference between the kind of universalism she advocates and that which is at the heart of Habermas's communicative ethics.

The universalism of Benhabib's interactive model of justice has to do not with the *judgment* reached by way of dialogue but with the conditions governing *participation in* the dialogue. Whereas Habermas regards his theory of justice as universalist to the extent that moral norms and principles are *generalisable,* Benhabib wants to give up this aspect of his dialogical model – partly at least in order to take account of the perspective of the concrete other. Universalism is no longer construed as the dialogically achieved agreement of each that a given norm or principle is valid for everyone but is rather interpreted as the conditions governing participation in this dialogue.[7] Benhabib herself notes the consequence of this shift of emphasis:

> ... when we shift the burden of the moral test in communicative ethics from consensus to the idea of an ongoing moral conversation, we begin to ask ... what would be allowed and even necessary from the standpoint of continuing and sustaining the practice of the moral conversation among us. The emphasis now is less on *rational agreement,* but more on sustaining those

---

[7] Benhabib puts forward two principles governing participation: (i) the principle of universal moral respect and (ii) the principle of egalitarian reciprocity (Benhabib, 1992, 29).

> normative practices and moral relationships within which reasoned
> agreement *as a way of life* can flourish and continue. (Benhabib,
> 1992, 38).

Despite my sympathy with this approach, I see it as having one significant, undesirable consequence. Both Habermas and Benhabib affirm that moral principles and judgments have a cognitively articulable kernel and reject approaches to justice that see these as mere statements of preference or taste. Ethical cognitivism is thus opposed to ethical decisionism (the reduction of ethical judgments to an 'I will' that cannot be further questioned) as well as to ethical emotivism (the conflation of statements such as 'murder is wrong' with 'I dislike chocolate'). However, although Benhabib regards her interactive universalism as a *cognitive* theory of justice (Benhabib, 1992, 49), it is hard to see in what sense it can lay claim to this. Clearly Benhabib's model represents an alternative to both ethical decisionism and ethical emotivism to the extent that it takes statements such as 'x is right' to mean that 'I can justify to you with good grounds why one ought to respect, uphold, agree with x' (Benhabib, 1992, 49-50). It is not clear, however, what entitles the speaker to claim that her grounds are good and, accordingly, why it represents a *cognitivist* position.

An ethical cognitivist must have at her disposal some means of demonstrating the validity of moral claims; more precisely she must provide some means of demonstrating the validity of the *knowledge or grounds* on which these claims are based. An ethical cognitivist can be a fallibilist: that is, she can acknowledge that knowledge now regarded as valid may be called into question in the future as a result of new arguments or evidence, but she must also believe in the possibility of distinguishing – at least in the here and now – between valid and invalid knowledge. This is not a problem for a dialogical cognitivist such as Habermas who defines a discursively achieved consensus as the *test* of the validity of the knowledge embodied in moral norms and principles. For Habermas proof of the validity of moral norms and principles is simultaneously proof of the validity of the grounds that justify them. In dispensing with the idea of consensus however, Benhabib has to find some other criterion of moral validity. For this she looks to the procedure of argumentation and the moral-practical presuppositions guiding it (at least in certain sorts of societies). What makes a moral claim valid on her conception is not the knowledge it embodies – the grounds that justify it – but the way in which it is reached. Interactive universalism must thus remain agnostic about the validity of the knowledge on which a statement such as 'x is right' is based, even where it recognises the validity of the procedure by which it is attained. It thus gives up the idea of justice as moral insight that is a crucial part of Habermas's conception. Habermas still believes it possible to distinguish between the validity and invalidity of the *grounds* supporting moral claims; Benhabib can do no more than distinguish between valid and invalid *ways* of reaching a decision with regard to the morality of claims. Benhabib's position is perfectly compatible with a plurality of moral perspectives with regard to a given issue. Whereas for Habermas if x is right in a given instance, a,b,c ... z must be wrong, for Benhabib not only x but also a,b,c ... z might be valid. One implication of this is that the critical thrust of her model is considerably weaker than that of Habermas's. Whereas Habermas provides a standard against which not just the way in which a decision is reached but the grounds on which a decision is based can be criticised, Benhabib's approach admits only the former possibility.

I think we lose something if we give up the idea of justice as moral insight. One consequence, as we have seen, is that the capacity for moral (and hence also social and political) criticism is weakened. This is something that must be of concern to feminists who write and act on behalf of the disadvantaged and the oppressed. Furthermore, the idea of moral validity as moral insight has traditionally been part of the ideal of autonomy, an ideal that many feminists have criticised but that they cannot, I believe, do without. In my view, feminist opposition to autonomy is based (for the most part) on objections to the various problematic ways in which it has historically been interpreted; I maintain that the ideal of autonomy has a valuable core that is indispensable to feminists in their struggles against oppression and discrimination (see Cooke, 1997b). For these reasons severing the link between justice and moral insight has unwelcome implications for feminists. Nevertheless we have to recognise the force of post-Enlightenment attacks on metaphysics, particularly on attempts to uphold ahistorical, absolute, overarching standards of truth and rationality. Is it possible to reject ahistorical metaphysical projections while retaining some notion of moral insight? As we have seen, Habermas attempts to develop a 'post-metaphysical' conception of rationality that would preserve the idea of moral validity while avoiding metaphysical projections; however, the resulting conception runs foul of feminist suspicion of abstract universalism and emphasis on the standpoint of the concrete other. Benhabib attempts to modify Habermas's theory in order to make it more sensitive to differences of identity, needs, modes of reasoning and contexts of moral judgment, but the price she pays for this is a considerably weaker conception of moral validity (and, consequently, of moral autonomy and of moral critique).

Is this unavoidable? I do not have an answer to this difficult question, not just because space does not permit. The attempt to reconcile universality with particularity is not a new task for political and social philosophy and it is not peculiar to feminist theory. The history of philosophy bears witness to its persistence, and it is at the heart of contemporary debates on multiculturalism and the politics of recognition. However, the problem has been reinterpreted and gained renewed urgency in light of feminist concerns. What I have wanted to do in the foregoing is to spell out one challenge facing a feminist theory of justice: how to retain hold of universalist ideas of equality and liberty while acknowledging the concrete demands of context and particular needs and ethical concerns – and how to do so without renouncing the idea of moral insight and the stronger notions of autonomy and critique that depend on it. This is a challenge facing everyone, not least those like myself who have been inspired by Fergal O'Connor to see justice as our concern.

References

Butler, J. 1987. 'Variations on Sex and Gender: Beauvoir, Wittig, Foucault', in Benhabib and Cornell (eds), 1987.

Benhabib, S. 1986. *Critique, Norm and Utopia.* New York: Columbia University Press.

Benhabib, S. 1987. 'The Generalized Other and the Concrete Other', in Benhabib and Cornell (eds), 1987.

Benhabib, S. 1992. *Situating the Self: Gender, Community and Post-modernism in Contemporary Ethics.* New York: Routledge.

Benhabib, S. and Cornell, D. (eds). 1987. *Feminism as Critique.* Minneapolis: University of Minnesota Press.

Cooke, M. 1993. 'Habermas and Consensus', *European Journal of Philosophy* 1:3.

Cooke. M. 1994. *Language and Reason: A Study of Habermas's Pragmatics.* Cambridge, Ma: The MIT Press.

Cooke, M. 1997a. 'Authenticity and Autonomy: Taylor, Habermas and the Politics of Recognition', *Political Theory* 25:1.

Cooke, M. 1997b. 'Habermas and Feminist Theory', in Dews (ed.), 1999.

Dews, P. (ed.). 1999. *Habermas: A Critical Reader.* Oxford: Blackwell.

Evans, J. 1995. *Feminist Theory Today.* London: Sage.

Fraser, N. 1986. 'Toward a Discourse Ethic of Solidarity', *Praxis International.* 5:4.

Gilligan, C. 1982. *In a Different Voice: Psychological Theory and Women's Development.* Cambridge, Ma: Harvard University Press.

Grant, J. 1993. *Fundamental Feminism: Contesting the Core Concepts of Feminist Theory.* New York & London: Routledge.

Habermas, J. 1982. 'A Reply to my Critics', in Thompson and Held (eds), 1982.

Habermas, J. 1990. *Moral Consciousness and Communicative Action.* Cambridge, Ma: The MIT Press.

Habermas, J. 1990a. 'Discourse Ethics: Notes on a Program of Philosophical Justification', in Habermas, 1990.

Habermas, J. 1990b. 'Moral Consciousness and Communicative Action', in Habermas, 1990.

Habermas, J. 1992. *Postmetaphysical Thinking.* Cambridge: Polity Press.

Habermas, J. 1992a. 'Individuation through Socialization: On George Herbert Mead's Theory of Subjectivity', in Habermas, 1992.

Habermas, J. 1993. *Justification and Application: Remarks on Discourse Ethics.* Cambridge Ma: MIT Press.

Habermas, J. 1996. *Between Facts and Norms.* Cambridge, Ma: The MIT Press.

Kohlberg, L. 1981. *The Philosophy of Moral Development.* London & San Fransisco: Harper and Row.

Meehan, J. (ed.). 1995. *Feminists Read Habermas.* New York & London: Routledge.

Moller Okin, S. 1989. *Justice, Gender and the Family.* New York: Basic Books.

Thompson, J. B. and Held, D. (eds). 1982. *Habermas: Critical Debates.* London: Macmillan.

Waugh, P. 1992. 'Modernism, Postmodernism, Feminism: Gender and Autonomy Theory', in Waugh (ed.), 1992.

Waugh, P. (ed.). 1992. *Postmodernism: A Reader.* London: Edward Arnold

Young, I. 1987. 'Impartiality and the Civic Republic', in Benhabib and Cornell (eds), 1987.

CHAPTER 8

Green Politics and Ecological Stewardship

John Barry

O
f recent movements in intellectual and civil life the 'green'
or ecological perspective has captivated the popular and
scholarly imagination. Unlike other movements such as
postmodernism, it has strong roots within civil society, being at the
forefront of some of the most important forms of political action
and ethical debates in Ireland and elsewhere.

The values, vision and approach of green moral and political
theory overlap in some significant respects with the basic political
and moral vision of Fergal O'Connor. Like others in this volume I
had the honour of being taught by Fergal, and looking back can
see how his influence had much to do with my interest and particular
approach to the study of green moral and political theory. Fergal's
emphasis on classical themes such as the centrality of the virtues to
the experience of the moral life, played a large part in how I
subsequently conceptualised the new and developing field of green
normative political theory. In particular, Fergal's attitude towards,
and conceptualisation of, 'technique' in its various forms in modern
life, and his abiding conviction of the necessity for virtue (partly in
response to the corrosive effects of technique) are themes I wish to
explore in this presentation of green political theory.

Green politics and modernity

One way to view green politics is to see it as a critical reaction to
modernity. More specifically, one can view green politics in terms
of its attitude to the two Revolutions at the heart of modernity:
namely the Industrial and the French Revolutions. The dialectic
between these Revolutions forms the historical origins and the

theoretical dynamic of green political theory. The Industrial Revolution marks the desire and possibility for humans to live better, in terms of the material conditions of life, through the systematic application of science, technology and the market organisation of the economy. The French Revolution marks the democratic imperative of modernity, in terms of popular sovereignty and universal citizenship. The dynamic between these two 'moments' of modernity frames what may be called the 'unstable narrative' of modernity, a narrative that, I argue, green politics seeks to re-write.[1] A green view highlights the potentially undemocratic as well as ecologically irrational dangers of the logic of the Industrial Revolution. The green claim is that there is an intrinsic connection between the achievement of an ecologically rational social environment relationship and the extension of democratic norms to more and more parts of society. This requires, as suggested later, a re-examination of some assumptions of the Industrial Revolution, particularly, its view of 'progress'.

Anthropocentrism and ecocentrism

In the popular imagination and, indeed, for many greens themselves, the novelty of green politics lies in its rejection of anthropocentrism in favour of an ecocentric worldview. Within green debates 'anthropocentrism' refers to the quality of human-centredness and the significance of human reasons and interests in social-environmental affairs. 'Ecocentrism' seeks to displace this human-centredness with a 'trans-human' ecological sensibility in which humans or their interests are no longer the be-all and end-all of moral concern when questions of social-environmental interaction are at stake. According to the radical green understanding of it, the anthropocentric worldview sees the natural world as simply there for human enjoyment. In its strongest form this view is expressed in an economic perspective that reduces the world to a store of

---

[1] This idea of modernity as a fall from grace has its roots in the late 18th and early 19th century 'romantic' reaction to the Industrial revolution, and is the origin of certain strands of ecological thought such as 'deep ecology'. From this radical green perspective modernity represents humanity's second fall, the first being humanity's banishment from the Garden of Eden. For a critical analysis of deep ecology see Barry (1993, 1995).

resources. This perspective is, in no small measure, responsible for the modern environmental crisis, in the view of many radical greens and environmental ethicists. They see the roots of the crisis in what Weber called the 'disenchantment of the world', a direct consequence of modernity. This refers to the transformation of the non-human world from a realm of meaning into a collection of material means, in which the natural world is valuable only in so far as it is useful to some human end. Thus for ecocentrics, anthropocentrism is synonymous with seeing the natural world as possessing merely instrumental and not also intrinsic value. Hence, 'radical' green politics rejects anthropocentrism as the dominant moral, economic and political worldview.

Ecocentrism privileges the protection or preservation of the environment over human use of the environment. It attempts to reverse the existing situation where the case for environmental preservation has to be justified or proved, while human use of the environment goes unquestioned. It seeks to replace an anthropo-centric presumption in favour of any human use of the environment with an ecocentric presumption in favour of the preservation of the environment from human use.

Three points may be made in response to this position. First, we should reject both presumptions because the normative status of social-environmental relations cannot be determined in advance of experience. We have to know something about the empirical world of humans and of nature before we can construct appropriate normative responses in light of the facts. For example, any normative account of social-environmental relations must include human productive and transformative relations with the environment. That is, how we ought to treat nature must start from, and be consistent with, recognition of the *fact* that humans must use nature to survive and flourish and that this is part of what it means to be human. This is related to the argument that the 'environment' with which human societies interact is a 'humanised one'. Against the more romantic greens, it should be said that the ecological niche in which we humans find ourselves is a transformed or intentionally human-ised dimension. We are the species nature did not specialise; hence we have no 'natural' ecological habitat. In holding this, green politics explicitly rejects the existentialist vision of human beings simply being 'thrown into' a hostile and indifferent world. The coevolutionary history of our species and our symbiotic relationship with the external world (which, as green politics points out, has increasingly become characterised by parasitism) demonstrates that the earth is indeed our 'home'.

Second, there needs to be recognition that contingency, risk, and uncertainty mark the ecological aspects of the human condition. This is why those versions of deep ecology that seek to find a single definitive answer to the relationship between humanity and nature go astray. My own view of the aim of green politics is much more modest, and perhaps more difficult. It is that green politics is concerned with the shifting dimensions and problems (moral, ecological, political and economic) of the concrete relationship between particular societies and their particular environments.

Third, the ecocentric position is based on a false and partial understanding of anthropocentrism. Ecocentric objections do not touch anthropocentrism as a moral perspective (i.e. one that sees things from our point of view, and notes the importance of human interests in moral inquiry). Their proper target is a metaphysical understanding of anthropocentrism in which the natural world is regarded as made for, and only valuable in relation to, humanity and its purposes. But without some very specific and controversial religious context, it is difficult to sustain the claim that the external world is created solely for human enjoyment. Once we distinguish between anthropocentrism as a metaphysical claim and as a moral outlook, the ecocentric-anthropocentric divide, which has generated the most controversy within green moral theory, becomes more apparent than real. Nevertheless, the ecocentric complaint about the instrumentalisation of the natural world has to be addressed in any plausibly 'green' political theory. The task is to develop an approach that can integrate a defensible anthropocentrism with green demands for ethically symbiotic and ecologically sustainable relations between human societies and their environments.

Ecological stewardship and virtue

My proposal (Barry, 1999) is that an idea of ecological stewardship is a fruitful way of formulating responsibility for nature within a framework of human concerns. The stewardship position holds that care for the environment cannot be independent of human interests. It suggests a mode of human interaction in which the vital human interest in managing and transforming the environment is characterised by moral and ecological concerns. However, the concern for the non-human world that underpins stewardship is not disinterested or impartial. Stewardship is motivated by concerns for future human generations along the lines suggested by the Amerindian saying that 'We do not inherit the earth from our parents, but borrow it from our children'. The point about this stewardship perspective is that it is a reformed, long-sighted anthropocentrism that seeks to fulfil human interests in a manner that does not illegitimately preclude the intrinsic value of the non-human world.

The advantage of the stewardship idea is that it is politically (as well as philosophically) superior to ecocentrism. First, it taps into existing (Judaeo-Christian) ideas about human stewardship over God's (not humanity's) 'creation'.[2] It can, therefore, draw on a widely understood, and to some (perhaps-considerable) extent shared, cultural common ground to build political support. Second, it directly addresses green concerns. From the green perspective, 'ecological stewardship' can be interpreted as an ecologically rational mode of individual and collective behaviour and interaction, in which long-term human interests are secured. Ecological stewardship, unlike ecocentrism, emphasises a self-reflexive, long-term, anthropo-centrism, as opposed to an 'arrogant' or 'strong' anthropocentrism. Thus it can secure many of the policy objectives of ecocentrism, in terms of environmental preservation.

The key to developing the stewardship perspective in a way that expresses ecocentric moral concerns is an understanding of our attitude to the non-human world as a matter of 'ecological virtue'. This virtue-ethics approach views the moral dimension of green concerns as having less to do with finding the correct set of moral rules by which we are to interact with nature, than with cultivating respectful, less 'arrogant' habits, dispositions, and characters as our modes of interaction with the non-human world. The approach aims to cultivate a mode of being and behaviour that helps us to cope and adapt to, rather than eliminate, the

---

[2] The idea of humans as God's stewards is not limited to Judaeo-Christianity but is a strong theme in other great 'agricultural religions' such as Islam, Hinduism and Buddhism.

contingencies and uncertainties of the human condition in relation to our environment. Unlike the approach of some greens who seek to find a determinate and final answer to the 'truth' of human-nature relations, a virtue-ethics approach is not an attempt to eradicate or 'solve' the problems and challenges of the 'human condition'. Rather the approach is a matter of cultivating a knowledgeable and sensitive attitude towards, and perception of, the non-human world, but one that does not lapse into a sentimental romanticism. A proper regard for the non-human world would be one that is scientifically informed but that also leaves room for emotional attachments to particular ecosystems, land forms, species or individual animals.

Virtue, being concerned with what is difficult for us, is particularly appropriate to the green case given the likely 'sacrifices' and re-orientation of dominant (materialistic) views of the good life that the achievement of ecological sustainability demands. A return to virtue is necessary in order to cultivate the habits and dispositions to resist the temptation of a 'techno-fix' view, that says that all environmental problems can (or at least soon will be) solved through technological developments. The emphasis on ecological virtue thus expresses the basic green point that the environmental crisis is at root a moral question and not simply a 'technical-material' one. The appeal to virtue implies that the resolution of social-environmental problems is a matter of cultivating more ecologically sensitive characters, and not just of buying 'green' products or developing more 'eco-friendly' forms of technology.

A great strength of the virtue-ethics approach to green moral and political theory is that virtue brings with it an idea of human flourishing, or wellbeing, that does not reduce to material or economic 'welfare'. Virtue ethics can also furnish a much-needed sense of proportion and humility to guard against the constant vice of hubris, indifference and disrespect to the non-human world. By cultivating ecologically sensitive modes of relating to the world, particularly in respect of human transformative relations and practices, the normative change that greens argue for acquires a cultural as well as a political character. Green political theory, centred on the cultivation of 'ecological stewardship', becomes a matter of integrating these modes of interaction so that together they constitute a stewardship mode. Taking a virtue-oriented position implies that a concern of green politics is to create modes of human interaction with the non-human world that are ecologically sustainable and morally symbiotic. The latter refers to fostering self-reflexive modes of human behaviour in which human interests, for which particular human uses of the non-human world are carried out, are considered as necessary, but not sufficient, to justify that use. Green political theory is then concerned with discriminating legitimate, worthy, or serious human interests from illegitimate, unworthy or trivial ones. The concern with virtue is thus related to discriminating 'symbiotic' from 'parasitic' human modes of interaction, and to fostering the former as an ecologically virtuous mode. At the same time, the classical view of virtue as a mean between extremes is also evident in the reflexive form of anthropocentrism. This reformed anthropocentrism is a mean between the extremes (vices) of deep ecological 'submissiveness' in respect to nature, and the 'arrogance' of 'strong' anthropocentrism.

Technique and enclosure in green politics

The illumination of the dangers of technique and professionalisation within increasing areas of human life was one of Fergal's constant themes. On this point the green view is firmly with those, like Fergal, who urge caution with regard to technique in all its manifestations. From a green perspective, technique requires moral judgment, and therefore ecological virtue, in order to distinguish 'permissible' from 'impermissible' uses of the natural world. One theorist who looms large in green theory is Ivan Illich (1971, 1975, 1981) because of his call for the 'de-professionalisation' of such central areas of human life as health, education, transport, housing and work. Agreeing with Illich, greens seek to return more and more areas of people's lives to the status of 'practices', with an instrumental view of institutions such as the nation-state and the market, that are to be judged in relation to their impact on social practices. Following MacIntyre we can define a social practice as 'any coherent and complex form of socially established co-operative human activity through which goods internal to that form of activity are realised in the course of trying to achieve those standards of excellence which are appropriate to, and partially definitive of, that form of activity' (1984, 187). The problem is the relationship between practices and institutions, for as O'Neill points out: 'Institutions ... not only sustain practices, they can also corrupt them. The pursuit of external goods – wealth, power and status – may come into conflict with the pursuit of internal goods and practices' (1993, 127).

Another way to put this, and one that is increasingly the language used by green theorists, is to talk of the necessity for the 'commons' to be re-appropriated and further 'enclosures' to be resisted. While many greens write passionately of the necessity to protect existing 'ecological commons' (Hildyard, 1993), green politics is also concerned with protecting the equally significant 'commons of everyday life' – the social practices – from the potentially corrupting influences of large-scale institutions. This is to be understood not as a complete rejection of institutions in favour of social practices on the grounds that the latter are always and everywhere ecologically, ethically and politically 'superior' to institutions. Rather the green concern with resisting enclosure of the commons is to be understood as arguing for a new balance between institutions and the social practices that make up the web of everyday life.

One area of life that greens are keen to see come under the rubric of a practice as opposed to an institution is the world of work. For greens there are sound ecological as well as moral reasons why work ought to be transformed into a practice in which internal goods as opposed to external rewards take precedence. At the individual level, the closing of the gap between production and consumption can be understood as an attempt to recapture some of the internal goods of production that are largely missing from modern forms of production.[3] One option is to alter or restructure

---

[3] It is interesting to note that concerns with the virtues of self-production arise in the west at a time when work is disappearing from its work-based societies, as a result of technological changes and the global division of labour, in the same way that the origins of an aesthetic appreciation of nature arose historically precisely at the time when human ability to destroy it also arose. As Williams has pointed out, 'An artistic reaffirmation of the separateness and fearfulness of nature became appropriate at the point at which for the first time the prospect of an ever-increasing control of it became obvious' (1992, 67). However, the difference in the case of the reaffirmation of the virtues and intrinsic value of self-production is that what is disappearing is formal paid employment, not 'work' as a valued, purposive, transformative activity. In this sense, the self-production ideal is a 'post-full-employment' phenomenon.

current productive conditions so as to allow the internal goods of work to be realised. This option includes worker participation schemes, flexi-time, multi-tasking, non-assembly line forms of production, and working from home. Such schemes can provide opportunities for the realisation of some internal goods of work such as autonomy, solidarity, creativity, education, self-esteem and self-confidence. The green aspect of this option is that a restructured productive sphere geared towards internal goods rather than criteria of efficiency and maximisation is more ecologically sensitive in making fewer demands on ecosystems. In short, work, as a trans-formative-intentional social practice is more likely to 'walk lighter on the earth' since it is regulated by qualitative and not just quan-titative considerations.

Another way to realise the internal goods of work is by encouraging self-production, both individually and collectively through informal economic practices. Self-production, in weakening the link between money and production, opens up the possibility of production becoming a site of freedom and not simply a sphere of necessity. As 'own-work' is not engaged in primarily as a means to secure money, it conforms to the ideal of a craft rather than an industrial mode of production. An 'external' or institutionalised understanding of 'work' is central to orthodox political economy premised on its view of work as 'disutility', something engaged in for monetary remuneration. Conceiving of work as disutility, to be entered into for monetary 'compensation' in the form of wages, further entrenches the central role of money within social life. Not only is money, as Chesterton said, like a sixth sense necessary to make use of the other five, but it is the primary reason for engaging in productive activity. Indeed, within orthodox economics only that which commands a monetary value, a price, is counted as 'productive'. Thus domestic labour, informal productive activity and mutual aid are by definition 'unproductive' since they do not show in the orthodox economic measure of a nation's economic activity. Historically the separation of people from resources, as a result of the enclosure of the commons, made the acquisition of money a prerequisite for fulfilling needs. At the same time the idea of work as 'disutility' entered into for monetary 'compensation' represents another act of enclosure. This enclosure may be understood as the transformation of 'work' into 'labour': the aim of economic efficiency coupled with the valuation of work primarily in monetary terms implies that there is no point in re-organising work to permit the introduction of internal goods.[4] This second enclosure is the enclosure of the informal economy by the formal, money-based and increasingly global one. Within green political economy, self-production as an organising principle of the economic life of society is an opportunity for the practice of virtue: the realisation of the internal goods of work. Self-production is thus also a matter of character formation and is consistent with a less 'consumerist' character typical of contemporary 'Homo economicus'.

Green political theory and progress

One of the defining themes of green political theory, and one that is so obvious that it often goes unremarked, is its attitude towards and concern with 'progress'. The whole tenor of early ideological accounts of green politics resonate with a perception that the costs of modernity, the modern view of 'progress' and economic modernisation, outweigh the benefits that are themselves suggested to be of questionable quality. From this position two equally unappealing understandings of green politics can be advanced. On the one hand, green politics constitutes a rejection of modernity's legacy of progress in both the socioeconomic and political spheres. On the other, green politics implies a rejection of industrial progress but the acceptance and radicalisation of 'democratic progress'. This more popular view of green politics sees it as anti-industrial, but pro-democracy. Now while the latter has obviously more to commend it than the former, the anti-industrial tenor of green politics and writing – much of it rejects 'consumerism', 'materialism', science, technology, and the market economy – needs to be questioned.

Gowdy (1994) represents the type of green view of progress that I wish to criticise.[5] According to him 'there is no convincing

---

[4] Since work as labour was conceptually viewed as 'disutility', a necessary evil, one would have thought that the economic aim was to minimise work by improving efficiency of production. On the whole, productive improvements have resulted in fewer people working harder, rather than less work per person.

[5] A more extreme version of this position can be found in Lasch's (1991) work.

evidence that past economic growth has led to unambiguous improvement in the human condition. Once we give up the idea of progress, we can concentrate on the making do with what we have rather than placing our hopes on some future material or ethical utopia' (1994, 55). Gowdy's injunction to abandon the idea of progress would, I hold, be a retrograde step. It is only if one equates progress with undifferentiated material economic growth that it makes sense from a green position to talk of abandoning progress. But progress does not necessarily equate with economic growth, as writers including J. S. Mill and the more sensible contemporary green critics, have emphasised. Green politics, I suggest, is concerned with re-defining and re-appropriating, rather than rejecting, the politically powerful idea of progress. Gowdy's extremely pessimistic advice to greens is that when they are accused of being 'anti-progress', to turn the tables on their opponents by rejecting the assumption 'that progress has taken place' (1994, p. 55). This is not only foolish but dangerous advice; to claim that no progress has taken place since the Enlightenment is to throw the baby out with the bath water, to say the least. Progress has taken place, albeit unevenly, unreflexively and, until now, largely without concerns for ecological sustainability or symbiotic moral relations with the non-human world. The rejection of progress is neither necessary nor desirable for green politics.

If green theory holds on to an idea of progress it may not enter debates about the necessity or utility of enclosing commons today, from a position that rejects enclosure, as a matter of principle. The green point is rather that while progress was premised historically on enclosing the commons, it is an open question whether further progress can be based on the patterns of past social development.

It is within this context that green political economy favours what may be termed a 'post-development' perspective. This arises out of a critique of the linear, one-dimensional version of social progress that equates progress with 'economic modernisation' after the model of western industrial societies. Progress, in the green view, can no longer be simply equated with ever increasing material affluence, the multiplication of desires, or the extension of market-based organisation of the human economy. This is the point about the green interpretation of 'sustainable development'. This is not about the continuation of present patterns of social progress on a more ecological basis, but for a different type of progress, a view of development that emphasises qualitative as well as quantitative indicators for judging social progress. In short what green politics invites us to contemplate is that the 're-embedding' of the economy within the ecosystem requires its re-embedding within, and circumspection by, democratic institutions and social practices.

Ecological stewardship and green citizenship

One of the main claims of green politics concerns the connection between a particular conception of citizenship as a constitutive aspect of a political process that I have termed 'collective ecological management' (Barry, 1999), and the cultivation of a 'stewardship ethic' that consists in the cultivation of ecological virtues and the avoidance of ecological vices. Stewardship as 'wise use' is not against human interests, but rather constitutes a mode of action in which future, long-term interests can be safeguarded against the temptation of immediate, short-term ones. Stewardship as a moral ideal of human excellence is most clearly expressed within the agricultural context within which this ethical tradition developed, where stewardship represents a set of interconnected character traits that 'good farmers' would hope to cultivate.

Within the family-farm social milieu, relations between humans and nature are characterised by sustainable and symbiotic modes of interaction. While the land is used and animals consumed, the former is not 'mined' or 'exploited' for short-term profit, nor are the latter treated purely as 'food resources'. In contrast to modern factory-farming, 'personal' as well as 'productive' relations exist between animals and humans within the context of agricultural stewardship. As an ideal one can see why it has appealed to many radical green critics of modern, urban life, who see in this ideal a way of directly 're-connecting' the people and the 'land'. Arguments for returning 'back to the land' have characterised green politics since its origins in the romantic backlash against the Industrial Revolution. Since the agricultural setting within which stewardship developed is no longer available to most people, clearly the virtues and character traits based on it will be difficult, though not impossible, to cultivate in an urban context.

It is a brute fact that city dwellers comprise the 'many' whose democratic endorsement of environmental policies green politics needs. The roles of individuals within urban modes of living are clearly different (in kind and degree) from those within the original agricultural setting of stewardship. Given the urban nature of contemporary life, and discounting green arguments that turn on the 'unnaturalness' of urban living, an ecological rather than an agricultural mode of stewardship has to be developed. Although the majority of people in modern society have no direct, trans-formative experiences of nature, this does not mean that the dispositions and attitudes constitutive of stewardship as a mode of action are impossible to cultivate in an urban setting. While eco-logical management within agricultural stewardship takes place in the context of farming as a social practice, urban-based forms of management are necessarily mediated by social institutions and forms of knowledge that do not presuppose a direct transformative experience of the environment. The most important of these social institutions are the (formal) market economy and the nation-state while scientific knowledge is the most important form of knowledge for ecological stewardship.

While the institutional framework is a necessary condition for modern environmental management, from a green perspective this needs to be supplemented with a focus on the individual's role in institutional processes and the development of social practices in which ecological virtue can be cultivated. A key aspect of the individual's role is a view of green citizenship as an integrative mode of human interaction. Green citizenship proposes a new combination of rights and duties, stressing democratic voice, institutional accountability, and citizen activism. The integrative role of green citizenship relates to its function to integrate other modes of human interaction, particularly those of consumption and production, within a stewardship mode.

The idea of green citizenship is vital to the green democratic position. Green citizenship is a necessary and desirable feature of collective ecological management. The nation-state and formal market cannot do all that is required to ensure an ecologically rational social-environmental symbiosis. Citizens will have to do their 'bit' in this collective enterprise. Citizenship as a mode of character thus transcends the purely 'political' or formal status and legal standing of citizenship, and comes to denote a way of acting that tends towards ecologically rational forms of action. Green citizenship becomes a way of transforming urban dwellers into ecological stewards, giving those who may have no direct experience of nature some responsibility for managing the relationship between society and the environment. One of the most important aspects of green citizenship in this respect is to educate individuals of the dependence of society (which includes them) on the environment, and the environment's dependence upon, and vulnerability to, society (including their actions). Green citizenship thus seeks to establish a 'citizen-in-society-in-environment' perspective as the appropriate basis for democratic environmental policy-making.

Conclusion

Aquinas wisely pointed out that it is better for a blind horse to be slow. Likewise it would be better for contemporary society, given the uncertainty that marks our dealings with the environment, coupled with the technological capacity to alter the conditions of life on earth as we know it, to moderate its demands for material consumption (ends), and adopt a more prudent disposition in the employment of its means. After all, we do not have exclusive ownership of the earth but share it with other species and future generations of humans, and while we transform it to fulfil our interests, we must be ever wary that we do not unjustifiably harm the interests of other species or those who will come after us. The earth was not made for us, but perhaps the reverse is true: that we were made for the earth.

References

Arendt, H. 1958. *The Human Condition.* Chicago:University of Chicago Press.

Barry, J. 1993. 'Deep Ecology and the Undermining of Green Politics', in J. Holder et al. (eds), *Perspectives on the Environment: Interdisciplinary Research in Action.* Aldershot: Avebury.

Barry, J. 1995. 'Deep Ecology, Socialism and Human Being in the World: A Part of, yet Apart from Nature', in *Capitalism, Nature, Socialism* 6:3, 30-39.

Barry, J. 1999. *Rethinking Green Political Theory: Nature, Virtue and Progress.* London: Sage.

Hildyard, N. et al. 1993. *Whose Common Future?* London: Earthscan.

Gowdy, J. 1994. 'Progress and Environmental Sustainability', *Environmental Ethics* 16:1, 41-55.

Illich, I. 1971. *Deschooling Society.* Harmondsworth: Penguin.

Illich, I. 1975. *Tools for Conviviality.* London: Fontana.

Illich, I. 1981. *Shadow Work.* London: Marion Boyers.

Lasch, C. 1991. *The True and Only Heaven: Progress and its Critics.* New York: Norton.

MacIntyre, A. 1984. *After Virtue* (2nd edn). Notre Dame: University of Notre Dame Press.

Nisbet, R. 1989. 'Progress', in D. Miller et al (eds), *The Blackwell Encyclopaedia of Political Thought.* Cambridge: Blackwell, 401-3.

O'Neill, J. 1993. *Ecology, Policy and Politics: Human Well-Being and the Nonhuman World.* London: Routledge.

Williams, B. 1992. 'Must an Environmental Ethic be Centred on Human Beings?' in C. Taylor (ed.), *Ethics and the Environment.* Oxford: Corpus Christi College.

CHAPTER 9

Prisons, Politicians and Democracy

Philip Pettit

Fergal O'Connor has always been outstanding among Irish political theorists for his capacity to relate abstract theory to concrete issues. To those of us who were lucky enough to be able to learn from him – in my case as a colleague at University College, Dublin – the first lesson he represented was the need to justify theoretical ideas by the perspective that they gave us on day-to-day questions. I am conscious of not having learned that lesson well enough but it is never too late to make amends. And so, in the spirit of his example, I start with lowly but pressing problems in penal practice and try to reveal a connection with issues in high democratic theory.

The prison problem

One of the most extraordinary features of today's democracies is that, regardless of other differences in their aspirations and achievements, they more or less uniformly rely on imprisonment as the principal response to crime. I say that this is extraordinary because it has long been a matter of common sense observation, and it is now a well-established finding of criminology, that prisons do not serve well the cause of combatting crime. Not much knowledge is required to see that prisons are brutalising and stigmatising institutions that deepen the alienation of offenders from the general society. And not much reflection is needed to see that they are likely to serve as recruiting and organising networks for those of dedicated criminal intent.

Why have prisons proved such a resilient feature of the democratic landscape? How have they managed to survive the growing evidence about their counter-productivity and the efforts of those professional and associational groups who have subjected them to a barrage of criticism? Criminologists, prisoners' rights groups, civil liberties associations, even victims' movements have subjected prison to withering criticism. And all to no avail. The resort to incarceration remains a steady and indeed a strengthening feature of many western democracies.

In searching for an explanation it may prove useful to move away from prisons, and even away from contemporary democracies. The Irish-Australian historian, Oliver MacDonagh (1958), is well known for his explanation of the emergence of the nineteenth-century administrative state. And that explanation, I want to suggest, offers a very plausible model of why imprisonment has proved so resilient.

The MacDonagh thesis is an attempt to explain the cascade of administrative reforms that emerged and stabilised in Victorian Britain: reforms in the mines and factories, in the employment of children, in the conditions on emigrant ships, and in a variety of other areas. The thesis is that those reforms materialised under the impetus of one and the same mechanism. The mechanism involved, first, the discovery of a scandal; second, the development of public outrage about the scandal; and third, a requirement on politicians to do something in order to respond to the scandal. We can call it the scandal machine.

According to MacDonagh, this scandal machine served in the first instance to introduce reforms in a given area and then, later, to reinforce and increase the effect of the reforms. As he describes the typical story, the machine initially had the effect of getting government to make an inquiry and to set up regulatory constraints; some years afterwards, when the scandal was found to have survived those constraints, it goaded government into establishing a regular inspectorate; and then a few years later, after the revelation of continuing scandal, it forced government to set up a proper bureaucracy to oversee the area in question.

The MacDonagh thesis is that we can explain the growth of the nineteenth-century administrative state by the cumulative effects of this simple but powerful mechanism. That state was not the intentional product of a Benthamite project of reform; it did not come of a utilitarian spirit sweeping through the halls of Westminster. It was the precipitate rather of a pattern that no one planned and that few understood. The growing administrative state was forced upon British democracy by systemic pressures, not by philosophical ideology or political will.

It is easy to reconstruct the elements that made the scandal machine so powerful. Nineteenth-century Britain was a more or less literate culture in which the press offered a ready outlet for the revelation of scandal; it was a more or less humanistic culture – the response to the Irish famine notwithstanding – in which scandal easily ignited outrage; and it was an increasingly democratic culture in which politicians had to prove themselves responsive to the feelings of the people. It was the combination of those forces, and not the vision or the leadership of any individual or group, that gave rise to the different aspects of the new governmental regime.

When we read MacDonagh's account of the rise of the administrative state it is easy to think of the mechanism at work as a sort of benign, invisible hand. Or at least that is easy for those amongst us who see the administrative developments that he charts as positive and progressive measures. But the scandal machine is not inherently benign in its effects, or so I now want to suggest. It can operate as often in the manner of an invisible foot as an invisible hand.

Consider the manner in which social work agencies are constrained by the scandal machine in their decisions as to whether certain children should be taken into care. If an agency decides that the children are better left with their parents or guardians then it runs a serious risk. Should anything bad happen, the newspapers and the television can be relied upon to reveal the scandal, to generate popular outrage and to call government down upon the head of the agency responsible. If the agency takes the children into care however, then short of large numbers being involved it can be more or less certain of escaping such bad effects. And this is so even if the reasons for taking the children into care are not professionally compelling: even if the option of taking the children away from their homes is a matter of just playing bureaucratically safe.

It does not take much imagination to see how in this type of case the scandal machine may operate like an invisible foot, not an invisible hand. The machine can easily ensure, at least in the absence of other safeguards, that social work agencies work for ill, not for good, in dealing with children at risk. It can have the result that children who would be much better left in their homes, perhaps under some sort of monitoring arrangement, are actually taken into institutional care.

We have seen what the scandal machine is and we have noticed that it may operate for good or for bad, depending on the circumstances in question. It is time, with these observations in mind, to return to the case of prisons. What I want to suggest is that the MacDonagh model provides a good explanation of what may be happening in this area. It does not need a lot of thought to see that the scandal machine operates with particular momentum in matters of criminal justice and that it can readily account for the resilience of the resort to imprisonment.

We can see how the scandal machine operates at the heart of penal practice if we ask ourselves what would be likely to happen in the event of a government reducing the maximum sentences available for given crimes, introducing new opportunities for early release, and arranging for a greater use of alternatives to imprisonment: say, a greater use of fines and community service orders. It is as sure as night follows day that at some point after the inauguration of such reforms an offender who would otherwise be in prison will commit some more or less sickening sort of crime. And it is equally sure that when such a thing happens it will constitute a matter of scandal, a cause of public outrage and a ground for calling on politicians to roll back the reforms which they had begun to institute.

There is no difficulty in seeing why such a crime would be a matter of scandal and outrage. We live in a society where the press and television have a vested interest in presenting people with the sensational and the shocking and in drumming up moralistic sentiment about the horrors involved. It is a well-tested Fleet street formula that people like savouring the scandalous and having their outrage pumped and primed; it is common wisdom indeed that they are willing to pay for the pleasure.

As there is no difficulty in seeing why the crime envisaged would be a matter of scandal and outrage, so there is no difficulty in understanding why it would force politicians, in all likelihood, to backtrack on the reforms they had initiated. When politicians are called upon to respond to the occurrence of a sickening crime, then there is only one plausible response they can make. They have got to show themselves as concerned and as angry as the most outraged in the community. And they have got to do that in the newspaper headline or the thirty-second sound bite. Let them fail to be sufficiently expressive of concern and anger and they will easily be upstaged by more vociferous opponents.

How can politicians be expressive in the required way? How other than by calling for a return to hard and harsh punishment? We will show these vandals, these vermin, what ordinary, decent folk think of such behaviour; the metaphors and the cadences will be familiar to every ear. We will crack down like government has never cracked down before on this sort of affront; the melancholy message is drearily predictable.

The reason why politicians are bound to be driven to this retributive, punitive response is that the forum in which they operate lends itself to no other language. The theatre of public responsibility and political will requires nothing less than an operatic display of fellow feeling and fellow outrage. Never mind if the words get lost. The audience isn't interested in what you are actually going to do; it wants to see and know that you care. Your job is to give the outrage voice and, in giving it voice, to orchestrate a chorus of demands for a return to the world where society is tough on crime.

If this line of thought is right then the criminal justice area is governed by the logic of the scandal machine and is subject to the control of an invisible foot. It is guaranteed never to move away from the pattern of counter-productive imprisonment that currently dominates our response to crime. Montesquieu (1989, 203) spoke over two hundred years ago of the danger that society would be subject, in its criminal laws, to what he called 'the tyranny of the avengers'. The scandal machine looks like a mechanism that ensures, unfortunately, that this sort of tyranny we will always have with us.

The depoliticising solution

But perhaps I should rephrase that message. The tyranny of the avengers looks like something we will always have with us, at least so long as decisions about imprisonment are made by democratically elected politicians under the pressure of public, theatrical demands. For just as democratic responsiveness played a part in ensuring that the scandal machine produced those positive reforms described by MacDonagh, so it plays a crucial part in ensuring that that machine produces the resilient pattern of imprisonment with which we have learned, at no small cost, to live.

The observation is important because it points us towards the only sort of feasible change that might save us from the tyranny of avengers. The change I have in mind can be described in a single word: depoliticise. If decisions about sentencing and penal policy were depoliticised, if they were entrusted to a network of expert and impartial committees that monitored the aggregate effects of every initiative taken, then – then and only then – there might be some chance of rationalising the way in which we run our criminal justice system.

Without going into the details of the change envisaged, it is clear why we might look to it with a degree of confidence. Think about how central banks have come to depoliticise various financial decisions in most contemporary democracies and think of the way in which this enables politicians to resist popular pressures to introduce what might very well be irresponsible policies. They can say that the issue is not one in their province. And they can say that it is an issue on which it would be improper for them, or for any amateur or outsider, to criticise the decision-making body. Thus they can protect themselves from media assault by passing the buck elsewhere and they can ensure that there is somewhere else to pass the buck – there are people willing to accept appointment to central bank boards – by arguing that those who are appointed for their expertise and impartiality are not fair targets of popular criticism.

The depoliticisation move is known in discussions of constitutional democracy as a gagging initiative: an initiative in which the politicians silence themselves, or have silence thrust upon them (Holmes 1988). I think that the failure to resist the pressure of the scandal machine in the criminal justice system, the failure to rectify manifestly irrational aspects of our criminal justice practice, shows that the only way to make ground in this area may be to gag the politicians and to transfer the decisions to non-political bodies. If war is too important to be left to the generals, criminal justice is too important to be left to the politicians.

I realise that I have not presented an adequate argument for depoliticising criminal justice decisions. In order to make a proper case for such a reform I would need to marshal the empirical evidence of current failure, I would need to canvass the problems with alternative possibilities of reform, I would need to detail the proposal I have in mind and I would need to establish its attractions by showing how well analogues work in other areas. Also I would need to plan an implementation procedure that would allow for bringing the strategy into play in stages, with evidence of the success of each stage being necessary for progressing to the next stage.

I hope I may be forgiven for assuming in the absence of a proper argument that the depoliticisation option would be better than the status quo. That assumption is not outlandish, if only because the status quo is so barbaric. For anyone familiar with the brutal practice of prisons on the one hand and the evidence of their counter-productivity on the other, the status quo in criminal justice must begin to look about as morally compelling as a system of slave-holding (Braithwaite and Pettit 1990).

Depoliticisation and democratic theory

One reason I may be forgiven for not arguing properly in favour of depoliticising criminal justice is that my interest in the proposal, for present purposes, derives from an interest in the theory of democracy. Assume, if not that it is certainly better to depoliticise criminal justice, at least that this is likely to be so. Assume, if you prefer, that whether or not criminal justice should be depoliticised, certainly depoliticisation is an attractive option in other areas of government: say, in the area of central-bank decisions. Any such assumption will serve to generate the question to which I now want to turn.

That question bears on how the theory of democracy can look with any favour on a depoliticising proposal. Under most accounts of democracy, the attraction of the arrangement is that it puts public decisions – say, decisions on matters relating to public goods – where they properly belong: in the hands of the people or in the hands of the people's representatives. The orthodox democratic theories suggest that good public decisions are decisions that express the popular will or, if not the actual popular will, at least an informed counterpart of that will: for example, the sort of will that might be expected to emerge among popularly chosen representatives who systematically debate the issues involved. In a democracy the people are politically sovereign, it is said, albeit they may cede legal sovereignty to their representatives (Dicey 1960). And under most assumptions that means that the polity works well, and the point of democracy is achieved, just so far as things are organised so that the sovereign's will is ... well, sovereign.

The problem with any depoliticisation arrangement is that on these will-based or voluntarist theories of democracy, it is not clear how such an arrangement could be justified. Depoliticisation involves taking decisions away from the people and away from the people's representatives. In particular, it involves taking away legislative and administrative decisions of the kind that belong with the people under established views of democracy: it is generally conceded that judicial decisions are reasonably left in unelected hands. And that suggests that if we endorse depoliticisation in any area of policy, then we are not true democrats but rather elitists of some kind. We wish to authorise not the people or the people's chosen spokespersons but rather, as it will be said, a corps of faceless, rational bureaucrats.

The challenge here is worth dwelling upon, even savouring. I remember attending a discussion among academics from different fields in Canberra about five years ago. The meeting was focused on some general political issues and a particularly forthright historian posed a problem for the gathering. He was a democrat, he said, or at least had always considered himself to be such. And yet he could not accept that decisions on a variety of matters – he mentioned capital punishment as one example – should be left in the hands of the people; he didn't even think that they should be left with representatives who considered themselves bound by the opinions of their constituents. The people, in his view, were just not up to making decisions of the sort envisaged. Was he inconsistent, he wanted to know. Did he have to make a choice between populism and democracy, on the one hand, or elitism and rationality on the other?

The issue before us is just the same. Can we endorse depoliticisation, in particular depoliticisation in the area of criminal justice, while claiming to be faithful to the ideal of democracy? I want to argue now that we can. It is true that voluntarist theories of democracy would represent depoliticisation as essentially inimical to democratic ideals. But voluntarist theories of democracy, so I want to suggest, are not the only game in town. There is an alternative vision of democracy – a critical or contestatory theory I call it (Pettit 1997) – and under this approach depoliticisation can often be just the sort of thing that democracy requires.

The contestatory theory of democracy

Where democracy exists then by almost all accounts the people as a whole enjoy a sort of collective autonomy that parallels the personal autonomy for which individual agents aspire. But there are two versions of the ideal of personal autonomy and they suggest, by analogy, two quite different versions of the democratic ideal.

The usual account of personal autonomy is voluntarist in character, like the usual account of democratic autonomy. What it suggests is that persons are autonomous just to the extent that they have taken charge of their own beliefs, their own desires and, consequently, their own decisions. They have tried, so far as possible, to suspend the formative influence of childhood and conditioning and they have sought to endorse only such beliefs and only such desires as they have found personally compelling. They have appropriated the intentional states that guide their behaviour, making them truly their own. They have achieved the sort of construction of the self for which existentialists yearned. They have become autonomous in the etymological sense of making the self its own nomos or law. 'Wo Es war', in Freud's expression of the idea, 'soll Ich werden'. Where there was just an impersonal process leading up to the formation of belief and desire – where there was It – there shall be a self in control: there shall be I.

While the voluntarist or existentialist ideal of personal autonomy has certain heady charms, it should be clear that it does not have any lasting appeal. It is entirely infeasible, since there is no one amongst us who is capable of the radical re-examination and reconstruction for which it calls. How can we probe into the origins of our every opinion and preference in order to decide whether it is the product of pathology or whether we can own it as the authentic property of the self? And even if it were feasible, we would still have reason to be unmoved by this voluntarist ideal. It gives expression to an atomistic longing to be isolated from community, particularly the intimate presence which community assumes in parents and teachers and other sources of authority and influence. It represents, as Sartre freely admitted, a desire for godhead: a desire to be thought thinking itself, in Aristotle's phrase; a desire to be one's own creator. It is a shallow, characteristically adolescent ideal, not something vindicated in adult experience.

But it would be a great mistake if disenchantment with the voluntarist ideal of autonomy led us to give up on the notion of autonomy as such. For there is clearly another version that the ideal may assume: a critical or reflective version rather than a voluntarist one. Under this picture of autonomy the history of a person's beliefs and desires – the fact that they originate in childhood and conditioning, for example – is neither here nor there. The important thing is not where the beliefs and desires came from but whether they are maintained in such a manner that the person is capable of critically reflecting on them and capable, should reflection so prescribe, of changing them in certain ways. The crucial achievement is counterfactual or modal, not historical; it consists in the ability, in the event of criticism revealing problems, to stand back and amend.

There are two dimensions, of course, to this critical ideal of autonomy. People will score high in autonomy so far as they are exposed to critical reflection, first of all, and so far as they have the capacity, second, to allow the results of criticism to impact on what they believe and desire. Exposure to critical reflection arises mainly from exchange with others, however; you can fail to achieve it only by sealing yourself into a solipsistic or monocultural shell. And so the more salient aspect of autonomy is the critical or responsive dimension. To be autonomous is to be attached to your ideas and values, not in the pathological manner that would make it impossible for you ever to rethink them, but in the rational way that leaves you open to the possibility of change. It is to be unhindered, at least in the main, by such traditional pathologies as those that we describe as compulsiveness, akrasia and weakness of will, prejudice, bias and dogmatism.

As there is a voluntarist and a critical version of personal autonomy, so there are two versions of democratic autonomy. We are accustomed to think of a community as autonomous and democratic to the extent that the will of the people rules: whatever is law is a matter of general consent, if only virtual or tacit or implied consent. But I suggest that we should think of a community as autonomous, not just to the extent that the people have chosen and endorsed everything that happens, but also to the extent that the people have a dual capacity in relation to whatever happens and whatever becomes law. They can challenge whatever happens – this parallels the possibility of critical reflection – and where the challenge is vindicated they can enforce a change: this parallels the possibility of critical reflection being effective.

The democratic ideal in question does not care essentially about where public decisions come from, any more than the critical version of personal autonomy cares about where a person's ideas and values originate. What is of primary concern from the point of view of this ideal is whether the people retain the ability to contest those decisions and to contest them with some chance of having an effect. The key feature of democracy consists, not in the fact of general consent and popular will – if there could ever be a fact about such matters – but in the capacity for people in every section of the community to raise a potentially effective challenge to any decisions that they judge to be inappropriate.

We can return now to the depoliticisation proposal and the problem that it raises for a voluntarist theory of democracy. For it should be obvious that if we go along with a contestatory component in our theory of democracy then we can take a very different view of such a proposal. Under the contestatory approach the important thing in the organisation of democracy will be to ensure in any given area of policy that there are channels whereby contestations can be raised and given a proper hearing: given a hearing in which the decision made can be reasonably expected to answer to our shared sense of the relevant considerations or, at least, to our shared sense of reasonable decision-making procedures. There is no reason in principle why the best way to establish this contestatory possibility may not involve a measure of depoliticisation.

There is every reason indeed to think that the only way to ensure the possibility of effective contestation in the area of criminal justice is precisely to depoliticise. Our argument in the first section, sketchy though it is, shows that there is little hope of politicians being able to hear and respond to the challenges of criminology and common sense to the barbarism and inefficiency of current penal practice.

Politicians are forced to hear those challenges in a forum where rituals of public outrage are also allowed and it is absolutely clear that in such a theatrical forum the challenges stand no chance of being taken seriously. The only hope of arranging for a proper hearing is to let the challenges be considered and assessed in a depoliticised environment: in precisely the sort of environment that might emerge under the proposal that we sketched.

The fact that we go along with the depoliticisation proposal, then, does not mean that we have to renounce democracy and accept that we are elitists. For while the proposal takes away power from the politicians, there is a real sense – a contestatory sense – in which it gives power to the people. Democracy and depoliticisation are not inherent opposites. They conflict with one another only under a voluntarist image of democracy, not under the image that we have sketched in this section.

Republicanism and the contestatory theory

But I would like to add a few words in order to emphasise that the contestatory theory of democracy is not a novelty – not an invention of my own – and not something disconnected from received values. The theory belongs with the long, republican tradition of thinking about politics (Pocock 1975, Skinner 1978, 1983, 1984). And that tradition has a powerful attraction in the contemporary scene.

The republican tradition is associated with Cicero at the time of the Roman republic; with a number of writers, pre-eminently Machiavelli – 'the divine Machiavel' of the *Discourses* – in the Renaissance Italian republics; with James Harrington, Algernon Sydney and a host of lesser figures in and after the period of the English civil war and commonwealth; and with the many theorists of republic or commonwealth in eighteenth century England and America and France. These theorists – the so-called commonwealth men (Robbins 1959) – were greatly influenced by John Locke and, later, the Baron de Montesquieu; indeed they claimed Locke and Montesquieu, with good reason, as their own. They are well represented in documents like *Cato's Letters* (Trenchard and Gordon 1971) and, on the American side of the Atlantic, the *Federalist Papers* (Madison, Hamilton and Jay 1987).

The key notion in the republican tradition, as I have argued in a number of other places (Pettit 1993, 1997), is the distinctive view of liberty or freedom that republicans maintained. Under this view, freedom does not consist in non-interference, as liberal theorists generally say, nor indeed in the power of participating in popular decision-making with which liberals like to contrast such freedom (Constant 1988). Republican freedom belongs neither with the negative image of liberty nor with the positive (Berlin 1958). It requires an absence of something, as does the liberal or negative ideal, but not the absence of interference. What it requires, rather, is the absence of what I call domination.

One person dominates another, on my account, to the extent that they have the ability to interfere on an arbitrary basis in that person's choices; they have the ability to interfere in those choices without having to be guided by the victim's interests or ideas. One person dominates another through standing over them, even if stand is all they do: even if they never strike. One person dominates another through having the other person under their thumb, even if they never press that thumb: even if they always stay their hand. Domination exists wherever there is subjection and vulnerability.

The republican ideal of freedom as non-domination delegitimates asymmetries of power such as those that have characteristically been associated with the relationship of employer to employee, man to wife, lender to debtor, bureaucrat to welfare client, and so on; in such relationships, after all, the stronger often has the capacity to interfere more or less arbitrarily with the weaker, even if that capacity is not likely to be exercised: even if liberals, therefore, would not be concerned about it. That is to say that the republican ideal is socially radical. But the ideal will appeal as an ideal for state activity only so far as we can be sure that in setting up the state we do not set up the sort of Hobbesian Leviathan that would represent the greatest dominator of all: that would dominate us more effectively than any dominators it might seek to inhibit. Can we do anything, then, to guard against the state being a mastering or dominating presence? The state will interfere with everyone to the extent that it employs coercive law: that is why liberals are so wary of it. But can we do anything to make sure that it is at least a non-mastering interferer: to make sure that its interference is forced to track people's interests and ideas?

The answer is that while there are a variety of things we can do

– republican proposals range from the rule of law to limited tenure in office to the separation of powers – the most crucial requirement is that we institute a contestatory form of democracy. That the government is democratic in the voluntarist sense is not going to ensure that it does not dominate people: the majority can be a more effective tyrant than any one individual. But that it is democratic in the contestatory sense will ensure an absence of political domination. It will mean that people in the society are in a position to contest any public decision – contest it with a reasonable chance of effectiveness – on the grounds that it is inimical to their interests and ideas: that it deals with them in a manner which any citizens in their position would be bound to reject. If people have such a power of contestation – and I am speaking of an ideal – then and only then will they be assured against domination by the state.

I hope that this connection with the republican tradition may add weight to the case for conceiving democracy in the contestatory image and, ultimately, to the proposal for depoliticising criminal justice practice. It should show that that image and that proposal belong with a long and well-tested tradition of thought, even if the tradition has had a bad run in the last century or so. Consider John Locke's (1965) argument that if government has the aspect of a legal contract – this connects with the voluntarist tradition – it also has the aspect of a legal trust. That argument led Locke to hold that the people have a right to challenge and resist a person in public office if the trust is not well discharged: if the person assumes a power, according to Tom Paine's (1989, 168) formulation, 'in the exercise of which, *himself*, and not the *res-publica*, is the object' (cf. Sydney 1996, 199-200). When we defend the contestatory conception of democracy we do no more than resurrect this republican way of thinking and give it a proper place in democratic theory.

References

Berlin, Isaiah. 1958. *Two Concepts of Liberty*. Oxford: Oxford University Press.

Braithwaite, John and Pettit, Philip. 1990. *Not Just Deserts: A Republican Theory of Criminal Justice*. Oxford: Oxford University Press.

Constant, Benjamin. 1988. *Constant: Political Writings*. B. Fontana (ed.). Cambridge: Cambridge University Press.

Dicey, A.V. 1960. *An Introduction to the Law of the Constitution.* E.C.S.Wade (ed.) (10th edn). London: Macmillan.

Holmes, Stephen. 1988. 'Gag rules or the politics of omission', in J. Elster and R. Slagstad (eds), *Constitutionalism and Democracy.* Cambridge: Cambridge University Press.

Locke, John. 1965. *Two Treatises of Government.* Peter Laslett (ed.). New York: Mentor.

MacDonagh, Oliver. 1958. 'The 19th century revolution in government: a reappraisal', *Historical Journal,* Vol 1, 1958.

Madison, James, Alexander Hamilton and Jay, John. 1987. *The Federalist Papers.* Isaac Kramnik (ed.). Harmondsworth: Penguin.

Montesquieu, Charles de Secondat. 1989. *The Spirit of the Laws.* tran. and ed. A.M. Cohler, B.C. Miller and H.S. Stone. Cambridge: Cambridge University Press.

Paine, Tom. 1989. *Political Writings.* Bruce Kuklick (ed.). Cambridge: Cambridge University Press.

Pettit, Philip. 1993. *The Common Mind: An Essay on Psychology, Society and Politics.* New York: Oxford University Press. Paperback edition, with new postcript, 1996.

Pettit, Philip. 1997. *Republicanism: A Theory of Freedom and Government.* Oxford: Oxford University Press.

Pocock, J.G.A. 1975. *The Machiavellian Moment: Florentine Political Theory and the Atlantic Republican Tradition.* Princeton: Princeton University Press.

Robbins, Caroline. 1959. *The Eighteenth Century Commonwealthman* , Cambridge, Ma: Harvard University Press.

Skinner, Quentin 1978. *The Foundations of Modern Political Thought.* 2 vols. Cambridge: Cambridge University Press.

Skinner, Quentin. 1983. 'Machiavelli on the Maintenance of Liberty'. *Politics* 18: 3-15.

Skinner, Quentin 1984. 'The Idea of Negative Liberty', in R. Rorty, J.B. Schneewind and Q. Skinner (eds), *Philosophy in History.* Cambridge: Cambridge University Press 1984.

Sydney, Algernon. 1996. *Court Maxims.* H.W. Blom, E.H. Muller and Ronald Janse (eds). Cambridge: Cambridge University Press.

Trenchard, John and Thomas Gordon 1971. *Cato's Letters.* (6th edn 1755). New York: Da Capo.

CHAPTER 10

The Civil Service – A Defence?

Frank Litton

Introduction

We Irish are curiously uninterested in the state. While we may contend over its outputs, we remain unconcerned with its nature, just as children squabbling over their parents' dispositions never think to question parenthood. The absence of any clearly discernible left-right split in the history of Irish politics shows our 'pragmatism' has little time for those 'ologies' that bring the state and our relationship to it into focus. The reception of the New Right is the most recent example of this indifference. Certainly there are a few voices who attempt to carry its arguments into public discourse. They receive scant attention: the voice of our common sense dispatches them as 'heartless' and 'Thatcherite', the bearers of a distinctly un-Irish virus. Once allowed into our bloodstream, problems of unemployment, poverty and inequality would remain endemic. This lack of interest in the New Right should please two groups. Those who believe the New Right are wrong can be glad error has found no audience, while those in the public sector, a special target of the New Right, can feel secure in their position and power. Although I belong to both these camps, I confess I feel no satisfaction that we in Ireland have escaped that serious debate on the role of the state that the emergence of the New Right has provoked in its challenge to the post-war orthodoxy. I hope to show that views coming from the New Right raise questions and draw attention to problems with the role of the public sector in our society. The questions are apposite, the problems real: the New Right fails only with its solutions.

Besides, the fact that we put ideas beyond the pale does not necessarily deny them influence. Notwithstanding the exclusion of almost all talk of socialism and planning in the fifties and sixties, we developed one of the most socialised economies in Europe.

Indeed of all the sectors in Irish society, the state has been by far the most successful. While the numbers employed in agriculture have declined and native industry grown only modestly, the state can boast of a record of consistent growth. In 1926 it accounted for some 16 per cent of GNP, today it consumes some 45 per cent of GNP and employs 25 per cent of the work force. In the late 1950s an industrial worker on average earnings would not have been liable to income tax; today a single person in similar circumstances is likely to find 44 per cent of his overtime pay going in taxation. The activities of the state impinge on almost every aspect of our lives. The shape and character of these activities are profoundly influenced by the organisations in the public sector that are charged with their design and implementation. The New Right provides a powerful case that the growth of the state has had more to do with the success of those organisations in advancing their own advantage than with either the citizens' wishes or any plausible construal of the public interest. Public servants are in this matter ably abetted by the politicians who likewise have an interest in a large and intrusive state and who act under a strong inducement to appease narrow interests at the expense of more general interests.

Pluralist democracy

The benign view of the operation of our political system goes something like this. We can place political systems on a continuum that runs from pure democracy to pure tyranny. The answer to the question 'why this law?' guides us to where a state lies on this spectrum. The answer is quickly given for either end. In pure democracy a law exists only because all the citizens consented to it; they foregathered under the spreading oak tree and found, in their deliberations there, the general will. In pure tyranny, laws reflect the whim of the tyrant: that he willed it to be the law answers the question. It is more difficult to answer the question in our kind of pluralist regime. Nonetheless, the typical shape of the answer is straightforward enough. We find that a particular law was passed because it served the interests of some group, or groups in society. A political party found it expedient to support them. However, the law, as finally passed, is unlikely to mirror exactly their interests.

As it moved through the legislative process, other groups asserted their influence to modify it in ways that accommodated their interests. To give detail to the answer we have to unravel the interactions between interest groups, political parties, and voters.

Interest groups play a crucial role in our system of government. Individuals who share a common interest bond together to defend and further that interest. The owners of restaurants, for example, share a common interest in shaping public policy in ways that advantage their businesses. So they are likely to form an interest group. The interest need not be so narrowly based: trade unions and federations of employers represent broadly based economic interests. Not all interest groups pursue economic goods; some are concerned with cultural objectives or to promote a moral vision. As society grows more complex and its division of labour ramifies, the number of interest groups increases. Political parties are a special form of interest group. While other groups are not interested in acquiring political power, remaining content to influence its exercise, political parties compete with each other for it. They attempt to identify common ground among interest groups and seek the votes of the electorate for their general programmes. The party, or combination of parties, that wins a majority of votes gets to exercise the state's power until the next election. They know, as they govern, that their performance today will affect their chances of re-election tomorrow. They must justify their policies in the face of criticism from opposition parties and the representations of interest groups.

The forces of electoral competition would seem to drive political parties away from too close a relationship with any particular interest: support the farmers and the urban vote is lost; support the captains of industry and your opponents will expose your partisanship. While a 'snapshot' of public policy at any moment may reveal nothing but policies pampering particular interests, under these pressures the trend will be towards outcomes that satisfy citizens overall. So it is that supply of public goods is brought into line with the demand. Nobody pretends that the system works perfectly. The inequalities in power and resources do advantage some interests over others, while the problems besetting some groups never get the attention that they deserve. Nevertheless, however imperfectly it may operate, we can be confident that the regime provides a structure of countervailing powers that prevents any one interest predominating.

Analysing interest group behaviour

I turn now to two analyses that give us serious reason for doubting this benign account. The first examines the behaviour of interest groups and the motives of those that join them, while the second explains what interests drive public servants, as they propose and implement policies, to satisfy interest groups. Taken together they amount to a very strong case against the public sector. Their style of reasoning is typical of the New Right. Can the public sector be defended against them? First, the case for the prosecution.

Mancur Olson (1971) invites us to consider the calculations that an individual might make when deciding whether or not to join an interest group. The important factors are the benefits of membership, the costs of membership and the strength of the relationship between the individual's joining and bringing about the outcome. What are the benefits? An interest group typically seeks some economic good for some category of persons. This may be a subsidy, a tax exemption, or some restriction on trade that weakens or removes competition. Such benefits are collective goods in that they are available to all who belong to the category regardless of whether or not they are members of the interest group. For example, restrictions on the number of taxi plates issued benefits all taxi drivers, not just those who are active in defending their interests. Apart from collective goods, interest groups can also supply what Olson terms selective incentives that go only to members of the interest group. For example, an interest group representing taxi drivers could organise some insurance cover advantageous to its members that was available only to them. The costs of membership range from whatever subscriptions may be involved to the time that participation may require.

Clearly an individual will not join an interest group if the costs exceed the benefits. However, he may not consider it worth joining even when the benefits outweigh the cost. If he believes that his membership will make little difference to the outcome, he will be disinclined to join. While he may devotedly hope that a group will emerge and the collective good be won, he is content to be a 'free rider' on this eventuality. The implications of this calculus are significant. The larger the numbers who share a common interest, the less likely is it that they will combine to pursue collective goods.

As numbers increase, the costs of organisation increase and the probability that a single individual decision to join, or not, will affect the outcome decreases. If four individuals have a collective good in their sights, the refusal of one to co-operate in its pursuit has an obvious effect on their chances of success. When four hundred... four thousand... forty thousand.... So it is that we are more likely to find taxi drivers organised than users of taxis, doctors than patients, publicans than pint drinkers, beef farmers than beef eaters.

The most obvious criticism of this analysis is to point to the existence of interest groups like trade unions that do represent large numbers. Olson acknowledges this criticism; his response is instructive. He explains large groups in terms of selective incentives. He points out, for example, that the earliest unions were based on crafts and membership was a condition of entry into the craft. The massive industrial unions emerged later. They found recruitment was greatly facilitated by physical intimidation. Unions in some European countries were extensively involved in housing provision and insurance for their members. A job, safety, security are all worthwhile selective incentives. None of this takes away from the fact that unions did, and maybe still do, defend the interests of their members, winning collective goods for large numbers who would otherwise be seriously disadvantaged. As Olson points out, membership of the state allows for significant collective goods; yet if income tax were voluntary who would pay?

However successful an explanation of unions along these lines may be, Olson's analysis certainly succeeds in explaining the behaviour of individual members. Typically only a tiny proportion of a union's membership attends branch AGMs and the activists are drawn from an even smaller percentage. Whatever reasons draw people into union membership, they are not sufficient to move them to active involvement. The average member is a free rider on the energy and commitment of a minority. From time to time groups will flare into action as some local issue awakens them from apathy. The union must champion their cause. Efforts to place it in a wider context, whether this be the condition of the industry or the interests of other groups in the union, receive scant support. It is too bad if changing circumstances require some major reformu-lation of the members' interests: there is no audience to hear, criticise, and be convinced of the new direction. Knowing they are nothing without the support of their members, the majority of whom are indifferent to all but those parochial issues where their participation counts and the stakes are high, union leaders find defence of the status quo the safest strategy.

The field of forces in which public policies are shaped comprises large numbers of small unrepresentative groups together with large groups that are unwieldy coalitions dedicated to the status quo. Important interests remain latent for the same reason they are important – the large number who share them. The result is a stream of policies that benefit small groups at the cost of the general welfare. Income is taken from those who succeed in producing what people want at a price they can afford, to be redirected in subsidies to those who conspicuously fail in that endeavour. Restrictions on competition keep prices high to benefit producers. Innovation is stymied as groups defend the faltering status quo. In his work *The Rise and Decline of Nations* (1982), Olson finds ample evidence to demonstrate his conclusion that states where interest groups are well entrenched in the policy-making process do significantly less well economically than states where these conditions do not prevail.

There is much talk of 'market failure' as justification for state intervention. Olson points to serious weakness in the 'political market' that determines the course of that intervention. The conclusion is straightforward: the less the state does the more likely it is that we will find economic success and the optimum distribution of resources.

The motivation of bureaucrats

Niskanen (1971) has produced a very influential account of the behaviour of senior civil servants who design and implement the policies in response to the demands of interest groups. His basic point is simple: the milk of human kindness is no different in the senior bureaucrats than in the private sector entrepreneur. They both want recognition, power and wealth. The entrepreneur working under market disciplines succeeds in his ambition by finding what consumers want and supplying it at a price they can afford. Senior bureaucrats do not work under market disciplines; their performance cannot be gauged by success at making profits. They win recognition, power and wealth by maximising their budgets. The larger a government department, the greater the range of its activities, the more money it has to spend, the more the influence and kudos enjoyed by its senior managers. So, Niskanen concludes, as senior bureaucrats decide how to respond to pressure from interest groups, they have a strong incentive to commit the state to levels of activity beyond those actually demanded. As they go about implementing policy, they have little inducement to concern themselves with the costs of their activities.

Of course bureaucrats do not have the final say in public policy. They work subject to the authority of the government, which in turn is accountable to the Oireachtas and through it to the people. Can they not be trusted to constrain the wholly understandable, if regrettable, ambitions of public servants? Niskanen's analysis can be seen as a particular example of the principal-agent problem. Lacking competence to engage in some endeavour important to him, the principal employs an agent to act on his behalf. How can he ensure the agent always acts in his interest as he proceeds? The reasons why he lacks competence – the reasons why he needs an agent – are also the reasons why he is in danger of exploitation by the agent. For example, someone extensively refurbishing a house attempts to safeguard himself by getting the widest range of estimates possible. He picks the most reasonably priced tender. Nonetheless, once the work starts he is at the mercy of the builder who, we may suppose, is keen to get as much from the job as possible. Unanticipated problems are uncovered that require expensive work, inexplicable delays slow the work, shoddy workmanship is explained away. Anyone embarking on such an effort is well advised to employ an architect. He transforms the relationship. He has no incentive to side with the builder and he has the expertise to defend the principal's interest. A minister typically lacks the information and expertise to formulate policy. His position is analogous to our house owner – except that the latter has the choice of a number of builders while the minister is dependent solely on his department. And there are no architects to advise the minister. Furthermore, it can be asked if the minister has any strong incentive to curb the budget-maximising ambitions of his bureaucrats. As a member of the government he may support cost effective policy making in the general interest, but as the minister of this department, seeking re-election in this highly competitive constituency and battling for public recognition?

Limitations to the New Right critique

These analyses fit comfortably into the New Right worldview. Humans are passionate creatures with only limited capacities for understanding the world. The selfish pursuit of interests, narrowly construed, is the human condition. The great merit of the free market is that under its discipline these selfish motives produce socially desirable outcomes. The free market is the form of social organisation best suited to human nature. While the state has an important role, it is a limited one. It holds that monopoly over the legitimate use of physical coercion necessary to enforce contracts and protect the territory from external threat and internal disorder.

These New Right themes, however modern their form of analysis, echo voices long heard in the western tradition of political philosophy. For instance, it is not too difficult to hear them enter the fray on the side of Thrasymachus as he propounds his theory of justice in Book 1 of Plato's *Republic* (Plato, 1991). The dialogue opens gently enough as Socrates probes conventional views of justice. While 'paying what you owe' is certainly just, there must be more to justice. We do not, for example, return a sharp knife borrowed from a friend, when he is deep in depression and intent on suicide. Nor is it satisfactory to claim that justice is 'doing good to friends and harm to enemies'. Who is an enemy? Who is a friend? What is harm? What is good? We should expect to find the answers by an art analogous, say, to medicine or navigation. To claim that mastery of that art involves doing harm is like saying that to practise navigation is to get lost. To know what justice is we must go beyond conventional opinions. It is at this point that Thrasymachus enters the dialogue. He launches a very different kind of attack on the conventional understanding of justice. What we call justice, he instructs us, is no more than the conventions of our society. And these conventions are imposed by the powerful in their own interests. We obey them only because the benefits of so doing outweigh the costs. Some are foolhardy and refuse to constrain their own self-interest. If they are unsuccessful, we call them

gangsters and throw them into gaol. If they act on a grand enough
scale and are successful, we revere them as founders of states.
Politics is all about establishing and maintaining protection rackets.
Our talk of justice conceals this reality from us. It soothes our
vanity as we submit to the will of the powerful.

I do not claim a total coincidence between the New Right and
Thrasymachus' position. Thrasymachus is concerned to offer an
account, or an unmasking, of justice, while the kinds of analyses I
have been reporting are not interested in justice. But that is the
point. The New Right's claim that political and social issues are
best understood in terms of self-interest, narrowly construed and
vigorously pursued, puts them in Thrasymachus' camp. He attacks
the notion of justice as an art that tells us of the good and how to
pursue it through politics. They provide an account of politics that
dispenses with justice so understood. This at least suggests that
Socrates' response to Thrasymachus can give us a critical perspective
on the New Right positions I have outlined.

The will to power and domination is common enough and the
similarities between states and protection rackets close enough to
support strongly Thraysmachus' position. It is plausible just as the
earlier views in the dialogue are plausible. Like them, it is not so
much wrong as incomplete. Socrates' questioning points to the fact
that since rulers could not survive without the wages for their
services, they must be about something more than simple robbery.
The image of the state as a protection racket fails to represent
reality. Socrates, in effect, asks what is involved in running a
successful polity. Why people may want to get involved in ruling is
one thing, how they get the power to do so, another; both are
different from and tell us nothing about what they must do as they
rule. There is an art – a body of knowledge of ends to be respected
and means towards them – of ruling and the leaders and the polity
prosper only to the extent that they are captured by its logic and
submit to its ends. 'The wholly bad and perfectly unjust are also
perfectly unable to accomplish anything' (352d).

All of this suggests that it would be a mistake to end our enquiry
into the growth of the state and the contribution of the civil service
to it with Olson and Niskanen. We need to go further and discover
those activities into which the business of rule has drawn the state
and its servants. I do this by first considering an explanation for the

growth of the state and then by focusing on the task of the policy-maker.

The business of rule

Douglas North, the economic historian and Nobel Prize winner, provides us with an interesting perspective on the growth of the state. He argues that a significant proportion of the state's business can be explained by its efforts to reduce transaction costs. These are the costs associated with making an exchange. They include, for example, the costs of drawing up and enforcing contracts: information, measurement, insurance, transport. Transaction costs are the friction in the economic system. If they are high, exchanges are inhibited and economic activity slows. Once you move to consider the dynamics that explain how economic systems develop and why it is that this development is so unequal across the globe, transaction costs reveal their importance. Successful economies are those that have managed to develop institutional arrangements and pursue policies that reduce transaction costs to manageable proportions.

Transaction costs have a clear relationship to the division of labour. In circumstances where there is little specialisation, tasks are readily comprehensible to those concerned and individuals are drawn together by ties of family and community as well as work, the exchanges that co-ordinate the division of labour will be simple and transaction costs low. No very elaborate institutional framework is required to sustain them. But our circumstances are very different. The division of labour that underpins our material wellbeing is complex in both the degree of specialisation and its geographical scope. The dynamics of economic growth drive it forward to ever greater ramification. In their survey of the growth of US government expenditures, North and Wallis argue that 'the wedding of science and technology in the late nineteenth century made possible a technology of production whose potential was only realisable with an enormous increase in the resources devoted to political and economic organisation – the transaction sector of the economy. A substantial part of this increase has occurred through voluntary organisation, and a substantial share has also been undertaken by government' (1982, p. 336). States are in a particularly advantageous position to reduce many transaction costs. Their monopoly over the legitimate use of physical coercion not only provides peace, it also underwrites laws that enforce contracts and regulations that set standards and provide sure parameters for the conduct of business. Nor is it an accident that states were involved in providing the physical infrastructures – roads, railways, telecommunications, airports – that provided the essential framework for developed economies. The scale of investment, the low rates of return in the short to medium term, and the legal complexities of acquiring land and rights of way, made these an unattractive proposition for the private investor. The state with its legal authority and command of financial resources could develop them.

Explanations of (and justifications for) the growth of the state are frequently couched in terms of market failure. The state has moved in – or should only do so – when markets fail in their allocative task. So it is that the state should control natural monopolies, or provide public goods that escape the possibility of effective pricing, or handle externalities. North's discussion suggests that this is only part of the story: state policy is called for not only to remedy failures but also to provide for success. The context in which ever more complex markets can operate must be sustained.

The state's provisions of social welfare contribute to this context. Left to their own devices markets generate inequalities of wealth and power that build resentments and fuel conflicts. While there are winners, there are also losers, some of whom may not command the resources necessary for a decent existence. Although overtime markets may produce an optimal allocation of capital in financial terms, lives can be wrecked in the process of adjustment. As capital moves to more lucrative investments, industries vanish and communities are dislocated. The assurance of a standard of living not too far from the average provides the ordinary person with the security that makes a market society acceptable.

The finding that the business of the state is best understood with reference to the division of labour is hardly new. Book 1 of Plato's *Republic*, which I have briefly considered above, introduces the problem 'What is justice?' As the investigation proper begins in Book 2, Socrates proposes that the character of justice is best sought by first looking at what it is like in cities where we find it writ large and clear to see. How do we find it in a city? 'If we should watch a city coming into being in .... would we not also see its justice coming into being and its injustice' (369a). To see a city coming into being is to watch the division of labour emerge. The character of justice is found in the problems and possibilities it brings. At the beginning of the modern age, Hobbes defined the central problem of politics in terms of 'transaction costs' or the creation of circumstances where covenants could be secure, while Rousseau, his profoundest critic, found the discovery of the division of labour to be the fall from grace. These political philosophers found the nature of politics in reflecting on the problems consequent on a division of labour that multiplies differences just as it magnifies interdependence.

Markets are among the most important devices for orchestrating a division of labour. As North shows, they can only operate in a space cleared and secured by politics. As political philosophers show, questions as to the size of the space and the laws and policies directed at it, call on understandings and goods not found within it. The New Right may be criticised both for their too ready assumption that markets can solve all or most of the problems in the division of labour and for absolutising the motives engendered within them.

Motivations other than budget maximising

I turn now to consider more closely the role of civil servants in this business of rule. As I observed above, the minister-senior bureaucrat relationship is one instance of a principal-agent relationship. I compared it to the dealings between a householder and a builder; I could just as well have compared it to the relationship between a patient and a consultant. The latter comparison is worth pursuing. A patient feels ill and visits his GP. The problem is serious; the services of a consultant are needed. Since the patient hardly knows what is wrong with him, still less who is most expert in its treatment, he is in no position to seek out the cheapest and best consultant. He goes where his GP advises. The consultant examines him and commits him to hospital. Several days later as he recovers consciousness, the consultant tells him that the operation, which removed several important bits and pieces, was just in time to save his life. Tears of gratitude fill the patient's eyes as he pays the bill.

The consultant retires to his villa in Tuscany for a well-earned break. The patient tells everyone how lucky he has been.

All those ingredients that can make the principal-agent relationship so hazardous are present here: the principal's urgent need, his almost total reliance on the agent's knowledge of what can satisfy that need, the practically nonexistent choice of agents. Yet we believe by and large that consultants do not exploit their patients. I suppose our confidence in doctors is based on the existence of a medical ethos respectful of patients, which is inculcated in doctors during their education and supported by the institutions they inhabit. This ethos does not mean that doctors are indifferent to 'villas in Tuscany' or the prestige and material comfort won by wealth. It does mean that they not believe exploiting their patients' ignorance is an acceptable route towards them. I do not think this confidence would be well grounded if this ethos amounted to no more than a list of 'thou shall nots' expressing 'core values' uttered by authority. We trust it because it is more than a prohibition of disreputable behaviour. It directs the doctor towards substantial goods. Medicine wins our respect because it is what Plato terms an 'art' or what MacIntyre, in his modern rendering of this classical concept, calls a 'practice'. A practice is, MacIntyre reports, 'any coherent and complex form of socially established co-operative activity through which goods internal to that form of activity are realised in the course of trying to achieve those standards of excellence which are appropriate to, and partly definitive of, that form of activity, with the result that human powers to achieve excellence and human conceptions of the ends and goods involved are systematically extended' (1981 p. 175). MacIntyre distinguishes between 'internal' and 'external' rewards. The latter are the money and respect that flow to practitioners as a consequence of the benefits the practice bestows on others; the former are the specific rewards of the practice. The villa in Tuscany is an external reward, the development and exercise of those abilities that can successfully diagnose and treat an illness, returning a patient to health, are internal rewards.

Could we not say that public administration is a practice, one centred on the public good? Thus we could dismiss Niskanen because his analysis does not recognise the motivating power of its internal rewards. MacIntyre, famously, does not believe we live in a time conducive to practices. Far from flourishing, they live a furtive existence and are always under threat from the prevailing worldview. He accepts, it seems, the common view that the modern world favours only two solutions to the challenge of orchestrating divisions of labour: markets or bureaucracies. Neither is friendly towards practices. Markets deal only in external rewards and are built around a negative reciprocity where individuals strive to get as much from each other in return for as little as possible. Market relations cannot handle divisions of labour involving complex interdependencies (Williamson, 1975). Hence the emergence of bureaucracies. The bureaucratic manager is one of the typical characters that MacIntyre identifies and analyses in elaborating his account of our *Weltanschaung* (1981, pp. 71-75). In the manager's world, a radical distinction is made between facts and values. The former describe reality. They provide the basis for those models of the world's working that allow us to manipulate it to our own ends. The latter are the feelings of approbation or disapprobation the world provokes in us. They are 'subjective' and so are beyond rational justification. The manager prides himself on his mastery of those techniques that guide him in the manipulation of systems and the people who comprise them. Though the ends to which these techniques are deployed cannot be rationally justified, they are not beyond conflict. In these conflicts, the managers seek the power necessary to proceed in their desired direction. Striving to persuade others of a mutual interest, they build coalitions that can give them control of the resources they need. The restless pursuit of power after power becomes the managers' guiding principle. It is obvious that their world, so understood, excludes the possibility of a practice. For within a practice the ends of its activities are an 'objective' good, part of the reality shared by the practitioners.

Since civil servants work within bureaucracies, how could their activities be construed as a practice? No one can deny that there is ample evidence for MacIntyre's account of management. It was, and to a considerable extent still is, close to the orthodoxy of management education. Nonetheless it is fairly described as Thrasymachean and is therefore open to the same kind of criticism that Socrates educes against Thrasymachus. Space does not allow me argue that this is true for management in general. So I will merely assert that some contemporary writing on management, straining against positivist prejudices in an effort to account for the experience of managers, supports the claim that management is successful to the extent that it approximates to what MacIntyre describes as a practice. What I will try to demonstrate is that policy-making and implementation can and should be construed as something like a practice. The first move is to observe that markets and bureaucracies do not exhaust the possibilities for orchestrating divisions of labour. Increasing attention is being paid to a third possibility – the network.

Book publishing is typically organised as a network. There are many steps in the production of books: they must be written, edited, copy-edited, designed, type-set, indexed, printed, distributed. It is very rare for publishers to employ specialists in all these skills. They employ commissioning editors who identify publishable authors with the help of a range of contacts, and production executives who organise the buying in of the services of freelance editors, copy-editors, indexers, designers and so on. Most Irish publishers are small businesses, though at any time quite a large number may be employed in the writing and production of books.

In markets, relationships are centred on contracts made under the sign 'caveat emptor'. In bureaucracies they are formed by standardised procedures, controlled by hierarchy, that co-ordinate the division of labour. The relationships that hold networks together cannot be understood simply in terms of contracts, nor are they controlled by hierarchy. Publishers, for example, will seek to establish a 'stable' of freelancers on which they can draw as circumstances require. The relationship among them is shaped by the recognition of a shared interest in the endeavour of publishing. Well-written, designed, proofed, indexed and printed books are recognised as an important good. All those involved appreciate and value the skills that must be combined to produce them.

While market forces exert their influence, commitment to the endeavour of publishing and its goods play a decisive role in shaping the relationships. Individuals know that a poor performance from them will be recognised as such, and shame rather than financial loss consequent on a breach of contracts is the penalty they most fear.

I make two moves. The first is to suggest that networks, and the motivations that hold them together, are best understood in terms of MacIntyre's concept of a practice. Networks work because they succeed in bringing internal rewards into play. The opportunism or 'self seeking with guile' that predominates when only external rewards are recognised is thus allayed. Trust becomes possible and, with it, patterns of relationships capable of handling the complexity inherent in the business to be done. The second move is to establish that policy-making and implementation is sometimes best understood as the facilitation of networks. The example of education must suffice to support this move.

A variety of groups are necessarily involved in education: children, parents, teachers, trade unions, first and second level schools, institutes of technology, universities, churches. The fact that almost all states are considerably involved in educational provision suggests it is not amenable to co-ordination through markets. Most believe that education, at any level, is dialogue rather that monologue, and as such it can only be structured to a limited extent. The effective teacher is continuously creative in finding instances and shaping events that open the students' minds. This creativity cannot be programmed, and so resists the standardisation of work practices that is essential to bureaucratic co-ordination. This, in any event, would be difficult because of the variety of subjects, levels, sites, and circumstances in which the endeavour is pursued. Education, it seems, has that variety and complexity that only networks can co-ordinate. Consequently, it must be seen as a practice.

The various groups involved find a basis for their collaboration in a shared commitment to the goods of the practice. Each group's claim for respect is grounded in its contribution to these goods. Awareness of their interdependence and shared commitments to these goods provides a basis of trust. This does not mean harmony is automatic. Conflicts are endemic in any division of labour. The specialisation it allows delivers different vantage points, each making a claim for the direction its limited perspective reveals. But it does mean that a central focus is possible that can bring the educational system as a whole into view. The government department (Education and Science), as the main supplier of resources and with its ultimate responsibility for setting standards, has a key co-ordinating role. Its major task is to devise, and work through, those arrangements that ensure that the goods of the practice regulate the management of interdependencies and the flow of resources. This entails assisting the practitioners to merge their horizons so that the common good of the endeavour comes into view. This is policy-making and implementation.

In the face of the world's injustice, Socrates could not convince Thrasymachus that justice was realised, only that it was real. I hope I have shown that it is reasonable to see that public-policy-making, at least in some circumstances, is really a practice. I do not underestimate the difficulties of constructing the institutions that would realise it as such. But the attempt to find them is more realistic than anything the New Right has to offer.

References

MacIntyre, A. 1981. *After Virtue*. Notre Dame, Indiana: University of Notre Dame Press.

Niskanen, W.A. 1971. *Bureaucracy and Representative Government*. Chicago: Aldine-Atherton.

North, D. C. and Wallis, J.J. 1982. 'American Government Expenditures: A Historical Perspective', *American Economic Review*, 72, 2.

Olson, M. 1971. *The Logic of Collective Action: Public Goods and the Theory of Groups*. Cambridge, Ma: Harvard University Press.

Olson, M. 1982. *The Rise and Decline of Nations: Economic Growth, Stagflation and Social Rigidities*. Cambridge, Ma: Harvard University Press.

Plato. 1991. *The Republic*, trans. Allan Bloom (2nd edn). New York: Basic Books.

Williamson O.E. 1975. *Markets and Hierarchies: Analysis and Anti-Trust Implications*. New York: Free Press.

CHAPTER 11

Public Policy and Social Partnership

Rory O'Donnell

Introduction

Since 1987 Ireland has conducted public policy by means of social partnership between the state and economic and social interests. This is embodied in the four partnership programmes, each setting out the parameters of pay and policy for a three year period. National deliberative institutions have played a significant role in these developments. The National Economic and Social Council (NESC) is an advisory body in which employers, trade unions, farmers and senior civil servants analyse policy issues and seek consensus on strategic policy directions. A notable feature has been the attempt to widen partnership beyond the traditional social partners. A new forum, the National Economic and Social Forum (NESF), was established and membership of NESC was gradually widened to include members of the Oireachtas ('first strand'), the traditional social partners ('second strand') and representatives of the unemployed, women's organisations and the community and voluntary sector ('third strand'). The fourth national partnership programme, Partnership 2000, was negotiated by this wider set of organisations. Alongside these national arrangements and institutions there has been a remarkable profusion of partnership approaches at local level, focused on local development, social exclusion and specific problems such as drug addiction.

Irish social partnership has been analysed from a variety of perspectives. There was considerable debate about the feasibility of macro-political exchange in Ireland, given that the structure of trade unions, business associations and political parties does not conform to that found in the classical European post-war cases of neo-corporatism.[1] While the period of social partnership has been one of unprecedented growth in output, exports and employment, liberal economists, such as Walsh and Leddin, have argued that partnership represents a rigid system that protects insiders at the expense of outsiders.[2] There has been debate on the effectiveness of area-based partnership in addressing social exclusion and promoting economic development.[3] This paper focuses on a fourth aspect of the analysis of social partnership: the ongoing discussion within the partnership process itself, motivated by perceived difficulties and opportunities.

Section 2 summarises the self-understanding of Irish social partnership as expressed by the NESC in 1996. Section 3 outlines a set of problems in the extended partnership process, identified in an NESF review undertaken during 1997. These problems raise important questions about the foundations, nature and potential of the partnership approach. Does partnership demand a deep level of agreement on the nature and direction of the economic and social system? Can it work in the absence of such agreement? Can it serve social ends and promote greater equality without a new ethical consensus for redistribution? Must all participants develop the structural and organisational characteristics of traditional social partners, such as trade unions, employers associations and government? Section 4 identifies three dimensions of partnership and argues that there are limited preconditions for effective social partnership. Section 5 outlines a new view of the nature of a social partner, and contrasts this with the concept used in earlier studies of post-war European neo-corporatist systems. Some conclusions are presented in Section 6.

---

[1] See Hardiman, 1988, 1992, Roche, 1992, 1994, O'Donnell, 1993, O'Donnell and O'Reardon, 1997, O'Donnell and Thomas, 1998, Teague, 1995 and Taylor,1996.

[2] See Walsh and Leddin, 1992, Haughton, 1998. For more positive views of the economic effects of social partnership, see NESC, 1990, 1993, 1996, O'Donnell, 1993, O'Donnell and O'Reardon, 1997.

[3] See NESC, 1995, Craig and McKeown, 1994, Kearney et al, 1994, Commins and Keane, 1994, Nolan, Whelan and Williams, 1998, Walsh, 1998.

The self-understanding of Irish social partnership

The development of social partnership since 1987 has involved a wide range of economic and political actors in a complex process of negotiation and interaction. Detailed, shared, analysis of economic and social problems and policies has been a key aspect of this process. For a variety of reasons, much attention has been paid to the partnership system itself. In order to develop the overall approach, and make it more inclusive, it was necessary to characterise the nature, purpose and goals of partnership. In its 1996 report, *Strategy into the 21st Century*, the NESC offered the following characterisation of social partnership, as it has developed since 1987.

    i) The partnership process involves a combination of consultation, negotiation and bargaining.

   ii) The partnership process is heavily dependent on a shared understanding of the key mechanisms and relationships in any given policy area.

  iii) The government has a unique role in the partnership process. It provides the arena within which the process operates. It shares some of its authority with social partners. In some parts of the wider policy process it actively supports formation of interest organisations.

  iv) The process reflects interdependence between the partners. The partnership is necessary because no party can achieve its goals without a significant degree of support from others.

   v) Partnership is characterised by a problem-solving approach designed to produce consensus, in which various interest groups address joint problems.

  vi) Partnership involves trade-offs both between and within interest groups.

 (vii) The partnership process involves different participants on various agenda items, ranging from national macroeconomic policy to local development (NESC 1996, p. 66).

This list can be seen as both a description of the partnership process, as it is, and a set of conditions for effective participation in the process. Indeed most of these principles were explicitly adopted by both the 'traditional' and 'new' social partners in the 1996 agreement, Partnership 2000.

However, the participants have continued their self-reflective examination of Irish partnership. This is so because of a set of problems that came to light during NESF's 1997 review of the partnership system and discussion of a future framework for partnership. In significant parts of the national partnership process there is limited shared understanding, diverse views on the extent and nature of interdependence, distrust of the differential participation on different policy agendas and a frequent absence (and some outright rejection) of a problem-solving approach – leaving only trade-offs.

Problems of extended social partnership

The limits of consensus
The first set of problems arises from the possible limitations of consensus. The emphasis on a 'shared understanding' and 'consensus', in the description of social partnership, can be misconstrued or exaggerated in ways that undermine the effectiveness of partnership.

In discussion of the rationale and methods of partnership it became clear that the emphasis on 'shared understanding' and 'consensus' was seen in different ways. The language of partnership can, if not carefully used, create an exaggerated notion of consensus. This encourages the idea that the process requires a very deep level of agreement on the nature and direction of the whole social and economic system. Given the large differences of power and resources that characterise society, it is validly pointed out that no such consensus exists. Indeed if partnership is premised on such a deep level of agreement, then some who are interested in reducing the inequalities of power and resources feel they must dissent from aspects of the partnership approach. The central argument of this paper is that partnership does not require that deep level of consensus. The preconditions for effective partnership approaches are much less than is sometimes believed.

A further limitation is that consensus can produce bland agreements, prevent innovation and, by producing lowest-common-denominator agreements, undermine the strategic choices which are necessary to good government. An excessive, or badly understood, attachment to consensus can lead partners and government to focus on agreement, rather than the mobilisation of people and resources.

Limited terms of inclusion

Significant steps have been taken to widen participation in Irish partnership beyond the social partners that were traditionally seen as essential to macroeconomic management. Nevertheless the widening of inclusion has, until recently, been partial. This created a number of problems. Among some groups it served to heighten the ambiguity and reservations about the idea of consensus. At the same time it created the possibility that the traditional social partners would fall back on a consensus established elsewhere, rather than engage fully. It served also to undermine the distinctive roles of different partnership bodies, such as NESC, NESF and the Partnership 2000 Monitoring Committee. Given their partial inclusion in the overall policy system, groups sought to undertake agenda setting and underlying analysis in the bodies to which they belonged.

The terms of inclusion may also have contributed to a perceived hierarchy of partnership bodies, in which NESC was seen as shaping the decisions made in national negotiations, and as having higher status than NESF. That view, in turn, encouraged a particular idea of 'strategy' and 'decision-making' and strong distinctions between strategy, policy and implementation – views which require critical examination.

The terms of inclusion also seem to sustain diverse views on the very logic of social partnership. As noted above, the idea of functional interdependence has figured prominently in analysis of Irish social partnership. This requires some discussion, because different views on it underpin different views of the logic of social partnership.

An overly narrow reading has encouraged the idea that functional interdependence consists only of the interdependence between government, employers and trade unions. Indeed some focus only on the macroeconomic outcome which they jointly shape. While that interdependence is clearly vital, it is not the whole picture. It is not helpful in addressing a range of issues that have subsequently emerged. These include structural reform, enterprise-level issues and, most of all, social exclusion and unemployment. One effect of the narrow view of interdependence is to see different aspects of social partnership as having distinct rationales: while partnership focussed on macroeconomic policy reflects the functional interdependence of government, employers and unions, partnership approaches to exclusion, unemployment and social issues rest on a moral claim. To the extent that this conception has taken hold, it might be seen as a major weakness in Irish social partnership, and plays a significant role in the problems under discussion.

It does not take into account the way in which inclusive social partnership allows discussion on the concerns, knowledge and interdependence that each group brings to the table. It is an inaccurate perception, because it overlooks the way in which the prosperity and good of the society are, in fact, connected with the degree of social exclusion. The functional interdependence in this case may be less immediate, less direct, but no less real for that.[4] The practical and functional effects of exclusion press moral considerations on all concerned with public policy.

The excessive distinction between 'issues of interdependence' and moral issues also sustains an excessive distinction between 'traditional social partners' and other groups, something I discuss under the heading 'a new view of what a social partner is' below.

The difficulty of linking national representation to local action
Among the social partners, a major concern is the difficulty of linking national representation to local action. This concern is expressed in many different ways. Some highlight the way in which participation in national partnership draws representatives away from the day to day problems within their sector. Some draw attention to the peculiar language used in national partnership and policy analysis, and the difficulty which members have in following it. Many cite great difficulty in communicating the purpose and meaning of national partnership reports and agreements to members on the ground.

A striking feature of this situation is the diversity of perception and the commonality of the problem. ICTU tends to see the difficulty as a reflection of the enormous size of the trade union movement and the particular content of the partnership programmes since 1987. IBEC tends to see it as a reflection of the diversity of firm types and the natural focus of businesses on market signals rather

---

[4] The fact that the functional inter-dependence is less direct and less immediate does have consequences. There is a need for a more thorough analysis of the many ways in which economic and social issues relate to each other.

than policy processes. Voluntary and community grou
inclined to see the problem as one peculiar to them: t
Women's Council because of the 150 separate organisations ....
to it; others as reflecting the depth of the difficulties that
disadvantaged citizens confront, the limited resources of voluntary
and community organisations and the limited content, and potential,
of social partnership agreements. Elected politicians in the NESF
see it as a reflection of the somewhat uneasy parallel existence of
partnership and the Oireachtas.

While it is clear that these particular views have some validity,
the more striking thing is that all groups face a similar problem:
how to link national representation and policy formation with action
on the ground. Of course, that problem is not purely a result of
participation in national-level partnership. Quite apart from national
partnership, organisations face a major challenge in supporting and
reflecting the creative, innovative, actions and beliefs of their
constituencies and members.

Limited effectiveness in achieving real change
All groups express frustration and disappointment at how difficult
it is to make partnership deliver real change. Members speak
persuasively about the need to 'get beyond the aspirational'. In
discussing the limited effectiveness in achieving change, four types
of explanation are commonly offered. The first is that it reflects
lack of real power or influence in national-level negotiation. A
second is that it reflects our limited knowledge of what works in
many difficult policy areas. A third explanation is that, even where
the partnership bodies (such as NESF and NESC) advocated certain
approaches, problems of implementation frustrated their realisation.
A fourth explanation emphasises the political will required to refocus
resources on new policy priorities.

All four explanations are relevant, and their relevance varies
across policy issues. If some of the arguments advanced above are
accepted, and if the case developed below is persuasive, then it
may be possible to find a path forward which increases effectiveness.

Indeed to these four explanations can be added a fifth, which
complements them. The limited effectiveness of social partnership
in achieving a reduction in exclusion and unemployment reflects
the limits of the shared understanding on these problems. While

there has been significant development of a shared understanding on the need for active labour market policies, this consensus does not embrace all aspects of the problems of unemployment, exclusion and inequality.[5] A shared understanding on other aspects of exclusion and inequality is urgently needed. How to achieve this is a critical issue in the re-design of the national partnership arrangements (NESF, 1997).

Proliferation of partnership bodies

Almost all studies of partnership and discussion with partners draw attention to the proliferation of partnership bodies as a problem. This is seen as creating a drain on resources, confusion about who does what and, in some contexts, dis-empowerment rather than empowerment. These are problems that arise in both national and local partnership structures.

Problems of monitoring

Although the creation of a central structure to monitor the implementation of national partnership agreements was an important innovation, the arrangement does give rise to problems. One person, deeply involved, says that the current arrangement – in which the social partners on the central monitoring committee interrogate civil servants, first, on what action has happened and, second, on what results have been achieved in some policy area – 'has becomes a farce'. In many areas of policy, neither the civil servants nor the social partners can get meaningful answers to their questions. To report these views is not to criticise those involved. Indeed, the purpose is precisely to move beyond praise or blame, to a serious discussion of what arrangements can assist more effective monitoring.

---

[5] This is evident in disagreement over the balance between active labour market policies and community development in the work of Area Based Partnerships, in the adequacy of existing concepts of exclusion to reflect womens' labour market experience and choices, and in divergent views about the mainstreaming of certain 'social economy' pilot projects.

The relation between social partnership and representative democracy

Discussion sometimes arises on the relationship between social partnership and representative democracy. The politicians who participate in NESF see a significant gap between social partnership and elected representatives. There has yet to be clear statement of what problems, if any, social partnership creates for representative democracy. A perceived decline in the significance of the Dáil should not be attributed solely to partnership, since many countries have seen the role of their parliaments decline relative to that of the executive. Nor can the reduced interest in party politics be attributed solely to partnership; many countries have experienced party political convergence. The 'gap' between elected representatives and social partnership varies. Government ministers have close connection with social partnership. The problem seems most acute at the level of local government where the emergence of many local partnership bodies is sometimes seen as a further erosion of local government. Although members of the Oireachtas and local councillors often describe this as a 'democratic deficit', a democratic deficit is normally something felt by the demos, not by party politicians. Those active in local partnerships fear incorporation in local authorities, on the grounds that bureaucracy will destroy their innovative approach and councillors will politicise (in the worst sense) their projects. Overall, the relationship between social partnership and representative democracy is linked to the question of devolution. While Ireland has adopted an unusual approach to that question, our problem can be seen as an acute version of a worldwide problem of democracy (Dorf and Sabel, 1998)

The limited conditions of problem-solving

The seven problems outlined above set a challenging agenda. Not only are there problems, but the perceptions of those problems differ significantly across the social partners. These differences extend to the rationale, nature and conditions of partnership. One view is that partnership demands of those who participate a deep level of agreement on the nature and direction of the whole social and economic system. This view can produce ongoing exchanges, between and within strands, that undermine the effectiveness of partnership. I argue in this section that partnership does not require so deep a level of agreement. The preconditions for effective partnership are fewer and less burdensome than this view suggests.

This argument is developed by distinguishing initially between two different conceptions, or dimensions, of partnership:

- functional interdependence, bargaining and deal making
- solidarity, inclusiveness and participation.

I go on to argue that effective partnership involves both of these, but cannot be based entirely on either. For there is a third dimension which transcends these two:

- deliberation, interaction, problem solving and shared understanding.

The preconditions for this are less than is sometimes believed. In particular they do not include a pre-existing consensus on the nature, direction or justice of the overall economic and social system.

The first dimension/conception of partnership – which emphasises functional interdependence, bargaining and deal making – has been discussed at some length above, and has figured in commentary on recent Irish partnership. Its most concrete manifestation is the mutual benefit of a core agreement between business, unions and government. However, for a variety of reasons, this hard-headed view is not adequate, on its own, to describe or understand Irish social partnership. Among the reasons that this is so is the fact that the performance of the economy does depend on resolving problems of exclusion and unemployment. Furthermore, the second dimension cannot be ignored.

The second dimension/conception emphasises solidarity, inclusiveness, and participation. This has been an important theme in many of the NESF reports. NESC also invoked this in its 1996 *Strategy* report when it said

> The Council believes that the widest participation in social life, economic activity and policy making are inseparable and fundamental requirements for the well-being of Irish society. The inclusiveness and quality of relationships in social life, communities, economic life and public governance are goals in themselves. These are desirable, quite apart from the fact that inclusive and co-operative participation is productive – economically, socially and in public policy terms (NESC, 1996, p. 175).

In addition it suggested that the partnership 'model of policy-making, business and industrial relations is also consistent with some enduring characteristics of Irish society' (NESC, 1996, p.65).

The partnership process, and the policy-oriented discussion of it, combines these two dimensions/conceptions. To acknowledge only the first dimension, and exclude the claims of the unemployed and marginalised as 'moral' issues with no functional consequences, would be to validate the claim that the process simply reflects the power of the traditional social partners. To focus on the second dimension is to adopt a naive inclusivist view that risks reducing the process to a purely consultative one, in which all interests and groups merely voiced their views and demands. Ironically this would lead, by a different route, to the same end-point; partnership would ultimately be no different from pluralist lobbying, in which the outcome favours those groups with the most resources.

These two dimensions are both present, but even together they are not adequate. While functional interdependence is wider than many think, it is certainly less immediate and visible in some problems than in others. The absence of a solid affective basis for social solidarity suggests that we resist the temptation to try to deepen and widen the partnership model by casting it as grounded in some organic characteristic of Irish society.

The view that partnership demands of those that participate a deep assent to the nature, direction and justice of the economic and social system would seem to be based on a particular combination of the two dimensions/perspectives outlined above. It is based, primarily, on a heavy dose of the hard-headed view that partnership is about deal making by powerful interests that cannot escape one another. The functional interdependence, which drives them to deal, includes unions, business and government, but does not include others. Since consensus follows self-interest, and is the pre-condition for agreement, it is hardly surprising that the consensus does not include the marginalised. Given the pre-existing consensus on the fundamentals, the agreement/compromise produced by national partnership is essentially about distribution. This hard-headed, even cynical, view is combined with a thin layer of the second perspective, which emphasises solidarity. Since partnership reflects pre-existing consensus, and since the claims of the marginalised are moral rather than practical, a social partnership that really included the marginalised is dependent on a new, and radically different, level of social solidarity.

There is a third dimension of partnership, which transcends the two discussed above. Although the concepts of 'negotiation' and 'bargaining' distinguish social partnership from more liberal and pluralist approaches, in which consultation is more prominent, they are not entirely adequate to capture the partnership process. Bargaining describes a process in which each party comes with definite preferences and seeks to maximise their gains. While this is a definite part of Irish social partnership, the overall process (including various policy forums) would seem to involve something more. Partnership involves the players in a process of deliberation that has the potential to shape and reshape both their identity and preferences. The idea that identity is formed in interaction is important. It is implicit in the description of the process as 'dependent on a shared understanding', and 'characterised by a problem-solving approach designed to produce consensus' (NESC, 1996, p. 66). This third dimension has to be added to the hard-headed notion of bargaining and to the idea of solidarity, to adequately capture the process. It is relevant to the question of exclusion, and to wider discussion of the nature of partnership.

The key to these features of partnership would seem to be the adoption of 'a problem-solving approach'. As one experienced social partner put it, 'The society expects us to be problem-solving'. A remarkable feature of effective partnership experiments is that the partners do not debate their ultimate social visions. The problem-solving approach means that these are, almost always, left unspoken. This problem-solving approach is a central aspect of the partnership process, and is critical to its effectiveness. This is not to suggest that partners abandon their social vision. Their action in partnership is definitely informed by, and consistent with, the deep commitments that motivate their work in the public sphere. Indeed the vision and values which attract people to join the voluntary associations of social partnership are probably more important now than in the past. Recognition of the prevalence of a problem-solving approach, and the limited debate on ultimate social visions, clarifies what has been said in the previous paragraph. Although the process can go beyond bargaining, and can draw the partners into a process of deliberation and action that can reshape their identity and preferences, not everything is at stake for those who participate.

This suggests that rather than being the precondition for partnership, consensus and shared understanding are its outcome. This, in turn, means that the shared understanding cannot be a static, once-off, condition. Indeed the extension of partnership in recent years has involved some groups coming to share the prevailing understanding of the macroeconomic constraints, but simultaneously producing and disseminating a new understanding of the policy problem which concerns them most, unemployment. That process of development and dissemination must continue, particularly on the subject of social exclusion.

Therefore an adequate account of the process, as it actually is, combines all three dimensions: first, pure interest mediation (as reflected in words like 'bargaining', 'interdependence' and 'trade-offs'); second, a commitment to inclusion and a degree of solidarity; and third, the process of deliberation by which partners come to a shared understanding, a process of interaction to which they submit themselves, in which they 'lose some of their sovereignty', and in which they risk some of their identity.

These arguments allow us to reassess the view that partnership is entirely dependent on pre-existing and widely shared beliefs. An approach that sees co-operation as standing on purely normative foundations confronts several difficulties. The most relevant of these is that such an approach overlooks the interactive nature of political, economic and social processes. Ironically, an excessive emphasis on the normative basis of social partnership – seeking to ground it in a thick set of shared values – may lead to more pessimism than the more pragmatic approach adopted by the actors in recent years. A sufficiently thick set of values is unlikely to be found. But all we need are attitudes and values that are good enough to sustain public co-operation. Behind this lies the possibility that the real deficit, or binding constraint, may not be limits to social solidarity, but knowledge of the institutional forms which will make solidarity and democratic governance effective in current circumstances.[6] This

---

[6] The main argument of this paper, and proposals in the 1997 NESF report, are not dependent on this possibility. It may be the case that, by enhancing the effectiveness of partnership and identifying innovations worthy of generalisation, the limits of solidarity will be revealed in resistance to the

highlights the key challenge: to explore institutional arrangements to make partnership more effective.

In the right institutional context, skilled actors engage with one another in ways that (temporarily and provisionally) resolve conflicts, which are undecidable in more general debate. They can even initiate practical measures of social solidarity and co-operation, for which no one can provide a compelling foundation. These can, in turn, disclose radically new possibilities for social and economic life. If this is correct, then the key task is discovery of the institutional arrangements that can assist this, rather than extended prior discussion of economic and social systems, democracy, solidarity and community.[7] Furthermore, both Irish and international experience suggest that the discovery of those institutional arrangements is itself an experimental and practical process (Sabel, 1994).

It is a remarkable, if not easily understood, fact that deliberation which is problem-solving and practical produces consensus, even where there are underlying conflicts of interest, and even where there was no shared understanding at the outset. It is also a fact that using that approach to produce a consensus in one area, facilitates the same approach in other areas. The key may lie in understanding what kind of consensus is produced when problem-solving deliberation is used. It is generally a provisional consensus to proceed with practical action, as if a certain analytical perspective was correct, while holding open the possibility of a review of goals, means and underlying analysis (see below). This type of agreement certainly involves compromise. But the word compromise is inadequate to describe it. 'Compromise' so often fudges the issues that need to be addressed,

It seems, then, that there are few preconditions for the partnership process. A problem-solving approach emerges as the main condition. What are the preconditions of a problem-solving approach? These also seem to be limited. Three points are made here:

---

change which would result. But that situation would still be preferable to one in which the achievements of social partnership are constrained by the six problems discussed in Section 3.

[7] Discussion, in other forums, of foundational questions concerning these matters may, of course, throw important light on social partnership.

- problem-solving relations between social partners can be helped or hindered by the design of the partnership bodies
- there are also internal conditions for a problem-solving approach, within each social partner
- a problem-solving approach is relevant at four different levels: agenda setting, underlying analysis, policy consensus, and implementation and monitoring.

That the design of partnership bodies can help or hinder relations between social partners is confirmed by the experience of the partners over many years. That problem-solving depends not only on relations between partners, but also on the internal organisation of each social partner, is demonstrated below where I outline a new view of what a social partner is now.

The third point provides an opportunity to clarify what is meant by 'a problem-solving approach designed to produce consensus'. The term 'problem solving' might be thought to refer only to action at the exact level at which a problem is experienced. This is not what is intended. Indeed the argument here is that a problem-solving approach is as relevant in agenda setting and underlying analysis as it is in implementation or monitoring. It may seem strange that a problem-solving approach can be adopted in doing the underlying analysis of a social or economic problem – and it certainly conflicts with the traditional 'scientific' approach, in which the underlying analysis is simply true or false. However, experience strongly suggests that certain analytical approaches are more likely to command agreement than others, and certain analytical approaches have more meaningful implications for action than others. A problem-solving approach involves working within these approaches, while staying true to the evidence.[8] Adoption of a problem-solving approach does not rule out fundamental differences of perspective, but it does involve using those differences in particular ways. A similar argument applies to agenda setting. Besides emphasising the role of a problem-solving approach in all stages of the partnership process (agenda setting, underlying analysis, implementation and monitoring), these points highlight the fact

---

[8] While this approach conflicts with an idea of 'scientific' social and economic study that had its heyday in the 1960s, it is consistent with a more sophisticated, and realistic, philosophy of social science (O'Donnell, 1992).

that the term 'problem-solving' is more than a platitude, or a synonym for 'good' or 'polite'.

It was argued above that to understand why problem-solving produces consensus, even where there are conflicts of interest, we should note what kind of consensus is involved. I observed that the unsatisfactory terms of inclusion encouraged exaggerated ideas of the nature and content of strategic agreement. It would be equally mistaken to focus only on the technicalities of government decision, and thereby underestimate the significance of strategic consensus. This calls for a careful and frank look at the kind of consensus produced in the deliberative bodies such as NESC and NESF, and at the role of that consensus in the overall system of public governance. The consensus produced in these bodies must be seen as a part of a complex process, which involves strategic orientation, policy making, implementation and monitoring (see below and O'Donnell and Thomas, 1998).

A definite characteristic of successful NESC and NESF reports is argumentation or reason-giving. In these reports the social partners and others present the society not with a deal, however good, but with the reasons why a certain perspective or policy initiative has commanded their agreement. It is to this problem-solving and the reason-giving that we should attribute whatever success these bodies have had. This contrasts with the view that attributes their influence to their apparent focus on high-level 'strategy' or 'policy-making'.

Discussion among the participants has made it clear that it is possible to participate in partnership, while holding significant reservations about the value of the whole project, relative to some alternative strategy. Those discussions also reveal that each partner is inclined to think that it is the only one in that position. This can encourage each to luxuriate in its own painful, but somewhat delicious, dilemma: 'Social partnership is alright for others, but is it consistent with the unique competitive pressures/historical mission/ radical powerlessness of our organisation?' The purpose of this discussion has not been to deny that the dilemma is real; nor to suggest that organisations talk to one another about it. The purpose is, first, to emphasise the possibility of participating while still questioning. And, second, to suggest that the fact that all groups face this dilemma should, at the very least, influence the way it is discussed within each.

A new view of what a social partner is

It was argued above that the unsatisfactory arrangements at national level have obscured a clear view of the nature of a social partner in the Irish context. In particular they have prevented recognition of the extent to which social partners face similar problems. These problems concern relations between national organisations and local members, and the difficulty of achieving tangible results from the partnership process. To explore this I set out a new definition, or description, of a social partner, emphasising process rather than structure, and information rather than force.

In developing and studying Irish social partnership arrangements, we have tended to adopt ideas from countries with a longer tradition of partnership-type policy systems. In international studies of neo-corporatist systems, there is a very clear idea of what a social partner is.[9] This traditional idea is summarised in the left-hand box of Table 1. A key idea is that to be capable of negotiating and delivering, an organisation must have 'social closure' or monopoly of representation of a given social group. For example unions were seen as having a monopoly of representation of workers, and business associations a monopoly of representation of enterprises. This monopoly gave them an authorised jurisdiction or charter. A second element of the traditional idea was the emphasis on their functional roles. They were seen to have a definite functional role in the economy or a clear regulatory role. Indeed many went so far as to say that only producer groups had the characteristics which make them capable of being social partners. The key activity undertaken by organisations with these characteristics was bargaining, with each other and with the government. In many respects, the logic of that bargaining is summed up in the next characteristic listed in the left-hand box: state intervention in the economy. It was because the state intervened extensively in the economy that it found itself deeply engaged with unions and employers' associations. Finally, each of the organisations was hierarchically organised and concentrated. This gave them a clear 'peak organisation', which was capable of both representing and disciplining a large number of individuals and sub-organisations.

---

[9] See Cawson, 1986.

Table 1. Traditional and new ideas of a social partner

Traditional idea of a Social partner	*New characteristics of a social partner*
• monopoly/authorised jurisdiction	• continuous mobilisation
	• co-ordination of functions
• function (economic or regulatory	• actors in civil society
	• information as key resource
• producer groups	
• bargaining	• new forms of public advocacy
	– analysis
• state intervention in the economy	– dialogue
	– shared understanding
• hierarchy	• actor, not just voice

Consciously or unconsciously, this idea of the nature of a social partner has influenced our thinking in Ireland. It underpins the idea, discussed above, that while the involvement of functional groups reflects power, the involvement of marginalised groups rests on a moral claim. It underpins the idea, held by some, that in order to participate effectively, all groups must take on the characteristics of traditional social partners. Ironically, it also underpins the contrary view, that there is an agenda to make voluntary and community groups like traditional social partners, an agenda that should be resisted.

The central argument of this section is that the traditional conception of the nature of a social partner has lost much of its relevance in Ireland. A careful examination of social partnership over the last thirteen years gives a very different picture. Furthermore, we get a picture which fits many of the voluntary and community organisations involved, not just IBEC, ICTU and the farm organisations. The characteristics are summarised in the right-hand box of Table 1.

The first is the fact that social partners are continuously mobilising citizens who have problems that need to be dealt with. Organisations cannot take for granted their role as representatives of a given group. They must offer practical achievements and a vision of a better economy and society. Rather than relying on fixed functional roles, their strength is in co-ordination: they assist in defining and co-ordinating functions. Their base is actors in civil society who have to respond to the unintended consequences of policy, economic change or action by other groups.

While the ultimate role of the traditional social partner was bargaining, and achievement depended on the power resources deployed in bargaining, this is no longer an adequate description. Economic change has fragmented these power resources and shifts in popular opinion have made traditional social partners uncertain about how, and whether, they can deploy them. By contrast, information is the key resource that a modern social partner brings to the table. They are needed, precisely because the information is generated within their organisational ambit.

In the place of the old form of bargaining, there are new forms of public advocacy. These are summarised in the right-hand box as analysis, dialogue and shared understanding. It is possible to bargain without discussing, and a lot of traditional bargaining was like that. At the other extreme, it is possible to analyse without putting yourself in the shoes of the actors, and a lot of traditional social and economic science was like that. In between there is a combination of discussion, analysis and deliberation, which might be called 'negotiated governance'. Irish social partnership, at its most effective, seems to be moving toward that model.

The final characteristic is that a new social partner is an actor, not just a voice. Mobilising, organising, delivering and solving problems (with others), seems to be a feature of effective social partners. Indeed these might be seen as conditions to be an effective social partner. The goals, methods and knowledge of organisations are shaped and reshaped in action. A continuous danger of the partnership approach is the slide to 'talking shops'. Critics, who describe social partnership in this way, often contrast it with the clarity and independence of traditional public policy, in which democratic decision is followed by executive implementation. That model is a lost paradise in many policy spheres, but this should not lead us to dismiss the danger of 'talking shops'. Involvement in action, as well as talk, is one way of preventing that danger.[10] This feature of a modern social partner is related to a weakening of the traditional distinction between political work, self-help, charity and labour organisation.

The importance of action also reflects the limits of representation. One of the effects of the many changes in the economy and society is to qualify the possibility of representation. This is discussed below. Its relevance here is that it underlines the increased role of action, and of organisations that create and co-ordinate action. Furthermore, within that there is an increased role of direct action by members, rather than action for members, or organisation for the purpose of representation.

This contrast between the traditional idea of a social partner and the new characteristics of a social partner is intended to highlight an important process of change. It is not offered as a definitive account of the origin of that change or of the extent to which it has occurred in various parts of Irish social partnership. This change is happening at a different pace, and to a different extent, in various organisations. Some recognise a definite decline in their role as representatives, and pressure for new forms of service provision to members. Others see a less distinct shift in that direction. While the right and left-hand boxes of Table 1 crystallise the pattern of change, they are of course too neat, and should not be read as two mutually exclusive categories. Indeed given that partnership combines bargaining, solidarity and deliberation, we should not expect all the traditional roles of social partners to disappear. Nevertheless, the new view of a social partner, outlined here, does open the way for careful reflection on the variety of organisations active in Irish partnership, and for a more constructive engagement between the three strands.

If this contrast is accepted, it has important consequences for a re-design of the partnership model. The purpose is not to naively assume that there are now no differences between partners with a major economic role (employers associations, trade unions and

---

[10] It turns out, of course, that to be effective in action it is necessary to do a lot of talking, both within and between organisations.

farm organisations) and other partners. The purpose is threefold. First, to abandon the misleading traditional distinction; second, to recognise the extent to which all partners face some common problems and challenges; third, to find arrangements that make partnership work better by helping each partner to address the particular difficulties they face.

The overall effect of these changes is a trend to convergence in organisational patterns, although, as noted above, that convergence is by no means total. We can now see that functional inter-dependence extends well beyond those involved in production. The functioning of the economy and policy now encompasses a wide range of social groups, and organisations in the voluntary and community sector must be added to the list of social partners. Those new organisations are taking on many of the characteristics of social partners. But, if the argument of this paper is correct, it might not be ideal if they took these characteristics off the old menu (the left-hand box in Table 1), rather than off the new menu (the right-hand box in Table 1). This is particularly so with regard to one function: representation. The old-type of community and voluntary sector had little role in representation. The blurring of the old distinctions between politics, community organisation, charity and self-help has, appropriately, brought the community and voluntary sector much closer to public policy. But, in moving closer to public policy, it may not be possible to become representatives, in the way that social partners were in the past. This is so because the older social partners are finding their role in representation declining, relative to their other roles.

To see this, we need to note that there is convergence in the opposite direction also. The 'traditional' social partners are taking on some of the characteristics of voluntary organisations. They can no longer rely on having an automatic membership; they must continually prove their relevance to their members, by demonstrating practical achievements and tapping into new forms of solidarity. Their members have opportunities for self-advancement (and self-development) not provided by the organisation. Their members value direct participation in decision-making, not just participation via representation. Their role as representatives is giving way to, or being balanced by, their role as service providers to their members. And the kind of services that they are asked to provide is changing.

All of these changes are pressing them to review and change their organisations.

One aspect of this new view is that neither the 'constituency' of a trade union or employers' association, nor the 'community' of a social organisation, can be taken as given. They are shifting, such that they need to be continually re-created. Consequently, all claims to 'represent' are contingent. No organisation can validly claim to 'represent' a given section of society forever, or without direct involvement of the relevant citizens.

This new perspective does not deny the existence of conflicts of interest between individuals, groups and the state. But it subtly alters the way we should understand them. Resolving these conflicts remains a key element of social partnership. Whereas the old model involved power bargaining with limited need for discussion, the new approach involves more interaction. A recognition of the role of interaction and deliberation has a most important, if surprising, consequence. In this interaction, each social partner is a stimulus to the other and must, therefore, be attentive to its own way of acting (Joas, 1993). Each partner must develop not only its own consciousness, but its self-consciousness: an awareness of how its statements and actions impact on others.[11] Consequently, while rethinking the relation between partners, the new perspective also draws attention to the, equally difficult, internal problems of group action. This shift in perspective is particularly relevant, given the striking commonality of the problem confronting all Irish social partners: the problem of linking national representation to local action .

Conclusion

The argument outlined above has a number of implications at both a practical and conceptual level. When combined with observation of other trends in public administration, it suggests ways of re-

---

[11] The practical relevance of this could be demonstrated by citing an organisation such as ISME (the Irish Small and Medium-sized Employers), not involved in Irish partnership, that has displayed a distinct lack of self-consciousness. The point is further underlined by recent news reports of debate within that organisation which suggest precisely a belated development of self-consciousness.

designing the deliberative institutions of social partnership. One such trend is a shift in the role of the centre and national government. The complexity, volatility and diversity of economic and social problems, and of social groups, is undermining the ability of central government to allocate public resources, direct the operation of government departments and public agencies, and administer complex systems of public delivery and scrutiny. Another trend is the changing relationship between policy making, implementation and monitoring, which places monitoring, of a new sort, at the centre of policy development. We urgently need examination of the practical successes and failures of policy, which is then used to revise both the methods and goals of policy. This demands a new fusion of policy-making, implementation and monitoring. National-level partnership arrangements cannot be effective if they are premised on an outdated view of the power, autonomy and effectiveness of central government.[12] At the same time, social partnership institutions are one obvious place to organise and co-ordinate the practical deliberation that is required. In the light of these arguments, the work of the NESF and the NESC is currently being revised to achieve a better combination of strategic analysis and problem-solving exploration of the success and failure of existing policies (NESF, 1997).

The argument goes some way to conceptualising the type of interest mediation or concertation which has emerged in Ireland – and some other European countries, such as the Netherlands – since the late-1980s, and which underpins those countries' relative economic success. The categories and ideas used in earlier studies of classical North European neo-corporatism seem inappropriate in understanding these recent experiments. From this may emerge a new concept of 'post-corporatist' concertation.

At a practical level, the argument, and the experience on which it draws, suggests the possibility of a policy system which combines some of the advantages of liberal pluralism and neo-corporatism, while avoiding some the weaknesses of each. The new social partnership may combine the openness and flexibility of liberal pluralism with the co-ordination of interests achieved by neo-

---

[12] These trends, and the issues they raise, are discussed in greater detail in NESF, 1997.

corporatism. It avoids the worst excesses of the 'pluralist bazaar' – in which those with the greatest resources win the lobbying competition – but also the closed and fixed set of interests typical of neo-corporatism. It cuts with the grain of the economic, social and technological changes that have reduced the effectiveness of government.

The argument also connects, obliquely, with wider debates in political philosophy and theory. In considering the relation between philosophy and politics, Rorty recommends 'that the pressure to rise to a higher level of abstraction should, so to speak, come from below. Locally useful abstractions ought to emerge out of local and banal deliberations. They should not be purveyed ready-made by philosophers, who tend to take the jargon of their own discipline too seriously' (Rorty, 1996, p. 71). The policy-oriented studies of Irish social partnership – driven by the participants' desire to understand and improve the process – have found it necessary to create and use certain 'locally useful abstractions'. Yet, in doing so, they have found themselves touching on, sometimes re-inventing, themes and ideas in both recent and earlier philosophy and political theory. There is a clear resonance with the emerging discussion of deliberative democracy and dialogical rationality.[13] There is close affinity with the exciting attempt to reconceptualise the nature of, and conditions for, problem-solving interaction in both business and public life.[14, 15] Most of all, the Irish discussion has echoes of an earlier exploration of the institutional arrangements that make co-operation possible and, more importantly, make it effective. As Dewey urged in *Freedom and Culture*, 'we have to analyse conditions by observations, which are as discriminating as they are extensive, until we discover specific interactions that are taking place, and learn to think of interactions instead of force' (1939, p. 39).

---

[13] See Cohen and Rogers, 1992, Dryzek, 1990, Hirst, 1990, 1994, Myerson, 1994, Gutmann and Thompson, 1996 and Elster, 1998.

[14] See Sabel 1994, Cohen and Sabel 1997, Dorf and Sabel, 1998, Piore, 1995.

[15] By contrast, the Irish partners have not drawn much, or at least not collectively, on the recent theoretical debates on the foundations of democracy, the legitimacy of political authority or the sources of moral commitments and social solidarity in politics. The focus has been on the *effectiveness* of democratic governance, rather than on these foundational issues.

References

Cawson, A. 1986. *Corporatism & Political Theory.* Oxford: Blackwell.

Cohen, J. and Rogers, J. 1992. 'Secondary Associations and Democratic Governance', *Politics and Society*, 20, 4: 393-472.

Cohen, J. and Sabel, C. 1997. 'Directly-Deliberative Polyarchy', in C. Joerges and O. Gerstenberg (eds), *Private governance, democratic constitutionalism and supranationalism.* Luxembourg: European Commission.

Commins, P. and Keane, M. 1994. 'Developing the Rural Economy: Problems, Programmes and Prospects', in *New Approaches to Rural Development.* NESC Report No. 97. Dublin: NESC.

Craig, S. and McKeown, K. 1994. *Progress through Partnership.* Dublin: Combat Poverty Agency.

Dewey, J. 1939. *Freedom and Culture.* Buffalo: Prometheus Books.

Dorf, M.C. and Sabel, C. 1998. 'A Constitution of Democratic Experimentalism', *Columbia Law Review.* 98, 2: 267-473.

Dryzek, J.S. 1990. *Discursive Democracy, Politics, Policy, and Political Science.* Cambridge: Cambridge University Press.

Elster, J. (ed.). 1998. *Deliberative Democracy.* Cambridge: Cambridge University Press.

Gutmann, A. and Thompson, D. (eds). 1996. *Democracy and disagreement.* Cambridge, Ma: London: Belknap Press.

Hardiman, N. 1988. *Pay, Politics and Economic Performance in Ireland 1970-87.* Oxford: Clarendon Press.

Hardiman, N. 1992. 'The State and Economic Interests; Ireland in a Comparative Perspective', in Goldthorpe, J. and Whelan, C.T. (eds), *The Development of Industrial Society in Ireland.* Oxford: Oxford University Press

Haughton, J. 1998. 'The dynamics of economic change', in Crotty, W. and Schmitt, D.E. (eds), *Ireland and the Politics of Change.* London: Longman

Hirst, P. 1990. *Representative Democracy and its Limits.* London: Polity Press.

Hirst, P. 1994. *Associative Democracy: New Forms of Economic and Social Governance.* Cambridge: Polity Press

Joas, H. 1993. *Pragmatism and social theory.* Chicago: University of Chicago Press.

Kearney et al. 1994. *EU Leader 1 Initiative in Ireland. Evaluation and Recommendations.* Dublin: Department of Agriculture, Food and Forestry/Commission of the European Communities.

Myerson, G. 1994. *Rhetoric, Reason and Society, Rationality as Dialogue.* London: Sage Publications.

NESC. 1986. *A Strategy for Development 1986-1990.* Dublin: National

Economic and Social Council.

NESC. 1990. *A Strategy for the Nineties: Economic Stability and Structural Change*. Dublin: National Economic and Social Council.

NESC. 1993. *A Strategy for Competitiveness, Growth and Employment*. Dublin: National Economic and Social Council.

NESC. 1995. *New Approaches to Rural Development*. Dublin: National Economic and Social Council.

NESC. 1996. *Strategy into the 21st Century*. Dublin: National Economic and Social Council.

NESF. 1997. *A Framework for Partnership: Enriching Strategic Consensus Through Participation*. Dublin: National Economic and Social Forum.

Nolan, B.,Whelan, C.T. and Williams, J. 1998. *Where are poor households?: the spatial distribution of poverty and deprivation in Ireland*. Dublin: Oak Tree Press in association with Combat Poverty Agency.

O'Donnell, R. 1992. 'Economics and Policy: Beyond Science and Ideology', *Economic and Social Review*. 24, 1, 75-98.

O'Donnell, R. 1993. *Ireland and Europe: Challenges for a New Century*. Dublin: The Economic and Social Research Institute.

O'Donnell, R. and O'Reardon, C. 1997. 'Ireland's Experiment in Social partnership 1987-96, in Fajertag, G. and Pochet, P. (eds), *Social Pacts in Europe*. Brussels: European Trade Union Institute.

O'Donnell, R. and Thomas, D. 1998. 'Partnership and Policy-making', in Healy, S. and Reynolds, B. (eds), *Social Policy in Ireland*. Dublin: Oak Tree Press.

Piore, M. J. 1995. *Beyond Individualism*. London: Harvard University Press.

Roche, W. 1992. 'The Liberal Theory of Industrialism and the Development of Industrial Relations in Ireland', in Goldthorpe, J. and Whelan, C.T. (eds). *The Development of Industrial Society in Ireland*. Oxford: Oxford University Press

Roche, W. 1994. 'Pay Determination, the State and the Politics of Industrial Relations', in *Irish Industrial Relations in Practice*. Dublin: Oak Tree Press.

Rorty, R. 1996. 'Response to Ernesto Laclau', in Mouffe, C. (ed.). *Deconstruction and Pragmatism*. London: Routledge.

Sabel, C. 1994. 'Learning by Monitoring: The Institutions of Economic Development', in Smelser, N. J. and Swedberg, R. (eds), *The Handbook of Economic Sociology*. New York: Princeton University Press.

Sabel, C. 1996. *Ireland: Local Partnerships and Social Innovation*. Paris: OECD.

Taylor, G. 1996. 'Labour Market Rigidities, Institutional Impediments and managerial Constraints: Some Reflections on the Recent Experience of Macro-Political Bargaining in Ireland', *Economic and*

Social Review. 27, 3, 253-77.

Teague, P. 1995. 'Pay Determination in the Republic of Ireland: Towards Social Corporatism?', *British Journal of Industrial Relations.* June, 33, 2.

Walsh, B. and Leddin, A. 1992. *The Macroeconomy of Ireland.* Dublin: Gill and Macmillan.

Walsh, J. 1998. *The Role of Local Partnerships in Promoting Social Inclusion.* Dublin: Combat Poverty Agency.

CHAPTER 12

'Share Value' and Shared Values?

Fergus Armstrong

'Did he who made the lamb make thee'?
– William Blake, 'The Tyger'

Introduction

Economic commentators have been assiduous in explaining the Irish economic miracle, but they did not predict it. So there is a general wariness about presuming on continuance of its benefits, especially in the wake of failures in emerging market economies. It remains to be seen whether the Celtic tiger can pass a dope test.

In the longer term the sustainability of recent advances in prosperity may owe as much to the quality and nature of the business culture that is being bred by current success, as to any other factor. The culture, in turn, may be influenced by the form of the legal, regulatory and governance regime that applies to new trading concerns. Irish success is not founded on any *Mittelstand* that compares with those interacting, flexible, technologically forward-looking, small scale companies built on family traditions, of the kind that served as industrial backbone in Germany and Northern Italy. The business style, in fact, is largely bought in. The significance of the overseas industry sector means that the American business idiom has been a dominant influence on the attitudes of new Irish entrepreneurs, many of whom have worked in US companies. The industrial model has however been overlaid with a significant 'social market' element, reflecting European thinking and official encouragement. Indeed the compact reflected in 'partnership' deals between employer, labour and other representative organisations has been credited by many as an essential ingredient in the Irish success story. Flashpoints have arisen however, as between Anglo-

American business dogma and the partnership ideal. Ryanair, a new generation Irish company, launched on the US capital markets, encountered intense hostility and expressions of ministerial disapproval when it sought to maintain a non-union policy, this being a liberty offered without question to any US company contemplating an investment in Ireland.

Whatever may be the relevance of social partnership to the success that has been achieved, one notable feature plainly observable in the approach of those entrepreneurs whose prosperity came with the tiger, has been a sharpening focus on the role of capital markets. Day-to-day management decisions are weighed, as never before, by reference to their effect on share value. This is true not merely of recent entrants to public share markets or for that matter the increasing number of major Irish public companies that have attained world class significance, but also for privately held concerns. The standing expectation is that there will come a day when the entrepeneur goes to market with the company. Venture capital providers, for their part, encourage this tendency in so far as they will normally expect to dispose of investments within no more than five years, either through a public offering of shares or a trade sale to a competitor or portfolio investor, and encourage management (typically director-owners) to conduct the affairs of the company accordingly. At times, new capital will be introduced, not because the business needs the money but because the share price achieved in the transaction will serve to ratchet up the asking figure on a flotation or sale.

These tendencies, already well evident over recent decades, have been accentuated by changes in rates of capital gains tax. The Finance Act 1994, as amended, allowed a preferential rate of 24 per cent for disposal of shares in modest-sized trading concerns where the shares had been owned for at least three years. The rate reduction from 40 per cent to 20 per cent effected by the Finance Act 1998 is not hedged in any way. The time horizon within which a new entrepreneur works towards disposal is often relatively short. One is seldom talking about a working life. 'Cashing In, Selling Out and Getting Rich' – a newspaper headline describes the process. The country has produced a significant crop of talented business people, with a decade or so of working life behind them, who will not need to work again. The enticement of a golf villa in Portugal, while still young enough to enjoy it to the full, has understandable attractions. So an influential factor in the day-to-day decisions of many owners and managers of new Irish companies is the intent that the business be readied up for sale. Not just the merchandise but the shop itself is on offer. To the extent that this tendency has been increasing, there may be important, if subtle, consequences, in terms of attitudes to business and relationships within companies.

Success in share disposals reflects a skill at which new Irish entrepreneurs have excelled, which is deal-making. This is an activity that seems to combine a variety of Irish talents – imagination, personal agreeableness (even as the hard bargain is struck), nimble ability to reckon up mentally the value of concessions obtained or made and persistence and good timing in bringing a transaction to a close, striking while the iron is hot. Recent success in building up expertise in sophisticated financial services attests to abilities of this kind.

Such skills are of course vital to business. Yet they involve talents that are different to those that are necessary for research, product development and the building of a knowledge base and sources of renewal in an organisation. A business culture that swings markedly in the direction of valuing deal-making could, in a time of difficulty, prove less robust or less well equipped with reserves of intellectual capital.

So far as corporate governance is concerned, Irish law is modelled closely on the English both in terms of content as well as form and legal drafting. While in certain areas resources have been applied to ensuring that legislative solutions actually fit Irish conditions, the fundamental principles in regard to company structure and organs are decisively British. The conduct and modes of governance in Anglo-American business have undergone review in the wake of excesses of the Thatcher years and the 'slash and burn' policies adopted in the massive waves of down-sizing that took place in the United States. This is happening even as major concerns in mainland Europe have seemingly become persuaded to some degree of the need to restructure in order to gain or retain the support of investors in global markets.

In this contribution I review briefly the trend of recent discussion of the arguments for a more 'inclusive' approach to corporate govern-ance and the stakeholder-versus-shareholder debate. I suggest that the questioning of shareholder dominance and market hegemony produced by this debate has not given particular enlightenment to help in addressing the serious issues of workforce cohesion that present in large organisations at this time. I then suggest some broader principles that bear on these issues and discuss the relevance of choices in corporate governance for a country whose business culture is still emergent, where avoidance of the dread spectre of the bubble economy may depend to some degree on the quality of the working relationships that apply throughout industry.

The stakeholder debate

The stakeholder discussion was founded on a concern that an overly narrow emphasis on accounting profit causes directors and managers to overlook essential elements of the internal dynamic of business organisations, vital to longer-term prosperity. A perceived tendency to become fixated on numerical results is usually attributed to the workings of the capital markets and the overriding significance which they accord to share values and shareholder interests. Resulting short-termism can mean that companies do not adequately plan for the future, make sufficient investment, stimulate innovation, develop the potential of their employees or relate optimally to customers and suppliers; they may also fail to engage appropriately with issues of significance to the health of the societies which sustain them, including environmental ones. In the case of quoted companies such shortcomings are attributed, at least in part, to apprehensions of takeover which, although thought to serve as salutary discipline to spur performance, can produce unhealthy distortion of the objectives of a management team.

Reichheld, a US writer, attacked today's accounting systems as 'loyalty's public enemy number one', suggesting that they mask the fact that 'inventories of experienced customers, employees and investors are the firm's most valuable assets. Their combined knowledge and experience comprise a firm's entire intellectual capital. Yet these invaluable assets are vanishing from corporate balance sheets at an alarming rate, decimating growth and earnings potential as they go' (Reichheld, 1996, pp. 3-4). 'Snapshot accounting', he says, must be avoided. Business pictures should be time exposures, seeing people as assets rather than expenses.

The stakeholder alternative proposes an acceptance that a company must be seen to have more than one class of stakeholder – its shareholders – and that management needs to give better recognition to the roles which others occupy – employees, customers, suppliers and society at large – in determining its courses of action.

For UK companies, the stakeholder debate may be said to have been opened by Tony Blair as opposition leader in a speech delivered in Singapore (8 January 1996), in which he said:

> The ... relationship of trust and partnership applies within a firm. Successful companies invest, treat their employees fairly, value them as a resource not just of production but of creative innovation. The debate about corporate governance in Britain is still in its infancy but has largely focused on headline issues like directors' pay and perks. We cannot by legislation guarantee that a company will behave in a way conducive to trust and long term commitment. But it is surely time to discuss how we shift the emphasis in corporate ethos – from the company being a mere vehicle for the capital market to be traded, bought and sold as a commodity – towards a vision of the company as a community or partnership in which each employee has a stake, and where the company's responsibilities are more clearly delineated.

This theme was taken up in an enquiry sponsored by twenty-four UK firms including such major names as Guinness, Cadbury Schweppes, Whitbread and Thorn/EMI which led to publication of a report entitled *Tomorrow's Company*. This identified several obstacles which, it was suggested, were preventing UK companies from becoming globally competitive. Apart from a measure of complacency and ignorance of world standards, blame was attributed to 'over-reliance on financial measures of performance' and what was described as a 'national adversarial culture' (Royal Society for the Encouragement of Arts, Manufacturers and Commerce [RSA], 1994, p. 4):

> As the world business climate changes, so the rules of the competitive race are being rewritten. The effect is to make people and relationships more than ever the key to sustainable success. Only through deepened relationships with – and between – employees, customers, suppliers, investors and the community will companies anticipate, innovate and adapt fast enough, while maintaining public confidence (ibid, p. 6).

The enquiry's vision for a successful future included the following:

> The companies which will sustain competitive success in the future are those which focus less exclusively on shareholders and on financial measures of success and instead include all their stakeholder relationships, and a broader range of measurements, in the way they think and talk about their purpose and performance. In short, it is this 'inclusive' approach which differentiates 'Tomorrow's Company' from yesterday's company. (ibid, p. 1)

The inclusive approach would, according to the report, be reflected in a company which, amongst other things, 'values reciprocal relationships, understanding that by focusing on and learning from all those who contribute to the business, it will best be able to improve returns to shareholders'. (ibid, p. 1)

It is interesting that primacy was here preserved for shareholder interests, in so far as the approach suggested is one which is seen as ultimately likely to advance them most successfully. This did not suffice to save the stakeholder concept from sharp attack. A pungent example was an assault from Samuel Brittan (Brittan, 1996).

> The stakeholder approach is simply to dissolve this problem in a general mushiness. Everyone is supposed to promote the interests of everyone else and no-one is really accountable for anything. Management is theoretically responsible not only to shareholders or even to workers, but to suppliers, customers and the public at large. In practice it is simply a charter for management to do what it likes .... Someone who is theoretically responsible to everyone for everything is in practice not responsible to anyone for anything.

A publication entitled *In Search of Shareholder Value – Managing the Drivers of Performance* authored by members of the PriceWaterhouseCoopers accountancy firm (now merged with a sponsor of the *Tomorrow's Company* enquiry to make PriceWaterhouseCoopers) was similarly dismissive of the 'stakeholder corporation' (Black et al [1998], p. 14).

> The management of a business must have one prime focus: maximizing the value of its equity. If it is accountable to more than one interest, it will sooner or later be faced with the problem of deciding between them, and it can only give preference to one or the other by using some further criterion. This is all the more

true in today's decentralized corporation where middle managers are continually taking decisions with value implications; for instance, should an investment that adds value and keeps customers satisfied – but reduces the workforce – go ahead? Corporate paralysis would ensue without a clear, common criterion. When interests conflict, such as those of employees and shareholders, a choice has to be made, and stakeholder theory offers no help in making that choice.

Even an insightful diagnostician of business culture of the standing of Charles Handy was sceptical of the value of the stakeholder concept. In a lecture entitled 'What is a Company For' delivered in 1995 (which provided the stimulus, it seems, for the *Tomorrow's Company* enquiry), he commented (Handy, 1995, pp. 67, 69).

> I do not myself like the idea. I don't really know who all the stakeholders are or who would properly represent them ... stakeholders' language is a nice way of talking about the balancing act that companies have to perform, but I don't think, myself, that it answers the question 'what is a company for?' except in a very blurred way. It is certainly difficult to see how one could give it any teeth.
>
> ... It may be analytically convenient to say that the company is working for all the stakeholders, but that does not tell you what to do or where to go if you are the chairman. Inevitably, one or other of the stakeholders has priority and, given our current system, that is going to be the shareholder.

The qualification may be noted – 'given our current system'. Some attempts have in fact been made to sketch out an alternative regime of corporate governance. Economists Kay and Silberston proposed a new Companies Act for the United Kingdom, to be made applicable to companies in the plc category (Kay and Silberston, 1995). In introducing their ideas they point out that the notion that a company is 'owned' by its shareholders represents, in fact, a popular misconception, not supported in statute law or judicial decision-making. Goldenburg (1996) concurs. Nor are directors simply the agents of the shareholders. The responsibilities of directors, and those of agents, belong to the same broad category, namely that of fiduciaries, but the two are not one and the same. An agent lives and breathes for a principal in a way that a director does not, in relation to shareholders.

Kay and Silberston suggest that no particular legal problem arises if a company is owned by no specific category of persons (and it is not under our system – owning shares is not the same thing as owning the company). They consider, moreover, that the concentration, which they regard as excessive, given by British and American public companies to shareholder interests is attributable in the main to just one reason – the threat of hostile takeover.

Their blueprint for a new Companies Act for plcs runs as follows: the key feature is that appointment of executive management would be effected by a process set at a remove from the levers available to the shareholding majority. The governance framework would involve a requirement for an independent chairman and at least three independent directors (independence being assessed in terms of not depending on the company for substantial remuneration whether in salary or dividends). The role of the chief executive officer and perhaps that of other officers would actually be defined in the legislation. The process by which they are selected would also be statutorily defined. The independent directors would play a key role in this but they would be required to appoint a selection committee with other independent members drawn from other businesses and professional advisers and would be obliged to consult employees, investors and suppliers and any relevant statutory agencies. The term of office for the CEO would run for four years and could be renewed no more than once.

Crucially, the power of nomination of directors – executive or independent – would rest with the independent directors, who would however be obliged to consult the variety of stakeholders in the company before appointing new independent directors.

Such a scheme would effect a major change in the constitutional structure of major corporations in so far as it envisages that the organs of corporate control would to some extent float free of the grip of shareholders.

Although corporate governance has been the subject of a number of high level reviews by committees comprising leading UK industrialists – Cadbury, Greenbury and Hampel – there has been no indication of an appetite to entertain any radical prescriptions for a change in the legal expression of directors' duties, relevant to stakeholder recognition. The Hampel Committee issued its final report in January 1998 (Committee on Corporate Governance, 1998).

Its treatment of the stakeholder issue begins with an acknowledgement that 'Good governance ensures that constituencies (stakeholders) with a relevant interest in the company's business are fully taken into account'. The report accepts the Cadbury committee's definition of what is meant by corporate governance as 'the system by which companies are directed and controlled', stating that this puts the directors at the centre of any discussion on corporate governance, linked to the role of shareholders, since they appoint the directors.

Addressing the aims of those who direct and control companies, it states the 'single overriding objective' for stock market companies as 'the preservation and greatest practicable enhancement over time of their shareholders' investment'. The report acknowledges that every company must develop relationships relevant to its success, including those with employees, customers, suppliers, credit providers, local communities and governments. Managements, approved and monitored by boards, are to develop policies which address these matters but 'in doing so they must have regard to the overriding objective of preserving and enhancing the shareholders' investment over time'. While directors are responsible for relations with stakeholders, they are accountable to shareholders since shareholders elect them. Echoing Samuel Brittan, the report concludes that to re-define directors' responsibilities in terms of the various stakeholder interests would produce a result that the directors were not effectively accountable to anyone. Game set and match to capital?

Companies of people

I suggest that the stakeholder discussion, as it developed, was useful in drawing attention to the importance for major companies of nurturing their significant relationships, at a time when sharpening competitive forces were producing more utilitarian attitudes towards suppliers of goods and services and a spot market regime whereby the lowest quote on the day always got the business. It is notable how frequently US firms now use the word 'partnership' to characterise their relationships with suppliers.

Yet the stakeholder principle is unlikely to make a formal appearance in any legal code and the attention given to it may well have occasioned a distortion of viewpoint in so far as attitudes to employees are concerned. No serious business person needed to be reminded to give attention to the quality of the employer-employee relationship and it can hardly be sufficient to see employees as just one other category of stakeholder with whom good relationships are to be cultivated.

It is noteworthy that, at a time when the significance of human capital is increasingly to the fore in modern knowledge-dependent industry, the pre-eminence afforded to the work of expanding monetary capital seems to exclude acceptance of any concept whereby people may be, in some sense, considered as constitutive of a business as opposed to mere resource (hence the phrase 'human resources').

The consequence of this prioritisation is marked in the case of companies whose shares are traded on public markets. Quoted companies operate on a treadmill whereon half-year by half-year (or, in the case of the US markets, quarter-by-quarter) earnings must show continuous growth or else disappoint shareholder expectations. Such an environment mandates a policy of continuous expansion. Given a rapidly changing marketplace for goods and services, initiatives of recent origin must often be quickly abandoned. Such developments are then found to throw up employee surplus. New objectives proposed to follow discontinued ones may call for a different range of skills. Even if this is not the case, there can be a temptation for managements driven by the need to stimulate share price performance to use occasions of retrenchment to reduce existing staff levels, thereby creating the possibility of going later to the job market to choose from the best on offer, at the keenest prices, the staff required to implement the next leap forward. A survey by the American Management Association noted that 'because of concurrent job creation, job elimination is no longer synonymous with downsizing' (AMA, 1996, p. 1).

The *Financial Times* reported on 18 February 1999 that H.J. Heinz, the US foods company, planned to cut 4000 jobs in a restructuring expected to impact mainly in Europe and involve the closure or sale of 15 to 20 factories, the scaling back of at least 10 more as well as expansion of 13 other factories. The restructuring was code-named 'Operation Excel'. Aftershocks from such initiatives often strike close to home, heralded by dramatic announcements from high technology companies that can tear at the fabric of whole communities.

The organisation for which (or for whose shareholders) only growth is acceptable always finds it difficult to accommodate, indeed tolerate, what may be ebbs and flows in demand for the product of different segments of its business. Instability of employment is in fact an inevitable concomitant of a doctrinaire commitment to earnings growth. Because such a credo engenders a perspective that sees people as fungible, it becomes increasingly difficult for major companies to hold the loyalty of their staffs. Francis Fukuyama pointed out (Fukuyama, 1996) that the newer forms of organisation, from which layers of management have been excised, and which are adapted for lean or just-in-time manufacturing, with teams of employees being given considerable responsibility to organise their own workplace, just cannot be made to work in the absence of trust. He contended that many American corporations having implemented radical downsizing and re-engineering and flattened managerial hierarchies pocketed the resultant productivity gains and used them to then fire half their workforces. The message sometimes went out from the CEO: 'Yes we're re-engineering and by the way you're out of a job but you still have to trust us and be loyal to the corporate team.' The *Tomorrow's Company* report (BSA, 1994) warned that those companies which have different messages for different audiences – for example, to providers of capital, employees are labour costs to be cut, whereas to employees 'you are our greatest asset' – should be seen as 'yesterday's companies'.

In such companies, amongst the ranks of those made anxious and insecure, it is possible to discern clearly a different kind of individual. This is the go-getter whose perspective on the organisation to which he or (occasionally) she belongs is buttressed by a barely concealed cynicism, who is confident of his own capacity to advance in whatever theatre and will always have an eye to the next move, whether within or outside the company. The timing of the move will depend on whether the requirements of the job continue to accord with his personal agenda. Work colleagues will mutter that he 'knows how to look after number one' with a mixture of admiration and resentment. When he moves along, those goals that he achieved which reflected positively on the bottom line need to be viewed along with detrimental effects on the organisational fabric and relationships within the firm.

The stark fact must be faced, that for the typical Anglo-American corporation, and perhaps too for some Irish enterprises

> the psychological contract between employers and employed has changed. The smart jargon now talks of guaranteeing 'employability' not 'employment', which, being interpreted, means don't count on us, count on yourself, but we'll try to help if we can. No longer can anyone expect to be able to hand over their lives to an organisation for more than something like six years. After that you are on your own again, either by your initiative or theirs, and can only hope that you are, indeed, as employable as it was promised. We are, in effect, all mercenaries now, on hire to the highest bidder, and useful as long as, and only as long as, we can perform (Handy, 1997, pp. 70-71).

It would be naive to fail to recognise the real dilemmas that managements face in controlling costs in conditions of intensified competition. Competitive forces impact on the price of a company's output and its ability to earn profit sufficient to remunerate capital, defend independence and retain executive skills in the face of lucrative third-party offers. The company that does not embrace the advances in information technology relevant to its business, including those which displace employees who may be its least skilled and most vulnerable, may quickly find its position eroded in the marketplace. The management team contending with these challenges may be unable to avoid workforce reductions from time to time. The incidence of such occurrences and their effects on morale and motivation will, however, be significantly influenced by management mind-set. This is sometimes revealed in the language that is used. I recall one businessman commenting about what he saw as a periodic necessity for job cuts, suggesting that in this matter one had to be 'clinical, but humane'. Dr Daniel Vasella, a physician who took charge of the organisation (Novartis) resulting from the combination of the Swiss drugs giants Sandoz and Ciba-Geigy, comprising 134,000 people, of whom ten per cent were likely to be displaced by the merger, commented that 'job cuts are like surgery. You know it hurts but that it will do some good. The worst is to cut slowly but not deep enough' ('Triumph of an Ingenue', *Financial Times* 9/10 March 1996). The medical analogy evokes the professional detachment expected of the surgeon towards a patient.

Detachment or distance between senior management and the workforce at large is underpinned by a widening divergence between average employee earnings and the rewards of those in senior positions. Growing disparities can be explained in part by a recognition that top executives give their loyalties less to the company as such, than to its shareholders. Indeed one of the commonest tools of higher level remuneration – the executive share option – is designed to have precisely that effect, in so far as reward is hitched to growth in share values. Options give managements a one-way bet on the fortunes of the company as measured by share price and ensure that their allegiance is decisively set in favour of share markets.

Attention has been focused in recent years on the 'survival of the fattest' phenomenon (Plender, 1997) and the extent to which it can prove destructive of morale in the workplace. In so far as abuse is attributed to the potential conflict of interest involved when directors are called upon to fix the remuneration of their colleagues, the antidote, coming forth from the reports of the Greenbury and Hampel committees, is full disclosure to shareholders. One suspects, however, that the levels of generosity typically sanctioned by shareholders reflect a reality that option and remuneration packages serve to direct management loyalty towards the interests of owners of capital to a degree that would not commend itself if they were left at liberty to pursue the long-term advantage and prosperity of the organisation in the most enlightened way. The shareholder tail can wag the management dog.

A place for internal values

I have suggested that the stakeholder principle does not give an adequate answer to the serious problem of organisational cohesion that is presented by the hegemony of capital markets in that it gives insufficient recognition to the prime issue of the quality of the relationships that obtain between the people who comprise a modern organisation. Businesses, according to Charles Handy (1997, p. 183) are 'communities not properties and their inhabitants are to be more properly thought of as citizens rather than as employees or human resources'. He suggests that 'effective ownership will gradually revert to those who hold the resources, who will employ those who previously employed them. Those on the outside who provide only one of the resources – finance – will inevitably see their effective power decline'.

Yet even if the respective bargaining strengths in this relationship are set to alter, it seems to me necessary to continue to recognise its pragmatic, transactional nature. Introduction of a communitarian dimension ought not to obscure the reality that the workings of any successfully functioning company will reflect a deal that is cut between capital and the people it employs. And the capital interest will be the one that scoops the pool in the sense of taking the residue. When the values of many Irish quoted companies rose in response to a plan for reduction of corporation tax to a rate of 12 per cent by 2003, there was no suggestion that this benefit should accrue to any stakeholder other than shareholders.

The picture gets more complicated, of course, when employees show up on both sides of the bargain. Recent finance legislation has encouraged a widening of employee share ownership. Reconstructed state-owned companies, Aer Lingus, Telecom Éireann and others have ceded substantial equity interests to employees. Such developments may attune employees to market demands for efficiency and competitiveness, but employees as mini-capitalists may not prove more obviously loyal to the organisation or have more cooperative relations one with the other. In many cases, the holdings will not be of a size to influence behaviour. There will be plenty of room for argument about relativities in share allocation and, where allowed, an incentive to cash out before the downturn.

Deals are everywhere in this. What matters, I suggest, is the context and culture within which they are made and remade. Preference for the measurable and a bias towards the instrumental 'fix' serve to divert time and attention from the softer (derogatory term!) issues that struggle to achieve a legitimacy that goes beyond lip-service and simplistic statements like: 'Our greatest assets are our people!'

A useful concept here, I suggest, is the idea of 'internal' values, that is to say shared values in an organisation which, unlike external ones (such as share value) are actuated in the manner in which day-to-day operations are conducted, values that make their appearance in the quality of the relationships within the business, the levels of trust and co-operation thereby achieved and in the inherent satisfactions to be derived from good work and shared endeavour, which find their justification at the level of the individual.

Alasdair MacIntyre has illuminated the distinction between internal and external goods, as seen in the context of any human 'practice'. Practice he defines as 'any coherent and complex form of socially established co-operative human activity through which goods internal to that form of activity are realised in the course of trying to achieve those standards of excellence which are appropriate to, and partially definitive of, that form of activity, with the result that human powers to achieve excellence and human conceptions of the ends and goods involved, are systematically extended' (MacIntyre, 1981, p. 175).

I suggest that the activity of modern corporations will frequently embody a variety of practices as so defined. The practice, MacIntyre argues, yields up two kinds of goods – external ones (readily identifiable in the world of commerce in terms of output or profit) and internal goods which have to do with achievement of excellence and the fruits of co-operative activity. These ideas are bound up with the notions of continuity, skills that are passed on, traditions of excellence.

As already indicated, the recognition of such goods or values ought to be facilitated, indeed mandated, by recent evolution in industrial methods and growth in significance of 'knowledge based' industries, such as telecommunications, microelectronics, software and biotechnology. In such fields (some of which are, incidentally, those very ones in which new Irish companies have distinguished themselves) what is frequently referred to as intellectual capital becomes, increasingly, the crucial ingredient of competitive advantage. Developing and guarding human skills becomes ever more important as does the maintenance of a context for work that is optimally conducive to co-operation. This is true not merely for researchers or experts with esoteric skills. The 'flattened' organisations that Mr Fukuyama describes comprise better educated, resourceful personnel, in charge of their own work, whose abilities are leveraged up by information technology and who work in sophisticated systems of interdependence. These teams are not mere instruments of the modern corporation or of any of its stakeholders. They are in a real sense its mind and heart.

Unwillingness to articulate and champion the worth of intrinsic values in an organisation is often excused by statements of resigned obedience to the 'logic' of the markets, leading to a conclusion that business activity as such is morally neutral at best. As a sideline observer of business clients over some years it has seemed to me that many could benefit from a more elevated sense of the responsibilities they carry and of the inherent ethical worth of their efforts. The reality is that corporations are readily distinguishable in terms of character and ethos. Some are felt by those who belong to them to provide a setting in which they can flourish as individuals and in which the spirit of co-operation is maximised. Others, including some who make extravagant claims as to how far they 'empower' their people (often with purely financial incentives) make environments in which the operating principles include a significant element of manipulation, in which people feel, in a real sense, reduced.

Once 'internal' benefits or inherent values are given a place in the scheme of things, however, measures under consideration for the advancement of an enterprise can be subjected to tests as to whether or not they support them. And once it is recognised that what is involved is the long-run health, stability and worth of the business, one may be starting to fill a void caused by the loss of that sense of satisfaction and pride that was one of the sustaining forces of the well-run family business, handed on through the generations. Retrieval of the sense that newcomers to an organisation, even ones who may be moving on quite shortly, build on the achievements of those who went before, develop and improve methods of operation passed on and share a satisfaction in their contribution to this continuum will yield a dividend in terms of better quality and more stable employment, in short, better business.

Legal choices for an emergent business culture

Irish law-makers have limited freedom to direct what the business culture is to be or what governance rules are to be made to influence it. A high proportion of industrial activity is owned by foreign incorporated, mainly US entities, not subject to Irish company law. This is true of IDA-enticed projects but also for the multitude of domestic businesses whose owners have encashed their holdings, so that they are now subsidiaries of overseas companies.

Yet it would be unwise to assume that the legal system is without influence. New Irish enterprises that go to the stock markets and seek to maintain their independence must submit to the terms of the Irish codes for the time being. Indeed, the requirements of the regulatory regime may have a bearing on their ability to maintain that independence. The suggestions for novel corporate governance rules made by Kay and Silberston raise difficult issues of board accountability and may be far removed from what is practicable for Irish circumstances. However they serve as a reminder that company law can serve as a creative instrument that influences the quality of business activity. Shortly after publication of the Hampel Report, the British Trade and Industry Secretary announced a wide-ranging review of company law, including the issue of directors' duties, which has led to the suggestion that the notion of fiduciary duty might be broadened to include responsibility for more than the financial welfare of shareholders.

In company law parlance, the word 'member' is largely synonymous with shareholder. This reflects a genesis whereby the privilege, given by legislation, of artificial personality and limited liability, was conferred on the members for the time being of a company. Such members were, typically managers and owners. With expansion of trade and capital hunger, separation of ownership and management has taken place. The legal system, perhaps, has not fully adjusted to the shift.

The Companies Act 1990, in Section 52, introduced what at first sight might be seen as a dilution of the commitment expected of directors towards the interests of shareholders, in providing that '[t]he matters to which the directors of a company are to have regard in the performance of their functions shall include the interests of the company's employees in general, as well as the interests of its members'. However the next following subsection indicates clearly the draftsman's caution lest this injunction should open Pandora's box: '(2) Accordingly, the duty imposed by this section on the directors shall be owed by them to the company (and the company alone) and shall be enforceable in the same way as any other fiduciary duty owed to a company by its directors'.

The expression 'accordingly' might have a soothing effect on a less than attentive reader interested to promote industrial democracy. In fact the confinement of rights of enforcement of the obligation just created to the 'the company alone', this being an entity effectively controlled by its shareholders, makes it safe to characterise the section as double speak. And in fact it has indeed been largely a dead letter.

In recent times, European social policy has mandated concrete measures to allow consultation rights for employees in relation to major developments in international companies by requiring the set-up of European Works Councils or other consultation procedures in companies to which it applies – a measure eschewed by the British industrial leadership until the Blair government abandoned the opt-out negotiated by its predecessor. In fact, however, the terms in which the relevant directive has been implemented in Ireland do not inaugurate any very demanding regime of consultation.

The Partnership 2000 document (Department of the Taoiseach, 1997) states as an objective the extension of what are termed partnership arrangements at enterprise level and a National Centre for Partnership has been established in furtherance of this aim. Partnership is defined for this purpose as 'an active relationship based on recognition of a common interest to secure the competitiveness, viability and prosperity of the enterprise. It involves a continuing commitment by employees to improvements in quality and efficiency; and the acceptance by employers of employees as stakeholders with rights and interests to be considered in the context of major decisions affecting their employment.'

It remains to be seen whether these developments may engender some mutation of practice in individual firms. A gathering consensus on the desirability of a more participative business culture may, at some point, prompt the question whether the corporate governance regime can be shaped in a fashion that supports this objective.

Many of the changes in company law introduced in recent years have been reactive in nature, whether to European initiatives or a desire for conformity with English legislation or to political pressures resulting from the latest scandal. Controversies such as those concerning trade union recognition in major companies may have less to do with productive social partnership than subtler questions as to how companies are to be governed and in what manner the Irish law encourages wholesome participation and respect for distinctively human values.

Proposals for change in corporate law are unlikely to advance,

of course, without support from the business lobby. And awareness, on the part of managers and directors, of what is at stake may
be of greater significance than any legislative measures. A simplistic
proposition that 'the purpose of business is to make money' will
often find easy acceptance. An alternative formulation, under which
profit is seen merely as necessary to the health and prosperity of a
trading concern, a means to further improvement and investment
and the source of rewards that recognise a legitimacy for wealth
creation in what are ultimately private hands, should be no less
capable of delivering competitive results. The Centre for Tomorrow's
Company (established in the wake of the report referred to above)
cites a study by Stanford University of those large US businesses
that appear to have been more or less consistently successful over
fifty years or more, and are today the undisputed leaders in their
industries – the lead examples include Merck, Hewlett Packard,
Procter and Gamble and Motorola (Centre for Tomorrow's Company,
1997). This identified the following as important contributors to
success: continuity of values; actions consistent with values; investment in people; objectives beyond profit and investment for the
long term. Emerging Irish corporates, drawn to the American way,
who look to select their role models, and industrial promotion
agencies seeking to choose winners, need to give heed to the statistic
that of the 500 leading American companies operating in 1970 only
one-third are still even in existence. A focus given to richer ideas of
collaborative enterprise should also be reflected in the quality of
directors appointed to contribute to policy in promising concerns
and in endorsement of the approach of those managers who do,
instinctively, in their daily decisions, and in the relations which
they engender with staff, support the broader ideal.

References

Black, A., Wright, P., Bachman, J. and Davis, J. 1998. *In Search of
    Shareholder Value: Managing the Drivers of Performance*. London:
    Pitman.
Brittan, S. 1996. 'The Snares of Stakeholding', *Financial Times* 1 February.
Centre for Tomorrow's Company. 1997. *The Inclusive Approach and
    Business Success*. London: Centre for Tomorrow's Company.
Committee on Corporate Governance. 1998. *Final Report of Committee*

on Corporate Governance. London: Gee and Committee on Corporate Governance.

Department of the Taoiseach. 1997. *Partnership 2000*. Dublin: The Stationery Office.

Fukuyama, F. 1996. *Address to the IBEC Conference*. Dublin: IBEC.

Goldenberg, 1998. 'Shareholders v stakeholders: the bogus argument'. *The Company Lawyer*.

Handy, C. 1995. *Beyond Certainty*. London: Hutchinson.

Handy, C. 1997. *The Hungry Spirit*. London: Hutchinson.

Kay, J. and Silberston, A. 1995. 'Corporate Governance', *National Institute Economic Review*, August 1995.

MacIntyre, A. 1981. *After Virtue*. Notre Dame, Indiana: University of Notre Dame Press.

Plender, J. 1997. *A Stake in the Future*. London: Nicholas Brealey Publishing.

Royal Society for the Encouragement of Arts, Manufacturers and Commerce (RSA). 1994. *Tomorrow's Company*. London: RSA.

CHAPTER 13

The Priest in Politics

Austin Flannery OP

I t was a coolish evening in Dublin towards the end of October 1962. For days the newspapers had been full of reports and speculation about what would later be known as the Cuban Missile Crisis. The world seemed to many to be teetering on the brink of nuclear war between the United States of America and the Soviet Union, with presidents Kennedy and Kruschev indulging in dangerous brinkmanship. Jack Dowling, a retired army officer, since gone to his eternal reward, was addressing an open-air meeting in central Dublin. He was trying to alert his small and restive audience to the danger and the immorality of nuclear war. He quoted Pope John XXIII. He quoted scripture. Suddenly a man in the audience spluttered in incredulous anger: 'Are you trying to bring religion into this?'

Jack was not a priest. The appellation would not have pleased him, nor would he have relished being perceived as a spokesperson for the Catholic Church. Still, he was attempting to do something which, in 1962, almost all Catholics would have seen as best left to the clergy. He was attempting 'to bring religion' to bear on a matter within the competence of the state.

Changing contexts: the weakening of the Catholic Church in Ireland

Since 1962 a number of factors have conspired to change any role which clergy might allocate to themselves in political matters – both the nature of the role and its effectiveness. For one thing, there was the gradual weakening of the Catholic Church in Ireland, graphically foretold in May 1962 by the well-known writer and social commentator, Desmond Fennell. Secondly, profound changes were brought about in the Church by the Second Vatican Council, the first of whose four sessions was taking place even as Jack Dowling spoke. Then there was the cultural transformation which began in Ireland in the 1960s, symbolised by Telefís Éireann's 'Late Late Show' which was first broadcast in 1962. Telefís Éireann itself began, in a real sense, in 1962, though the first broadcast took place on the very last night of 1961, the station thereby just barely achieving the promised starting date.

I can still remember the surprise which greeted Desmond Fennell's suggestion that the number of Catholics in Ireland was bound to decline, in 'Will the Irish stay Christian?' (*Doctrine and Life*, May 1962). 'There is no reason to suppose', he wrote, 'that the Irish Catholic people will continue indefinitely to be believing Christians'. At that time few people were aware of advance indications that within a few decades a very large proportion of Irish men and women would cease to attend church regularly, to believe many of the church's teachings, or to accept its guidance in the realm of behaviour. Fennell argued, however, that what had happened elsewhere in Europe was all too likely to happen in Ireland also: 'In Europe during the last one hundred and fifty years the majority of people have abandoned Christian belief and practice; there is no reason why the same should not happen here.'

When Mr Fennell wrote his article, almost all Irish Catholics went to church on Sundays and a very high proportion went on weekdays as well, especially in the cities, where weekday attendance was more feasible than in rural areas. A large proportion of men and women were members of confraternities of one kind or another. Most men and women went to confession regularly, thanks in considerable measure to the influence of the confraternities. Parish missions were frequent and well attended. Among Catholics registry-office marriages were almost unheard of and for couples to co-habit without benefit of clergy or registrar was as abnormal as driving on the right side of the road. The future of the Catholic church seemed assured: churches were full and the flow of vocations to the priesthood and the religious life seemed unending.

Now, thirty-eight years later, we are witnessing a continuing and accelerating abandonment of Christian belief and practice by a sizeable proportion of our people. Mícheál McGréil illustrated the rapidity of the decline in weekly Mass attendance as follows: in

1974, 91 per cent of Irish people went to Mass every week; over the next ten years the figure dropped by 4 per cent. Over the following five years, however, the decline became more rapid, with weekly Mass attendance dropping by 5 per cent (in *Doctrine and Life*, January 1992, p. 5). There is little reason to suppose that this rate of decline has slowed in more recent years. The fact that the decrease in church-going is most marked among young urban dwellers has ominous implications for the future of Catholicism in Ireland, since our society is becoming increasingly urbanised and since a very large section of the population is young, more so than in any other EU country. Many of the non-practising Catholics between the ages of twenty-one and thirty-five are to be found among the better educated. They are numerous among those who work in the media. They are especially to be found in the working-class areas of the larger cities, particularly where large numbers of people are unemployed. Here the decline in church attendance is very marked. As a writer in the *Irish Times* put it a year or so ago, there are working-class housing estates on the outskirts of Dublin where 'the vast majority of people, nominally Catholic, no longer go to church.'

The fact that people do not go to church regularly, or even at all, does not of course imply that they have totally repudiated the church, or that they no longer regard themselves as Christians, or that they no longer aspire to live by the Christian moral law. There is, however, one area of morality where there is widespread rejection of the Catholic Church's teaching: sexual morality. It is not just that many Catholic men and women ignore the church's teaching on contraception, abortion, sex before marriage, and re-marriage after divorce. It is that in their eyes all of this is deemed to be acceptable and indeed eminently sensible behaviour. This implies a far-reaching repudiation of the church's authority, dangerous for the church, especially since church authorities have placed so much emphasis on sexual morality, sometimes unwittingly conveying the impression that it was the only morality that really mattered. In the estimation of many young men and women, this tends to leave the church stranded in yesterday's world, with no part to play in the world in which they themselves live. All of this – the point scarcely needs mentioning – has enormously diminished the ability of the clergy to influence political developments. And as if 'all of this' were not sufficient, there came the clerical scandals, especially the sexual abuse of children and of juveniles. The numbers of clerical offenders was not very great. Huge shock waves, however, spread from the disclosure of the suffering and psychological damage which their activities had inflicted on vulnerable young people.

It was not always so. Keogh (1966, pp. 104, ff.) describes the close relationship between priest and people and between priest and politician from the early 1920s until recent times. From the early 1920s, he tells us, 'Irish Catholicism ... sought ... as one of its major objectives to reinforce the legitimacy of the new state'. For much of the state's history, according to Keogh, it was not so much a question of the Catholic Church trying to exert pressure on politicians as of politicians from time to time asking the advice of bishops and priests on matters which posed problems for their Catholic consciences. Nor should this be surprising. Bishops, priests and politicians came for the most part from similar backgrounds. Almost all the politicians were Catholics, many of them devout Catholics. It was not uncommon for clerics and politicians to be close friends and 'the majority of politicians shared as Catholic an outlook as the hierarchy' (Keogh, 1996, p. 107).

Recent Catholic thought on church and state

The loss of the church's power to exert political influence does not distress thoughtful priests nowadays. They believe that separation of church and state is healthier for both parties and are aware that the church has sometimes had to pay a price for a close relationship. For the objectives of the state do not necessarily coincide with those of the church or of the Gospel. It is obviously desirable if church and state can coexist peacefully in a manner that is of mutual benefit. This is stated clearly in an article, 'Church and State' (in Komonchak et al., 1987, pp. 206-9), which describes the two institutions as 'central but incomplete embodiments of the religious and political concerns of human beings' and urges readers to be 'sceptical of generalisations' and to appreciate 'the pragmatic adjustments which different societies have made to resolve conflicts in this area' (p. 206). The First Amendment to the American Constitution, prohibiting the establishment of religion and guaranteeing its free exercise, 'set up the classic American pattern of church and state'. And as the article goes on: 'American political life has remained open to strong religious influences and American levels of religious practice and belief are among the highest in the industrialised world' (p. 208).

The author of that article, an American Jesuit, John Langan, points out that 'American Catholic leaders became articulate exponents of the principles of religious liberty, preparing the way for the eventual acceptance of the fundamental right of persons in Vatican II's *Declaration on Religious Liberty ...*' (p. 204). It is not surprising that a similar mind-set should be clearly discernible in what Vatican II had to say about relations between church and state, in the Pastoral constitution on the Church in the Modern World, *Gaudium et Spes*. Fr John Courtney Murray, one of the American exponents of the principles of religious liberty of whom Fr Langan speaks, had a major influence on the drafting of the portions of conciliar documents which deal with church and state. *Gaudium et Spes* declares:

> The political community and the church are autonomous and independent of each other in their own fields .... Their service will be more efficient and beneficial to all if both institutions develop better co-operation according to the circumstances of place and time .... The church, for its part, being founded on the love of the Redeemer, contributes towards the spread of justice and charity among nations and in the nations themselves. By preaching the truths of the Gospel and shedding light on all sectors of human activity through its teaching and the witness of its members, the church respects and encourages the political freedom and responsibility of the citizens (in Flannery, 1996, pp. 260-61).

Whatever the degree of closeness between church and state, certain kinds of relationship to government are forbidden to clerics. The new *Code of Canon Law* states that there are certain kinds of involvement in politics which are forbidden to Roman Catholic priests – to all Roman Catholic clerics in fact – and that for certain other kinds priests need special permission. Thus the *Code* states: 'Clerics are forbidden to assume public office whenever it means sharing in the exercise of civil power' (in Sheehy, 1995, 285, §3). However, a bishop could dispense from this regulation, allowing a priest to assume such public office if he judged 'that it would serve a spiritual purpose' (ibid). The Code also states that clerics 'are not to play an active role in political parties or in directing trade unions unless, in the judgment of the competent ecclesiastical authority, this is required for the defence of the rights of the church or to promote the common good' (Sheehy, 1995, 287 §2).

One will look in vain in the new *Code of Canon Law* or in the *Catechism of the Catholic Church* for a statement that clerics may not engage in armed rebellion. The reason is that Canon Law assumes that taking life is something foreign to the clerical state. Thus, the Code states that a cleric ought not to volunteer for military service without the permission of his bishop (in Sheehy, 1995, 289 §1) – it accepts that in some jurisdictions clerics may be conscripted into military service. It also asserts that occupations such as 'executioner, bodyguard, etc' are 'unbecoming for a cleric' (285, §1, commentary) and that it is 'impossible to justify clerics … indulging in acts of violence or major civil disobedience, even for what purports to be a good purpose' (287 §1, commentary).

Prophesy versus acquiescence

Meddling in politics, of course – indeed being up to one's neck in it – does not necessarily mean joining a political party, or taking part in government. Nor does it necessarily involve resorting to condemnation, protests, marches, speeches, pamphlets, or whatever. One can be up to one's neck in politics simply by acquiescing, by accepting government policy, or by sharing a consensus. It is widely accepted that it is wrong to acquiesce in the practice of evil. But such widespread awareness usually focuses on events which took place in the remote or recent past, and in another country. How widespread was the awareness among ordinary people in Hitler's Germany that he was perpetrating evil? Hindsight comes equipped with twenty-twenty vision, but things were not always clear on the ground at the time. Except perhaps for the more perceptive. Except for the prophets in society, some of whom have been priests.

One of the most effective prophetic sermons of all time was preached on the Sunday before Christmas 1511, in what is now Haiti, by Fr Antonio Montesinos, a Spanish Dominican. He rounded on the Spanish colonists of the island for their outrageous treatment of the native Indians. He put the following questions to them: 'With what right and with what justice do you keep these poor

Indians in such cruel and horrible servitude? Are these not men? Do they not have rational souls? Are you not obliged to love them as yourselves?' (in Griffin, 1992, p. xxi). In the congregation was a Spanish colonist and slave owner, Bartolomè de Las Casas. The sermon affected him profoundly. Some time later he gave his slaves their freedom and, dedicating himself to the defence of the Indians, joined the Dominicans. His subsequent work for the Indians earned him the title, 'Defender and Apostle of the Indians'. According to Anthony Pagden, Montesinos' last three questions 'were to become the referents of every subsequent struggle to defend the rights of the indigenous people of the Americas.' And for Las Casas, he adds, the very last question 'was to guide his actions for the rest of his life'.

The most famous prophetic preacher in our day was Archbishop Oscar Romero of El Salvador. He preached trenchantly, almost daily, against the oppressive policies of the right-wing government and was shot by a death squad while celebrating Mass. And, as we shall see later, a large number of Jesuits have also been killed in Latin America in recent years because they preached against injustice. The activities and the fate of Romero and the Latin American Jesuits, among others, are the most visible signs of a deep commitment to combatting injustice on the part of very many, but not all, Catholics after the Second Council of the Vatican. In Ireland the most visible sign of such commitment is the work of Fr Sean Healy and Sr Brigid Reynolds of the Conference of Religious of Ireland. Year after year they have offered well-researched and cogently argued critiques of government policy with regard to justice. And if it is particularly appropriate to mention here the work of Fergal O'Connor too, it should be noted that this work began even *before* Vatican II. The work of those mentioned and that of many others denote a profound change from bettering the lot of the poor to changing the structures that cause it.

From private charity to social justice

It is worthwhile to look more closely at how that change came about, because in due course it would have a significant effect on how priests, or a certain proportion of them, would understand their ministry and the part that work for justice should play in it.

According to Dorr (1983, p. 256) the change began in 1961 with the publication of John XXIII's *Mater et Magistra*. In previous pages Dorr recalls briefly the changes which had taken place in papal social teaching from Leo XIII's *Rerum Novarum* to Pius XII, within an abiding commitment to betterment of the lot of the poor. During the seventy-year period from 1891 to 1961 the church theoretically espoused 'a third way', which was neither capitalist nor socialist, but 'in practice it gave solid legitimation to the "free enterprise" model of society. Its protests against the excesses of capitalism … had become muted during the later years of the papacy of Pius XII. The church still challenged the ideology of liberal capitalism; but its opposition to socialism was far more explicit, systematic and effective' (Dorr, 1983, p. 255). Granted its opposition to socialism, it was to be expected that the church, especially under Pius XII, would side with western democracy. As Dorr puts it: 'Pius XII gave tacit support to the capitalist economic model that went hand in hand with the Western political system' (1983, pp. 254-255).

In Ireland this kind of relationship between church and state persisted more or less intact for several decades. However, things had begun to change by the early 1950s. James Ryan, Minister for Health in a newly-elected Fianna Fáil government, began implementing the 'Mother and Child' scheme which the previous government under John A. Costello had attempted to introduce, but which the hierarchy had strenuously and successfully opposed. They attempted to oppose Dr Ryan's implementation of the scheme too and wrote a letter to the newspapers to that effect. However, Eamon de Valera, head of the government, got in touch with his friend Cardinal John D'Alton and the letter was withdrawn. Other politicians during the latter part of the 1950s began to take 'a more independent and assertive position' vis-à-vis the hierarchy (Keogh 1996, p. 133). As I indicated earlier, Dorr traces the beginnings of the change to John XXIII's 1961 encyclical, *Mater et Magistra*. He suggests that for Pope John it was a matter of effecting not so much a move to the left as 'a decisive move away from the right.' As a result the church's social doctrine 'could no longer be invoked to give unilateral legitimacy to the values of a "free enterprise" approach; and the right to private property no longer held a uniquely privileged place in Catholic social teaching' (Dorr, 1983, p. 256).

In this connection it is instructive to recall that in the early 1960s two young Irish laymen, both to become prominent politicians later, showed themselves more responsive to changing church teaching on justice than did many of the Irish clergy. They were Declan Costello and Garret FitzGerald, who urged churchmen to make their voices heard in the cause of social reform. The church, Costello insisted, 'must act as a social conscience and speak out, not with a still quiet voice, but if necessary a large and strident one. If civil authority has failed to bring about social justice, it can, and I suggest, should, point out the failure.' And Garret FitzGerald wrote in *Studies* of Ireland's need to develop 'an internally consistent philosophy of our own, appropriate to the needs of the time in which we live, and clearly superior to the excessive conservatism sometimes found in Catholic attitudes, as well as the wishy-washy liberalism common in Britain and the doctrinaire socialism of other countries' (in Keogh, 1996, p. 157).

Linden too traces the beginnings of change in Catholic social attitudes to the early 1960s. Before answering his own question, 'Did something radically new begin in the church in the 1960s?', he points to the long tradition of charitable activity in the church and suggests that the church has always had in mind what has more recently become known as the 'preferential option for the poor', adding 'it is equally clear that having had it in mind, for long periods and in many places the church – though not all the church – forgot it'. From the 1890s, he goes on, Catholic social teaching 'recommended ... the protection of the marginal and the poor, albeit first viewed though a European prism of the consequences of the industrial revolution'. But he adds:

> What characterised the 1960s, though, was the growth of a vision of the church's mission that went beyond charity, understood as unconditional love expressed in charitable activity, towards a concept of working for structural change implied in the term 'social justice'. It was a movement from what was pejoratively called 'ambulance ministry' towards some form of political engagement in social movements .... The movement was world-wide but it was particularly Latin American liberation theology that provided its powerful impetus (Linden, 1996, p. 138).

The developments thus summarised by Dorr and Linden set the scene for the possibility of a quite dramatic change in relations between Catholic priests and politicians, more especially in parts of the world plagued with oppressive governments. To see how this came about one needs to look more closely at developments which have taken place since Vatican II.

It is my belief that the thinking which we rightly associate with Vatican II can to a certain – largely unrecognised – extent be traced back to the motivation behind the French Priest Worker movement some ten to twenty years before Vatican II and, before that, to the writings of J. Loew OP, Cardinal Emmanuel Suhard, H. Godin and Y. Daniel. The Priest Workers, as they were called, did not just play at being manual or blue-collared workers. They shared the conditions of workers and joined sometimes militant trades unions. Inevitably there was street theatre, at which the French excel, and occasional violent clashes between police and striking workers. When photographs appeared in French newspapers of priests who had not only joined trade unions but who were involved in confrontation with the police, conservative opinion was alarmed and many began to feel that something had to be done.

It was. The Vatican condemned the movement in 1954. The theologians to whom the movement looked for guidance – the Dominicans Yves Congar, M.-D. Chenu, H.M. Feret and the Jesuit H. de Lubac – were removed from their teaching posts. It had been a mould-breaking initiative which had linked the preaching of the gospel with work for justice. The condemnation of the Priest Worker movement and the sacking of its theological mentors did, however, have outcomes not intended by the Vatican. It outraged important sections of French Catholic opinion, who thought the movement an admirable attempt to take the gospel to de-christianised French workers. The novelist François Mauriac spoke for many French Catholics when he said that the Vatican might as well have destroyed one of France's beloved medieval cathedrals. The condemnation also ensured wide scale publicity for the movement and its ideas, not just in France but in other European countries too. Few things attract newspaper headlines as surely as does a condemnation or, as we shall see later, a martyrdom. It also ensured the dissemination, even if in attenuated form, of priest workers' ideas. Their dedication and the calibre of the theologians to whom they looked for guidance made a profound impression on thoughtful Catholics in France and elsewhere.

Developments since Vatican ll

While accepting what Dorr (1983, p. 256) has said about the role of John XXIII's *Mater et Magistra* in changing the Catholic church's thinking on social justice, I think it also has to be said that a more assured process of change was set in train after the publication in 1965 of Vatican II's *Gaudium et Spes*, or 'Pastoral Constitution on the Church in the Modern World', to give it its other title (in Flannery, 1996, pp. 163-289). That process would instil in Catholics – though of course not in all Catholics and not everywhere – the conviction that work to achieve social justice is part of the preaching of the gospel. That conviction was not stated explicitly in *Gaudium et Spes*. However, the latter's opening sentence, which was in tune with it, became familiar to many, thanks to frequent repetition: 'The joys and hopes, the grief and anguish of the people of our time, especially of those who are poor or afflicted, are the joys and hopes, the grief and the anguish of the followers of Christ as well' (in Flannery, 1996, p. 163). It is widely accepted that the document helped create a groundswell in favour of greater involvement with the poor and greater concern for justice. The 1971 Synod of Bishop, of which more shortly, said that in *Gaudium et Spes* the church had shown that 'as never before ... [it] understood the situation in the modern world, in which Christians work out their salvation by deeds of justice' (in Flannery, 1982, pp. 705-706).

Three years after the publication of *Gaudium et Spes*, Latin American bishops assembled at Medellin in Colombia. In the course of a document which had major repercussions in Latin America and which is widely associated with the beginnings of Liberation Theology they said: 'The Church – the People of God – will lend its support to the downtrodden of every social class so that they might come to know their rights and how to make use of them' (O'Brien and Shannon, 1977, p. 558). Many would say that the statement by the 1971 Synod of Bishops, headed 'Justice in the World', was crucial to the development of the church's thinking on social justice. According to Land, 'Nothing in recent times has so commanded the Catholic conscience [with regard to justice] as the Synod of 1971, with its reliance on the unmodified word justice' (in Komonchak et al., 1987, p. 551). And, writing on the 32nd General Congregation of the Society of Jesus (see below), McPolin (1976,

p. 56) says that the Synod's statement was 'probably the strongest influence in shaping the [Congregation's] decree' on the promotion of justice. The key passage on justice in the Synod's document reads: 'Action on behalf of justice and participation in the transformation of the world appear to us as a constitutive dimension of the preaching of the Gospel, or, in other words, of the church's mission for the redemption of the human race and its liberation from every oppressive situation' (in Flannery, 1982, p. 696).

The 32nd General Congregation of the Society of Jesus, under the inspired leadership of Pedro Arrupe, was held from December 1974 to March 1975. It was then that the Jesuits made their crucial commitment to the promotion of justice. The Congregation's central document is headed: 'Our mission today: the service of faith and the promotion of justice.' McPolin (1976, p. 57) writes: 'This justice is a willingness to recognise the rights of all, especially the poor and the powerless, to work to secure those rights, to encourage and to join with the laity in this task.' Pedro Arrupe said at the time that if the Jesuits were faithful to what was enacted in the 32nd Congregation they would have martyrs. That his words were prophetic would later become all too tragically clear.

An underestimated document, Pope Paul VI's *Evangelii Nuntiandi* (in Flannery, 1998, pp. 711-61), published nine months after the Society's 32nd General Congregation, played a major part in the spread of awareness of, as Pope Paul put it, 'the links between evangelisation and human advancement'. He pointed out that 'the person to be evangelised is not an abstract being but a person subject to social and economic factors', that the plan of redemption 'extends to the very practical question of eradicating injustice and establishing justice.' 'How can the new law be proclaimed', he asked, 'unless it promotes a true, practical advancement of men and women in a spirit of justice and peace?'.

The decisions which the Jesuits took in their 32nd General Congregation were of momentous importance for the Society of Jesus and for many other religious orders and congregations. As Arrupe assuredly felt they would, Jesuits were faithful to the fourth decree, especially in Latin America, in countries where this was to invite more bullets than plaudits. And his prophecy came true: thirty-five Jesuits were murdered in the space of fifteen years. The most gruesome and the most electrifying happening for the Society and for thousands of other religious was the shooting down by government agents of six Jesuits and two laywomen on the night of 16 November 1989 in San Salvador. A few days later, five hundred priests gathered in the church of the Gesù in Rome to celebrate Requiem Mass for the eight victims: a day or two later six thousand students attended another Requiem Mass in Munich. Because murders, especially of priests, still attract banner headlines, even the secular newspapers unwittingly helped spread awareness of the connection between evangelisation and work for justice.

Conclusion

The title which provided my remit for this piece is one of diminishing applicability to this island, simply because ordained priests are diminishing in numbers at the same time that they are becoming less clerical. By that I mean that they are ceasing to see themselves as members of a privileged caste, and are endeavouring to see themselves rather as servants of God's people. They are also, in many areas, making space for different forms of lay ministry in the church. Increasingly, clergy and laity are becoming more deeply aware that together they form the church.

Any such development will have to cope with a neo-conservatism, both secular and religious, in the Western world as a whole and in Ireland in particular. Keogh speaks of 'the growth of neo-conservative ideas during the 1970s and 1980s' and of the 'relative strength of conservatism in Irish society' (1996, p. 170). My own impression – based, as Jack Dowling used to say, on experience and report – is that there has been a regression to pre-Vatican II attitudes on the part of many (younger) priests and lay Catholics in Ireland in recent times. Keogh quotes Fr Bill Cosgrave to the effect that there has been 'a definite rowing back from the Vatican II perspective ... and we are in the midst of a "restoration" of pre-Vatican II emphases and attitudes, something that is quite evident in the Vatican's relation to local churches around the world' (1996, p. 174).

While no survey has revealed any widespread desire to jettison altogether clerical leadership in Ireland, it is certainly true that Irish priests and bishops have suffered a considerable loss of authority in recent years. In Keogh's words, 'the cumulative impact of the response to the handling of the scandals – had created a major credibility problem for the Irish hierarchy, probably unprecedented in the history of twentieth-century Irish Catholicism.' So, what of the ministry of Irish priests and work for justice? Are Irish priests, like priests in other parts of Europe and the United States, something of an endangered species? For one thing there will not be so many of them around in the years to come. Priests of any sort will be in short supply in Ireland and only a small proportion of their dwindling number is likely to be 'in politics'. If what has been happening in Ireland recently is anything to go by, in future we are more likely to be talking about Catholic lay people – rather than priests – in politics.

References

Dorr, Donal. 1983. *Option for the Poor, A Hundred Years of Vatican Social Teaching*, Dublin: Gill and Macmillan.

Flannery, A. (ed.). 1996. *Vatican Council II: Constitutions Decrees Declarations*, Dublin: Dominican Publications.

Flannery, A. (ed.) 1998. *Vatican Council II: More Postconciliar Documents*, Dublin: Dominican Publications.

Griffin, Nigel (ed. and trans). 1992. *Bartolomè de Las Casas: A Short Account of the Destruction of the Indies*, with Introduction by Anthony Pagden. London: Penguin Classics.

Keogh, D. 1996. 'The Role of the Catholic Church in the Republic of Ireland 1922-1995', in *Building Trust in Ireland: Studies Commissioned by the Forum for Peace and Reconciliation*, Belfast: The Blackstaff Press.

Komonchak, J.A., Collins, M. and Lane, D.A. (eds). 1987. *The New Dictionary of Theology*. Dublin: Gill and Macmillan.

Linden, I. 1996. 'Religious and Social Justice', *Religious Life Review*, 35, pp. 138-146.

McPolin, SJ, J. 1976. 'Jesuits Renew their Mission: The 32nd General Congregation', in *Religious Life Review*, 14, pp. 51-63.

O'Brien, David J. and Thomas A. Shannon (eds). 1977. *Renewing the Earth: Catholic Documents on Peace, Justice and Liberation*. New York: Image Books.

Sheehy, G. (ed.) 1995. *The Canon Law, Letter and Spirit: A Practical Guide to the Code of Canon Law*, Dublin: Veritas.

Index

group equality, 117-19
need, 112-13
political equality, 115-17
putting into practice, 120-2
respect, 113-14
women's search for, 41
Equality Studies Centre, UCD,
118, 121
eros, 17, 21, 27
Ethics and Politics, Department
of, UCD, 96
ethnic cleansing, 59
ethnocultural communities, 58, 59
Etzioni, Amitai, 90n
European Union, 1, 4, 67, 119
future of nation-state, 53, 56
social policy, 231
European Works Councils, 231
Evangelii Nuntiandi, 245
Evans, J., 128n
executive share options, 226

F
family, 89
'family values,' 106, 108
Fergal O'Connor on, 108-9
Plato's view of, 106-7
and the state, 95-110
structures, 83-4, 121
view of Hobbes, 104-10
feminism, 7-8, 41, 47, 80
and justice, 124-38
care v. justice, 125-6
contours of a feminist theory,
129-34
generalised and concrete
others, 126-9
interactive universalism, 134-8
Fennell, Desmond, 234-5
Feret, H.M. OP, 243
Fianna Fáil, 108
Finance Acts, 215
Financial Times, 223, 225
Finnis, J., 77n, 84

FitzGerald, Garret, 242
Flanders, 52
Flannery, Austin, 11-12, 244
France, 51, 166
cultural nation, 61
Priest Worker movement, 243
Fraser, Nancy, 47, 113, 128
Frazer, E. and Lacey, L., 80
French Revolution, 60, 140-1
Freud, Sigmund, 163
Fukuyama, Francis, 224, 228
functional interdependence, 191-
2, 197-8

G
Garvin, Tom, 70
Gaudium et Spes, 238, 244
'generalised other,' 126-9
Germany, 61, 214, 239
Gilligan, Carol, 125-6
globalisation, 4, 54, 55
and break-up of nation-state,
67-8
Goldenberg, 220
good, the. *see also* common good
collective goods, 173-4
individual conceptions of, 35-7
search for, 21-5
state as neutral between
conceptions of, 44
Good Friday Agreement, 52
Gorgias, The (Plato), 20
Gowdy, 149-50
Grant, J., 129n
green politics, 8-9, 140-53
anthropocentrism and
ecocentrism, 141-3
ecological stewardship and
virtue, 143-6
green citizenship, 151-3
and progress, 149-51
technique and enclosure in,
146-9
Greenbury Committee, 221, 226